e-Human Resources Management:
Managing Knowledge People

Teresa Torres-Coronas
Universitat Rovira i Virgili, Spain

Mario Arias-Oliva
Universitat Rovira Virgili, Spain

IDEA GROUP PUBLISHING
Hershey • London • Melbourne • Singapore

Acquisitions Editor: Mehdi Khosrow-Pour
Senior Managing Editor: Jan Travers
Managing Editor: Amanda Appicello
Development Editor: Michele Rossi
Copy Editor: Maria Boyer
Typesetter: Jennifer Wetzel
Cover Design: Lisa Tosheff
Printed at: Yurchak Printing Inc.

Published in the United States of America by
    Idea Group Publishing (an imprint of Idea Group Inc.)
    701 E. Chocolate Avenue, Suite 200
    Hershey PA 17033
    Tel: 717-533-8845
    Fax: 717-533-8661
    E-mail: cust@idea-group.com
    Web site: http://www.idea-group.com

and in the United Kingdom by
    Idea Group Publishing (an imprint of Idea Group Inc.)
    3 Henrietta Street
    Covent Garden
    London WC2E 8LU
    Tel: 44 20 7240 0856
    Fax: 44 20 7379 3313
    Web site: http://www.eurospan.co.uk

Library of Congress Cataloging-in-Publication Data

e-Human resources management : managing knowledge people / Teresa Torres-Coronas,
Mario Arias-Oliva, editors.
    p. cm.
  Includes bibliographical references and index.
  ISBN 1-59140-435-5 (h/c) -- ISBN 1-59140-436-3 (s/c) -- ISBN 1-59140-437-1 (eISBN)
 1. Personnel management. 2. Information technology--Management. 3. Knowledge
management. I. Torres-Coronas, Teresa, 1966- II. Arias-Oliva, Mario, 1968-
  HF5549.E14 2005
  658.3'00285'4678--dc22
                         2004016385

British Cataloguing in Publication Data
A Cataloguing in Publication record for this book is available from the British Library.

Dedication

As we were writing this preface, Madrid went through one of the worst days in its history. This is why we want to dedicate this book to the memory of those who are no longer with us, to the memory of those who lost their lives in the bomb attack on a train in Madrid on March 11, 2004. They were going to work, struggling to balance work and life; they were part of our human capital; they were inimitable, irreplaceable, and very special assets...they should be here.

e-Human Resources Management:

Managing Knowledge People

Table of Contents

Preface

Aim of This Book

In 1998, a highly innovative film, *Antz*, directed by Eric Darnell and Tim Johnson, was released. In the first scene of the movie, Ant Z 4195 is talking to his psychoanalyst and saying:

"...and my job, don't get me started on, cause it really annoys me...I feel physically inadequate, I, I, my whole life I've never been able to lift 10 times my own body weight and when you get down to it, handling dirt is...yuck, you know is not my idea of a rewarding career. It's this whole gung-ho super-organism thing that I, I, you know I can't get, I try but I can't get it. I mean you know, what is it, I'm supposed to do everything for the colony, and what about my needs, what about me? I mean I gotta believe there's someplace out there that's better than this! Otherwise I'd just curl up in a larva position and weep! The whole system out there just makes me feel...insignificant!"

Z 4195 is striving to reconcile his own individuality with the communal work of the ant colony. Our unhappy and depressed ant is working for a traditional hierarchical organization, where people are not treated as valuable assets and IT systems are not yet implemented. Even worse, he is currently working for an organization that may have neither examined people management practices, nor made a real connection between people and organizational performance. While this behavior is still prevalent in many of today's companies, we are presenting a book about e-HRM, about how IT is changing traditional HRM functions, about how e-HRM practices are implemented. Could this be a paradox? We hope so, because as Junipier (1996) pointed out: "Paradox is an excellent creativity facilitator; it delivers a seismic jolt to dominant ideas, themselves the most efficient suppressor of original thinking" (p. 19). We need creative facilitators to develop the new e-HRM landscape.

The above presents one of our oldest concerns about managing people: Most organizations are far from considering people as their most important asset. They are also far from applying common sense practices such as those to be found in Pfeffer's book, *The Human Equation* (Harvard Business School Press, 1996). These organizations are now entering the knowledge era, using IT solutions to solve their old HRM problems in one out of 10 cases, and in an uncreative way. Those in the world of HRM are being accused of living in an ivory tower, managing the human side of their organizations in ways that lack relevance in the new information era. The impetus for the HRM change comes from recognition of recent developments in the HRM profession and a realization that current practices do not reflect those changes, especially those concerning IT strategies. The problem often results in policies, practices, and strategies that may be outdated.

Organizations are progressively incorporating ITCs into their processes, using different tools and solutions. These tools are applied in a wide variety of ways (i.e., manufacturing resource planning, office automation, computer-supported cooperative work, distributed teams, supply chain, enterprise-wide resource planning, or virtual integration). The entry into service of the first high-capacity transatlantic cable in 1956 and the launch of Sputnik in 1957 marked the beginnings of the era of global information exchange. In 1956, for the first time in history, the number of white-collar workers exceeded that of blue-collar workers (Naisbitt, 1984).

The factor we would stress in this growth in TICs is not the increase in the amount, capacity, or inter-connectivity of technology in organizations. The strategic key lies in the organization's ability to integrate these technologies into their current business processes, and also in their ability to reorganize the said processes (Orlikowski, 1999, p. 3). And this is what this book is all about.

Content of This Book

e-HRM: Managing Knowledge People responds to the challenge of documenting recognizable, innovative, and creative approaches to e-HRM. Its aim is to define and carry forward the debate in a complex and versatile matter.

Future research will continue the process of clarifying and documenting the evolution of e-HRM. In the meantime, however, human resources management researchers, faculty, practitioners, and consultants may find the ideas and experiences offered in this book genuinely helpful and illuminating.

This book is presented in four sections — the first intended to be more general in nature, the following three devoted to specific aspects of the HRM field in the new information era. Section I, *The Cutting-Edge in HRM,* presents an overview of how ITCs are modifying general HRM processes and functions. This is the aim of the first three contributions.

In the first chapter, *Web-Based Organizing in Traditional Brick-and-Mortar Companies: The Impact on HR*, Jaap Paauwe, Elaine Farndale, and Roger Williams, based mostly on their personal experience, focus on how old economy organizations are developing new business models. These models are changing both customers' and suppliers' relationships with the organization and, of course, e-commerce strategy as a whole. With these new models being implemented, the potential implications for HRM need to be explored. The effects of Web-based organizing in HRM, including workers' selection, training and development, learning, trust-building within an organization, and knowledge sharing, among others, are discussed. One relevant conclusion of their analysis is that "internal improvements, necessary for the successful transference of business to the Internet, will enable the HR function to justify its existence in financial terms."

Scott A. Davis and Robert F. Calderón, in their chapter *Integrating Handheld Computer Technology into HR Research and Practice*, present potential applications of handheld computers for HR practice and research. They anticipate major improvements and widespread implementation of wireless networks with resulting implications for worker mobility, availability, and communication. These factors will impact work planning, schedules, conducting meetings, organizational data sharing, and an optimum balance between work and life. Their model, which integrates empirical research and practical knowledge, will be useful for those researchers and practitioners eager to explore handheld computer technology applied to strategic HR planning and management.

Mousumi Bhattacharya and Christopher L. Huntley's chapter, *Social Network Mapping Software: New Frontiers in HRM,* discuss the connections between social network mapping software and the effectiveness of HRM programs. Their study is based upon research into social networks and the effects of these networks on both business processes and HRM. The authors clearly show the uses of information on social networks in HRM processes and what information is generated by social network mapping software (SNMS). They classify the functionality offered by SNMS in the categories of data collection, descriptive modeling, and decision support. They also discuss how each of these functions provides information relevant to different HRM functions.

Section II, *Redesigning HR Administrative Processes*, explains how some HRM functions, such as e-recruitment and developing appropriate systems for employee relationships, are being implemented in the knowledge era.

As hiring qualified employees is a critical organizational decision in the knowledge-based economy, In Lee, in his chapter *E-Recruiting: Categories and Analysis of Fortune 100 Career Web Sites*, analyzes the corporate career Web sites of the Fortune 100 companies. He identifies 33 attributes that characterize corporate career Web sites and groups them into four major areas: recruiting methods, job search tools, job application tools, and information on organizational attributes. Knowing how other organizations are using Web sites to recruit their human capital is a first step towards finding breakthrough ideas for one's own organization.

In the next chapter, *Employee Self-Service HR Portal Case Study: Access, Content, & Application*, Andrew Stein and Paul Hawking examine the development of the human resources (HR) ESS portal. Without any doubt, the added value in this chapter consists of the case studies of three Australian organizations that have implemented an ESS portal. The authors show the information and process focus of these organizations' ESS portals, which are used to place the organizations into Brosche's (2002) portal development model.

Focusing on the development of human resources, Constant D. Beugré's chapter, *Human Resource Portals and the Protean Career: A Three-Factor Model*, develops a three-point model (individual attributes, characteristics of the human resource portals, and organizational factors) to describe the factors in the effective use of Web-based human resource services. On the basis of this model, he argues that the effective use of Web-based human resource services plays an important role in the management of the protean career.

As organizations have started to recognize e-learning as having the power to transform the performance, knowledge, and skills landscape (Gunasekaran, McNeil, & Shaul, 2002, p. 44), Section III, *E-Learning Strategies*, concentrates on the e-training and e-learning world.

Pamela D. Sherer and Timothy Shea, in their chapter *Keeping Up with the Corporate University: Resources for HRM Faculty and Practitioners*, discuss the major factors that influence the growth and role of the corporate university within organizations: in terms of strategy and human resources, knowledge management, and technology and e-learning. They also include in their chapter an annotated compendium of key resources in each of these areas, especially Internet resources. These resources are a good starting point to begin digging deeper into this rapidly changing subject.

E-Learning Strategies of Italian Companies, a chapter by Anna Comacchio and Annachiara Scapolan, is devoted to the empirical study of country-specific e-learning models, focusing on the e-learning experience of Italian companies in the pharmaceutical and banking industries. How are companies implementing e-learning? How are they analyzing the most important features of the e-learning strategies: users, contents, infrastructure, and service and support? The two cases presented will help the reader to answer these questions.

Section IV, *Managing IT and Organizational Changes*, discusses the processes for achieving success when implementing IT solutions within organizations.

In the chapter, *Is Organizational e-Democracy Inevitable? The Impact of Information Technologies on Communication Effectiveness,* Bernadette M. Watson, Gavin M. Schwarz, and Elizabeth Jones consider the relationships between social identity and e-democracy. They also discuss the inevitability of organizational e-democracy in organizations pursuing information technology changes. They investigate perceptions of changes in effective communication during the implementation of organizational change in a hospital. Their findings are discussed in terms of the implications that arise for HR practitioners.

Finally, Joseph Logan, in his chapter *Managing and Practicing OD in an IT Environment: A Structured Approach to Developing IT Project Teams*, outlines a framework for improving success in IT projects by leveraging the organization development (OD) practitioner's expertise in fostering cooperation and learning in teams. In the author's opinion, failures in IT projects are caused by a lack of integration of OD and IT.

In summary, this book's content sets out to highlight the trends in theory and practice which are likely to influence human resource management practices in the IT era, to examine innovative e-HR strategies from a variety of empirical and theory-based perspectives, to provide insightful analysis, and to promote the discovery and dissemination of innovative theories and best practices. But there are important strategic HRM issues missing, such as, for example: e-work and teleworking, the development of new industrial relations models, managing the e-workforce in multinational organizations, e-ethics, or managing values and IT. Of course, some critical reflections on competencies and abilities should have been considered (i.e., IT competencies for an HR manager, e-leadership and e-team skills, e-facilitation and e-coaching, e-trust, or e-creativity — developing skills of creative application of IT on organizations). So, there is still a lot work to do!

The Book's Audience

e-HRM: Managing Knowledge People presents insights gained by leading professionals from the practice, research, and consulting side of the e-HRM field. This book should be useful to a variety of constituencies who are interested in the interrelationships between human resources management and IT, including managers who treat their personnel as a key factor for organizational success, leaders wishing to develop the human side of their organizations, IT experts, human resources managers, researchers, consultants, and practitioners. Each audience may have different levels of interest in the theoretical concepts, practical experiences, and empirical data presented in this book. As we are exploring an evolving discipline, we assume that any of these readers will begin, but not complete, an exploration of the e-HRM new world. Enjoy the reading and enjoy the learning!

References

Brosche, C. (2002). *Designing the corporate portal.* Masters Thesis, Department of Computer Science, University of Gothenburg, Sweden.

Gunasekaran, A., McNeil, R.D., & Shaul, D. (2002). E-learning: Research and applications. *Industrial and Commercial Training, 34*(2), 44-53.

Junipier, D. (1996). Human resource and creativity. *Work Study, 45*(7), 15-22.

Naisbitt (1984). *Megatrends.* New York: Warner Bros.

Orlikowski, W. (1999). The truth is not out there: An enacted view of the digital economy. *Understanding the digital economy—Data, tools, and research.* Washington, DC: U.S. Department of Commerce.

Acknowledgments

With gratitude, love, and respect we thank…

Our publisher, Idea Group Inc., who supported this project and, of course, Jennifer Sundstrom, for her great job during the complex work of editing this book. Both our contributors and reviewers. The contents of this book were made possible because of contributors and the generous cooperation and valuable suggestions given by the reviewers. We are indebted to them for sharing their knowledge with us. All those working to expand and enhance scientific knowledge in the field of human resources management and IT, and who have contributed — and continue to do so — to the development of guidelines to achieve more efficient, effective management.

And last but not least:

To my beloved husband Jordi and my charming sons Arnau and Jordi, who have made my life a fascinating journey. (Teresa's special thanks)

To my wife, Mar, who has always supported me. (Mario's special thanks)

Teresa Torres-Coronas & Mario Arias-Oliva
March 11, 2004

Section I

The Cutting-Edge in HRM

Chapter I

Web-Based Organizing in Traditional Brick-and-Mortar Companies:
The Impact on HR

Jaap Paauwe, Erasmus University Rotterdam, The Netherlands

Elaine Farndale, Erasmus University Rotterdam, The Netherlands

Roger Williams, Erasmus University Rotterdam, The Netherlands

Abstract

This chapter introduces the notion of how old-economy brick-and-mortar firms are adapting their HRM policies and practices and the roles of their HR departments in light of newly introduced Web-based business-to-business transaction practices. It argues that the Internet has introduced three new business models in old-economy companies: the Internet as a marketplace, the Internet as a supply chain integrator, and the Internet as a catalyst for business model redefinition. These innovative ways of organizing are providing HR with opportunities to rise to new challenges and increase their added value to the firm.

Introduction

The so-called new economy has taken a beating over the past few years. The dot.coms have come — and many have gone again. Even the last great hope of the new revolutionary age, Enron, filed for bankruptcy. However, the phenomenon known as the Internet is not going to go away; it just keeps expanding. Slowly but surely more and more individuals and companies are coming to rely on it for doing business. Maybe the changes will be more gradual than originally predicted. But the changes are happening. The purpose of this chapter is to look at some of the possible consequences of these current developments for HR.

The Internet can, of course, be used for different purposes. Through the use of e-mail and similar derivatives, it is a messaging medium par excellence. However, it is more than mere communication: it is also a medium for entertainment and information. Moreover, the Internet can be used as a medium for transactions, for buying and selling. Although all applications have implications for the utilization of an organization's human resources, this chapter concentrates on the area likely to impinge closest on most organizations: the medium of *transactions*.

The largest growth in transactions using the Internet has been in the area of transactions between businesses; the so-called business-to-business (B2B) sector. Since the end of the 1990s when global e-commerce was worth a little more than $150 billion (*The Economist*, February 26, 2000), the growth rate has slowed, but is still continuing strongly. Forrester (www.forrester.com), a respected research organization in the field, expects this sector to reach $7 trillion or 27% of total U.S. trade by 2006. It is hard to know how seriously to take such a dramatic prediction, but major growth in this area — despite the downturn both in the world economy in general and in Internet-related stocks in particular — seems inevitable.

One particular area of growth in B2B transactions is taking place in old-economy firms. These companies are involved in transactions within the new economy in different ways. Firstly, they can invest in and even take over new economy companies. Secondly, they can start up their own subsidiaries to operate within the new economy. Thirdly, *they can attempt to incorporate the new economy into their old-economy organization.* It is this third area that is probably most interesting from the point of view of the utilization of human resources. This is because old-economy companies, which start up their own new economy companies, normally run them as separate entities. Clearly financial reasons play an important part in this decision, but so do organizational considerations. New economy companies may require a different organizational structure and culture than the parent company, and hence running new economy companies as separate entities minimizes any possible cross-contamination from the new to the old or vice versa. However, when old-economy companies attempt to integrate business-to-business e-commerce into their existing organization, solving the problems that arise can provide new challenges and opportunities in HRM. It is on this third way of organizing that this chapter concentrates.

Because this B2B growth area is concentrated in old-economy companies that are the majority employers, it is likely to have a significant impact on HRM. Most HR professionals are still concentrated in these medium-sized and large, old-economy companies, and this is where the HR function is subject to radical and dramatic change because of the implications of Web-based organizing. The new economy start-ups, those still around, hardly use the HR function in spite of the proclaimed importance of their people to their success. This chapter therefore focuses on the consequences of Web-based B2B transactions in medium-sized and large, old-economy companies, and discusses the implications for HRM and HR professionals.

However, before we begin our exploration, we will give an overview of the striking characteristics that distinguish Web-based transactions from more traditional transactions. We will then continue with a discussion of the different ways in which old-economy companies are attempting to integrate elements of Web-based organizing into their current business and the resultant implications for HRM. We must remark though that there is a lack of reliable information about this whole area. Most publications at the time of writing have been based more on personal experience than research and tend to focus on the same few companies that are often not only reorganizing to accommodate the new Internet economy, but are also intimately involved in selling equipment or services related to it. This chapter is therefore based on personal experience of working in the field, interviews with others more experienced than us, and a review of the available literature sources.

The Effect of the Internet on Business Transactions

The Internet is having a major impact on business transactions because of the different opportunities it offers. A number of significant differences distinguish transactions using electronic markets from what has gone before. These include the opportunities for global sourcing and selling, mass-customization, and networking (Timmers, 1999). By lowering the costs of transactions and information, technology has reduced market frictions and provided a significant impetus to the process of broadening world markets (Greenspan, 2000). This means that considerations about where to locate become secondary, whereas price competition increases. Internet technologies also allow specification design and pricing online, which again increases price competition. This facilitates meeting customer needs, often through a network of multiple business partners able to deliver value more quickly and cheaply direct to the customer. Experts have argued that transactions using e-commerce come far closer to the economists' ideal of perfect competition than transactions using traditional media, as barriers to entry are lowered, transaction costs are reduced, and buyers have improved access to information (see Shapiro & Varian, 1999; Wyckoff, 1997).

There are three main responses to the developments in business-to-business transactions via the Internet being observed (Wright & Dyer, 2000):

- **E-commerce:** buying and selling via the Internet;

- **Supply chain integration:** collaboration throughout the total value chain; and

- **Fully integrated e-business:** internal and external integration sharing real-time information (resulting in 'bricks-and-clicks' or 'clicks-and-mortar' hybrid organizations).

Wright and Dyer also identify a fourth derivative, enterprise resource planning (ERP), however this focuses on developing an intranet for internal integration within a firm, and less on relationships between businesses. Here we shall focus on the three B2B outcomes identified.

Firstly, the Internet is seen as an extension of normal market channels for buying and selling. In this approach, companies primarily use the Internet in order to improve the quality and speed of customer service, and as a medium to buy and sell more products or services cheaper. Thus for every business, the Internet — at the very least — offers opportunities for reducing operating cost levels and enhancing service levels (Venkatraman, 2000).

The second way in which old-economy companies attempt to integrate the new economy is by using the Internet to expand and improve their current collaborative relationships among their key suppliers; the Internet can encourage close integration between the partners through total value chain integration (Timmers, 1999), establishing virtual marketplaces within the supply chain primarily to reduce transaction costs.

Finally, the third approach, which is much more fundamental, requires that old-economy organizations totally rethink their business models before deciding on their e-commerce and supply chain strategies. This approach requires management to re-examine why customers buy from them, look at all stages in the processes involved, and consider how the Internet could impact each stage of the processes. Then, if necessary, new business models can be developed to fully integrate the new economy principles. This implies organizational revolution.

Alongside this rise in e-business, there is a lack of reliable data on the people issues arising from a move from a traditional brick-and-mortar business model to an e-business model. The changes however imply a need to learn to use these new technologies and to embrace a climate of constant change. Some specific outcomes might be a need to adopt more aggressive recruitment campaigns to attract the necessary technical staff when competing against the dynamic dot.coms. There may also be a resultant culture clash when the new 'techies' join the company on high salaries, compared with existing non-technical staff, which might lead to resentment and perceived unfair treatment.

In a review of the potential implications, Wright and Dyer (2000) have suggested six broad HRM principles in response to the issues e-business is raising:

1. The company should promote individual autonomy and personal accountability at all levels of the organization through the process of work design, to make the company more flexible to change.

2. Shared organizational vision and values should be reinforced through HRM policies and practices, particularly recruitment and training, to maintain a sense of community in times of change.

3.　The company needs to ensure employees understand the business strategy and context so that they can see where they fit into the whole. This can be achieved through communication, participation, training, and performance-linked reward in particular.

4.　There is a need to develop a learning organization, sharing the responsibility jointly between employees and the company to keep competency levels at the leading edge.

5.　It is also important to develop a sense of belonging, trust, support, and commitment throughout the organization. This entails arranging appropriate induction, providing access to information, investing in employee development, being a responsible employer with regard to work-life balance, and being honest regarding job security.

6.　And ultimately, rewards must be provided which are perceived to be commensurate with the effort applied.

These implications could be argued to apply across multiple types of organization; however, we explore these implications in detail in the context of the e-business model throughout this chapter. Each of the three responses to the Internet economy is now explored in turn, shedding further light on the major changes taking place in both HRM practices and within the HR department.

Companies Buying and Selling on the Internet

The first major developments in this area started in the mid-1990s and saw major U.S. firms such as Wal-Mart and General Electric moving to buying and selling online to cut costs and speed supplies. The aims of cutting paperwork and time may have been simple, but the results were impressive (see Box 1).

The initial rapid spread of business exchanges was followed by a realization by many large customers that if they combined their individual buying power with that of their large competitors into a separate buying and selling exchange, then this might have a major effect on their procurement costs. For example, General Motors, Ford, Daimler Chrysler, and Renault-Nissan merged their individual exchanges in 2000 to create Covisint, a virtual marketplace for the automotive industry. Later they were also joined by PSA Peugeot Citroen. In 2001, Covisint handled procurement transactions worth more than $45 billion (*Financial Times*, November 13, 2001), and in 2003, the Covisint user base expanded by 178% (*www.covisint.com*). Covisint provides the global motor industry with a common connection to its suppliers and customers based on common business processes, reducing costs, increasing efficiency, enhancing quality, and improving time-to-market.

Large companies can use the Internet for buying and selling to put themselves at the center of new e-business eco-systems that transform their way of doing business and their way of organizing. The interconnectivity demanded externally influences how the company is organized. For example, order-taking systems have to be made very customer-friendly and closely linked with planning and production systems in order to ensure just-in-time delivery and zero stocks. Hence we might expect the marketing function to increase in status and power at the expense of the sales function, as customer relationships become more important and more and more direct sales are taken over by the Internet.

Procurement will also have to be online to ensure adequate supplies. Closer links within the whole administrative system will also be required to ensure that, as far as possible, the whole paper chain from order to invoice to payment should proceed automatically. Finally, logistics and distribution must also be linked to the system, as delivery windows agreed with customers have to be met. These functions are thus also likely to gain in status and importance. But what of the impact on the HR function?

Box 1. GE saves time and costs by using the Internet

GE has built up a trading process network, which is a Web-based link to suppliers so that they can bid for GE components' contracts. This global supplier network links 1,500 corporate buyers and around 16,000 suppliers. According to information issued by GE in 2000, the system cut procurement cycles in half, processing costs by one-third and the cost of goods purchased by between five and 50% (*The Economist*, March 4, 2000). Every GE company now has targets for e-auctioning of around 60-70% of total spending, and this e-procurement model is applied not only to indirect spending, but to many services as well (*Financial Times*, December 5, 2001). Indeed GE's CEO, Jeff Imelt, has been reported as going even further in suggesting that his managers should either digitalize or outsource all parts of their business that do not touch the customer directly (Useem & Watson, 2001).

Implications for HRM

The implications for the HR function of large companies doing business through e-hubs have not been as immediate as those observed for the marketing and distribution functions discussed earlier, but they are becoming clearer. Many Western-economy companies need to lower their costs as global competition increases from developing countries with lower operating costs. In order to avoid being classified as just another commodity supplier, they also have to endeavor to add unique value by being able to offer exceptional levels of customer service and customized products and services.

Companies aiming to reduce costs, while at the same time increasing flexibility and speed of response to customer wishes, are forced to adopt innovative practices. These new practices fall under three broad headings:

- the introduction of flexible working practices to meet flexible production requirements;
- an agile production approach, focusing on minimizing buffers and concentrating on a just-in-time supply approach; and
- globalization of the marketplace and workforce.

An overview of each approach is presented next.

Flexible Working Practices

Introducing flexibility to the working practices of a company can have multiple meanings in different contexts (Brewster et al., 2001). Cost savings can be achieved by matching working hours as closely as possible to fluctuations in supply and demand. This can also improve productivity by enabling people to work the hours that suit them, often leading to lower levels of absence among employees. Long-term uncertainty for the company can be reduced by focusing on non-permanent employment contracts and external resourcing arrangements. Companies are also offering new patterns of working to tap into areas of the labor market previously ignored where essential skills and manpower are available. Further flexibility can be achieved by renegotiating the range of tasks existing employees are expected to undertake. Finally, in order to reduce uncertainty for the company, flexible forms of financial reward linking individual and company performance enable salary costs to represent financial performance more closely.

The extent to which each of these practices is adopted relates largely to the organizational context: the company's strategic choices, the norms within the sector, and the national level regulations and standards in force. For example, decisions regarding the introduction of such schemes as profit sharing or share options are most commonly closely related to the tax laws within a country. There may also be regulations through employment law or standards across a sector regarding the type of contracts a company is able to issue.

A final warning regarding the introduction of more flexible working practices involves the notion of a company creating a core and periphery workforce (Atkinson & Meager, 1986). The core consists of those employees on traditional permanent contracts, while all those on non-standard contracts make up the periphery. Extra attention needs to be paid on how the company manages this form of organization: how it communicates with employees who are not present throughout the week, how it motivates periphery employees so that they do not feel like second-class employees, and how people working non-standard hours are actually supervised. All these challenges raise new issues for the HR department to master.

Agile Production Techniques

Cost and quality issues have dominated production manufacturing environments throughout the last decade, resulting in the idea of lean manufacturing emanating from practices in place in the Japanese motor industry in particular (McCurry & McIvor, 2002). Characteristics of lean manufacturing include integrated production flow, low inventory, quality enhancement, flexible working practices, a problem-solving focus, and flat organization structures. These have led to linked HRM practices in the form of high performance work systems (HPWSs). These high performance or high involvement HRM systems focus on four core practices: employee development, flexible job design in terms of employee participation and teamwork, incentive-based payment systems, and investment in recruitment and selection (Boselie & Dietz, 2003). Team-based organizational change programs (such as 6 Sigma, Quality Circles, and TQM) have also been associated with this approach to HRM. These programs emphasize process management, customer focus, organizational learning, and self-managed teams (Wood, 1999). However, the literature is not unequivocal to the benefits of lean production, and criticism of the original Japanese approach has been voiced (Cusumano, 1994).

More recently, attention has switched to developing an agile production system. Lean production systems were seen as limiting innovation (McCurry & McIvor, 2002), which is undesirable in the fast-moving B2B transaction world. More attention is paid under the agile model of production to readiness for change and forming virtual partnerships. Agility is described as focusing on customer rather than market needs, mass customization rather than mass or lean production (Sharp, Irani, & Desai, 1999). This means that agility entails more than just the production system — it is a holistic approach incorporating technical, information, and human resource considerations. In essence, an agile production system implies a very fast and efficient adaptive learning organization, encouraging multi-skilling, empowerment, and reconfigurable teams. Under such a system, HRM practices focus particularly on employee development, the encouragement of learning, and knowledge management. These issues are discussed further in the following section, exploring in more depth the virtual partnerships being formed within the e-business community.

Globalization

Finally, as a further outcome of the globalization of the marketplace, we might also expect to see a globalization of the potential workforce for companies involved in e-commerce. The apparent boundaries between countries appear to be lowering, and as opportunities for buying and selling products and services across these boundaries increase, new opportunities for international expansion or the hiring-in of non-home country nationals who have a better understanding of international markets might be expected to occur. This means the introduction of international HRM practices, a new area of expertise for HR professionals used to operating in a single country. The national culture and institutions — including laws, standards, and common practice for the different countries — need to be considered alongside any international business strategy to ensure effective HRM (Harris, Brewster, & Sparrow, 2003).

Implications for the HR Department

To meet the need for cost savings and improved speed of service, there is an obvious need for better, faster, and smarter HR solutions. Alongside a requirement for a broadening of the expertise portfolio of HR professionals to cover flexible working practices, high performance work systems, and globalization issues, there is also a demand for increased flexibility of systems, providing more services online, streamlining administration, and supporting the process-driven work systems environment.

HR has for a long time been locked into transactional activities (administration) and traditional activities (such as recruitment, selection, and training) which take up the majority of time (Wright & Dyer, 2000). Many HR departments are so bogged down in such activities that they have no time for higher value-added services such as knowledge management, culture management, and strategic redirection and renewal. However, information technology is changing things. Transactional tasks are now largely carried out using IT systems either in-house or outsourced. Traditional and transformational activities are also gradually moving this way with the increasing introduction of e-enabled delivery of HR (e-HRM), saving more cost and time with online recruitment and training systems in particular. This e-HRM trend appears to be set to continue in the context of the Internet/intranet business model (Ruël, Bondarouk, & Looise, 2003). This point of view is, needless to say, shared by those who supply such e-HRM systems and who predict that Employee Relations Management (ERM) packages market will be a best seller (Siebel, 2001).

The resultant impact of e-HRM on the roles of HR professionals has been explored by Van den Bos and Methorst (2004) in relation to the roles of Ulrich's (1997) well-known model that divides out people and process-oriented activities, and operational and strategic activities. The use of IT to support operational processes can increase the amount of information available to people by providing online access to HRM policy and practice handbooks. Strategic processes can be streamlined through online notification of events such as holiday or sickness, and online selection of options such as training course registration and cafeteria-style benefit systems. Internet- or intranet-based operational activities focusing on people can facilitate collaboration between individuals through discussion groups, video-conferencing, and communities of practice, as well as giving people the opportunity to carry out their work at remote locations through tele-working facilities. Finally, at the strategic level, e-HRM can be applied to help people be constantly ready for change, encouraging online training and learning activities, as well as 360° feedback systems and internal vacancy application systems.

Hansen and Deimler (2001) describe such an e-HRM system as a fully integrated B2E (business-to-employee) enterprise portal. This form of realizing major cost reductions has already been undertaken by a number of large organizations such as Cisco Systems, Coca-Cola Co., and Delta Air. These B2E systems combine traditional e-HRM with online business processes (employee interaction, information searches, work scheduling) and community services (balancing work and home life by allowing people to deal with certain personal tasks at work, for example, discount deals and services through different companies).

Implementing e-HRM does however require difficult decisions to be made regarding the extent to which the new systems should be outsourced to gain the relevant expertise and cost-savings, and the required balance between techno-logical and personal service delivery (Van den Bos & Methorst, 2004). In order to realize potential savings, the company also needs to ensure its managers and employees understand the benefits of the new system and are actually prepared to use it; this is an important task for HR to adopt to ensure successful implementation.

Virtual Supply Chain Communities

Another way in which old-economy companies are reacting to the new challenges and opportunities posed by the growth of business-to-business transactions using the Internet is either to set up or join supply chain commu-nities. Such communities are most commonly a vertical chain of all the key suppliers involved in servicing one major customer.

The supply chain is a major cost to companies, accounting for 60-80% of many companies' total costs (Bovet & Martha, 2000). It is therefore logical for companies to focus on extracting greater value from these operations. The ultimate aim of any manufacturer is to build-to-order and not to carry stock, since the financial savings are potentially massive. This goal has probably only been attained by a few companies such as Dell Computers and Cisco Systems (see Box 2) (Hartman & Sifonis, 2000). However, it has been reported that although it takes on average between 60 and 100 days to make a car and deliver it to the customer, manufacturers such as General Motors and Toyota are planning systems to bring this down to five days (*The Economist*, January 8, 2000). Cutting cycle time to this extent will result in taking around 50% out of overall inventory for car manufacturers. With at least $20 billion in parts on hand at any one time to support assembly systems, the savings on carrying costs

Box 2. Cisco Systems' total value chain integration

Cisco Systems is a classic example of a manufacturer using a total value supply chain network. Cisco develops and manufactures high performance networking products that link geographically dispersed local and wide area networks. The company has created an elaborate web of partners on the Internet, including manufacturers, assemblers, distributors, original equipment manufacturer strategic partners, and sales channels. Products are conceived, designed, developed, manufactured, sold, serviced, and enhanced from multiple locations all on the Web. Cisco transfers its strategic knowledge (customer requirements and company strategy) and product knowledge assets to its strategic partners. In return Cisco receives system design input and planning knowledge from these partners. With Cisco's active encouragement, participants lubricate the system by freely exchanging knowledge and opinions. This community enables dramatically lower product cycle times, reduced costs, and fast innovation. Cisco's value network is drenched in intangible value exchanges that create its strategic advantage in the market (Tapscott, 1999).

alone could add up to several hundred million dollars per year (*The Economist*, August 26, 2000).

If an organization is to be successful in becoming a member of a virtual supply chain community, it will have to maintain the high performance work systems we mentioned in the last section, while continuing to develop in other areas as well. There needs to be a balance between the rationality and order resulting from the HPWS techniques, and a willingness to constantly consider change and implement innovation quickly as in the agile production model discussed earlier. This balance is difficult for any organization to achieve, yet it is not impossible. For example, the definitive study of why Toyota was able to achieve such a dominant position in the world automotive market concluded that this balance was the major reason for its success (Fujimoto, 1999).

It is obvious that such fundamental change requires innovation not just in a firm's own systems, but also in its whole supply chain. Web-based links need to be formed between both internal departments and suppliers and customers right through the chain. It also means integrating the whole value chain into virtual business communities (Timmers, 1999), virtual value chains (Rayport & Sviolka, 1995), or value nets (Bovet & Martha, 2000) depending on the preferred terminology.

Close and trusting collaboration between partners is essential in such a chain. No business involved can afford to have even one weak link in the chain because, increasingly, a firm's competitiveness does not depend on its own resources and capabilities alone, but is decided through its ability to mobilize its whole value chain. Hence, it is value chains rather than businesses that are competing against each other (Cool, 1997). In a virtual supply chain community, the relationship between partners will be one of collaboration, based on long-term relationships and joint involvement in new product development. Such value chain collaboration is critically dependent on affiliation, loyalty, and trust (Van Alstyne, 1997).

The ability to consider change and innovation in the context of a virtual supply chain is thus complex. It requires the development and maintenance of *a climate of trust* between network partners, both internally and externally. *Learning* both at individual and at organizational levels will also have to be of a high order in order to facilitate the necessary continuous improvement and innovation. Developing and supporting both trust relationships and a learning climate simultaneously thus appears to be the crucial competence required by companies.

The academic literature on trust among individuals has a distinguished history and, recently, the high incidence of mergers, alliances, joint ventures, and outsourcing interesting work has also been carried out at the organizational level (e.g., Blois, 1999; Child & Faulkner, 1998).

A major reason why trust is important in the context of a virtual supply chain is as a possible governing device. Traditionally the most popular governing device in relations between customer and supplier has been the legal contract. Unfortunately, legal contracts rely on being able to prescribe what should happen in all possible eventualities for their effectiveness. Thus, the more unpredictable the situation, the less effective any legal contract will be (Nooteboom, 2000). Virtual supply chains, in particular, operate within unpredictable dynamic situations. If a partner relies on methods of governance other than legal formality, this sends a clear message to the other partner; therefore, to trust someone or something is to accept risk, vulnerability, and uncertainty. It is not a state to be entered into lightly. Nevertheless, a relationship of trust can be economically sensible because the opposite — mistrust — may, in fact, add to the transaction costs involved in a relationship.

There are important distinctions in organizational trust between technical or competence trust, and intentional or motivational trust (Nooteboom, 1996). These distinctions are somewhat similar to those made by McAllister (1995) who, at the individual level, has split trust into cognition-based and affect-based trust. Cognition-based trust is related to confidence in the partners' technical work-related abilities, whereas affect-based trust is primarily dependent upon a personal emotional relationship. Partners will seek to heighten both kinds of trust so that the relative value of the partnership is raised, thus increasing the switching costs that would be incurred by moving to a different partner.

Cognition-based trust affects individuals at a transactional level. If a partner proves incapable of doing the job, delivering as promised on time, quality, and price, then a mistake has been made in assessing their technical capacity; however, there has been no personal betrayal. Affect-based trust on the other hand involves individuals personally. They feel a sense of personal loss if they can no longer work together. If this affect-based trust is broken, then the deep emotion of betrayal is felt. Affect-based trust thus takes a long time to develop but is more resilient. As Braunschvig (1998) has pointed out, alliances between individuals and groups develop more intensely in an unstructured situation, such as a virtual supply network, than in a clear command and control environment.

Implications for HRM

This new emphasis on trust relationships between organizations needs similar trust relations to be encouraged among managers within organizations. As the organization becomes less hierarchical and structured, so the manager's role changes. As a consequence of having to trust people to perform to the best of their abilities, managers have to become facilitators, creating the conditions under which employees can and want to give optimum performance. This clearly poses a major challenge for HR to support managers in these new roles.

Given our earlier discussion of creating a more flexible workforce to meet production and service requirements, the issue of trust is particularly pertinent, as this is becoming the key mechanism (rather than control) required for managing a workforce that is more dispersed in both location and time (Handy, 1995).

In attempting to develop a climate of trust, certain bundles of HRM practices can be adopted to support such an endeavor. For example, Whitener (1997) emphasizes the issues around the psychological contract between the employee and employer: alongside explicit contractual obligations such as appropriate pay and benefits in return for work carried out, there are other developmental and emotional obligations relating to job security, training and development, loyalty, commitment, and meeting promises such as overtime or support.

The level of trust and respect individuals have for their immediate supervisor also influences perceptions of justice and fairness, for example, in performance management systems. It is important to create systems that support both procedural and interactional justice, providing sufficient feedback and appeal opportunities, as well as treating people fairly and consistently. These are all skills that supervisors at different levels within the company need to be able to master, alongside the creation of appropriate HRM policies. The wording of such policies also reveals a company's attitude towards its employees and the levels of trust it is displaying; for example, an overemphasis on control and monitoring systems in policy documents can undermine any attempt to build trust relationships by individuals (Shockley-Zalabak, Ellis, & Winograd, 2000).

Other ways of facilitating trust in the work environment include focusing people's attention on small groups of workers with whom they work on a regular basis, such as through teamwork, to foster trusting relationships and encourage membership of a community (Handy, 1995). Particularly during times of extensive change, as we will discuss in the following section, a company needs to monitor trust levels among employees to anticipate how people are likely to react to the changes being introduced (Shockley-Zalabak et al., 2000).

Finally, considering briefly the other key aspect of supply chain integration, namely *innovation*, a company needs to focus on developing HRM practices that encourage organizational learning. However, learning both within and between organizations has proven difficult to manage. Many organizations are still struggling to realize any value from knowledge exploitation (Grimshaw, Breu, & Myers, 2002). And as Seely Brown and Duguid (2000) point out, experience has shown that knowledge and best practice is hard to disseminate even within the same organization, let alone along a supply chain, unless very closely guided and encouraged.

Although creating learning experiences from explicit knowledge sources is relatively straightforward, to acquire learning from the tacit knowledge held by individuals is more challenging. To learn most effectively, individuals must have sufficient prior knowledge to be able to understand the complexities of a new situation. Otherwise they will be slow to process and retain new facts and concepts because they will lack an ability to interpret and classify information based on pre-existing schemas and frameworks (Cohen & Levinthal, 1990). In other words, one must belong to a world in order to know it (Baumard, 1999). Immersion in the appropriate practice is thus the best way to gain access to this tacit knowledge.

In addition to creating a learning organization, other HRM practices can also be useful to encourage a culture of innovation. For example, reward and performance evaluation systems can be devised to encourage rather than punish risk-taking. Suggestion schemes can also be introduced for individuals to put forward their ideas on how processes might be improved, regardless of their position in the company. These activities — in combination with an environment that encourages knowledge sharing, learning, and development — can significantly improve a company's creative talent.

Implications for the HR Department

In practical terms for the HR department, guiding and encouraging knowledge exchange both within and between organizations can be considered a three-stage process (Seely Brown & Duguid, 2000). The first stage is to find out where interesting experience might be available. HR departments have a role to play in identifying organizations to which their own company can relate, which have useful experience in facing and overcoming the issues in which they are interested. So if the corporate aim is to develop and maintain more trusting relationships with suppliers and customers, HR needs to be aware of other relevant organizations from whose experience they could learn. The second stage is then gaining access to this experience through collaborative discussions, and the third stage is deciding if and how the experience can be exploited to fit the company's situation. The latter can best be done through setting up communities of practice, that is, bringing together similar people with similar interests facing similar problems.

A typical example of how the HR function might operate in this context would be as follows. The company aim is to switch a portion of its current investment in R&D to more venture capital type activities; it aims to take stakes in or take over young start-up companies with innovative ideas and technologies relevant to the basic business, instead of trying to grow them in house. However, the success rate of mergers and acquisitions is known to be low, and especially troublesome are takeovers where the objective is obtaining technological expertise (*The Economist*, August 5, 2000). So the company wants to learn how to improve its success rate in this important field.

Knowing, for example, that Cisco Systems has been practicing for some time a highly successful strategy based on growing primarily through acquisitions, many of which have been small innovative start-ups, and that much of this information about the Cisco approach is in the public domain, this would be a good starting point for HR to explore. For example, Bunnell (2000, pp. 64-76) outlines the Cisco acquisition process in some detail, showing the importance of the many different systems used. But no story, however well told, can cover the whole situation. In order to fill out the total picture, contact needs to be made between relevant individuals in both companies: the learner and the example company. Relevant individuals need to be able to talk with their equivalents, thus forming a community of practice. And it is of course the development of precisely such communities that has been facilitated by the growth of the Internet (Seely Brown & Duguid, 2000). The HR department thus has a powerful role to play in the development of organizational learning.

The moves we have outlined above towards a new balance between innovation, trust, and learning on the one hand and new forms of discipline and control on the other will not be easy. They will require a refocusing of role for HR professionals. HR roles have been widely discussed (see for a current over-view: Paauwe, 2004), but one of the most well known is Ulrich's (1997) model of four roles, namely strategic partner, change agent, administrative expert, and employee champion. However, these roles are not independent of each other. For example, both change agency and high-level strategic advice are required in converting a company from traditional supply chain processes to those immersed in the virtual supply chain economy. This becomes clear if we think, for example, about people in positions of power who have achieved their status through competence and expertise relevant to different aspects of the value chain. Moving to a virtual chain means that the power structure will have to be dismantled and rearranged. Therefore, institutionalized systems and extant political power structures are likely to resist change. We discuss in further detail the implications of managing this significant change situation for the HR department in the following section.

Organizational Revolution

The third and final possible reaction of old-economy companies to the growth of the Internet economy which we will discuss here is for the company to step back and reassess how the Internet might affect its business. Schwartz (1997) indeed argues that the major opportunities posed by the Internet economy lie first in de-constructing the value chain in order subsequently to reassemble it, if necessary with new roles and new business actors. Companies are thus being counseled to rethink the strategic fundamentals of their business.

For example, it is argued that information defines existing supplier relationships (Evans & Wurster, 1997); having a relationship means that two or more companies in a supply chain have established certain channels of communication and information. However, the economics of information are changing. The Internet enables this information to be unbundled from its physical carrier, hence reaching a wider community very cheaply. This has the potential to undermine established value chains. Many companies thus need to rethink their information strategies fundamentally — a process that often results in unraveling vertically integrated value chains.

What a company needs to examine is how transacting its business using the Internet might help add new forms of value to the company. Rethinking thus starts with the customer. It involves going right back to the fundamental value proposition and understanding what motivates end-customers to buy from the company and not from the competition. Once this is established, all aspects of the organization must be analyzed, such as the goods or services offered, the key business processes, the financial and human resources required, the organizational structures, and the major systems and procedures. These are the building blocks that can be redesigned, added to, and reconfigured to transform the value proposition using the new opportunities offered by the Internet.

The need for this radical rethinking of strategy and unraveling of vertically integrated value chains is particularly high in distributive networks (Tapscott, Ticoll, & Lowy, 2000). Distributive networks use mediating technologies to facilitate exchanges across time and space (Stabell & Fjeldstad, 1998). Hence they are the key organizations supporting business transactions via the Internet; they allocate and deliver goods — be it information, objects, money, or other resources — from providers to users (see Box 3).

In Europe, distributive networks such as power companies, postal and telecommunications services, and railways used to be government-regulated monopolies. They reflected a physical capital asset-based mindset — a view that to deliver value to a customer, the company should own its entire value chain. In the case of electricity supply, this would incorporate generating facilities, transmission lines, local distribution networks, and access to end-customers. Rethinking the strategy by concentrating on the opportunities and threats posed by transactions using the Internet raises opportunities for redefining the generation, transmission, and marketing businesses. This process

Box 3. The transformation of a distributive network: Federal Express

Federal Express started life in 1971 as a transportation company using trucks and roads to deliver goods. As early as 1979 it was using a centralized computer system to manage people, packages, vehicles, and weather scenarios in real time. Following a name change to FedEx in 1994, it has since moved further ahead into the Internet age. In late 1998, FedEx decided that its physical distribution system of trucks and airplanes was less valuable than its Internet-worked information resources: its digital capital was gaining value over its physical capital. FedEx decided to focus on value-added context services like online package tracking and logistics outsourcing and leave the actual driving jobs to outsourcers; hence, the company began selling its transport network, marshalling a web of truck and air transporters to handle the physical delivery. In the process, it created a $16 billion transportation powerhouse (www.fedex.com).

is currently underway in a number of countries, with one resultant international initiative being the setting up of an electronic marketplace for the utilities industry, Eutilia, similar in nature to that of Covisint in the automotive industry discussed earlier.

It is clear that business model redefinition can be a radical revolution. Thus, despite the enthusiasm with which some consultants propagate it, it is a high-risk strategy, as Enron found out to its cost. However, for some businesses, doing nothing may mean a higher long-term risk. The key to success for high-risk strategy such as value proposition redefinition lies in the way the whole process of redefinition and subsequent repositioning of the business is managed. This is likely to be a highly threatening organizational change process, leaving many managers and employees facing an unpredictable future in comparison to the relative security to which they were accustomed.

Such redefinition can be a highly threatening exercise for employees, and particularly senior management. These people may need strong encouragement before they are willing to undertake such an exercise. For example, in 1999, GE recruited an estimated 100 external top e-commerce experts to be used as 'black belts' or team leaders of a program entitled, "Destroy Your Own Business" (Floyd, 2002). These teams were set up in every GE business unit with the objective of redefining how the Internet could be used to annihilate the unit's mainstream business. The task proved very difficult. Many units were run by senior managers who, for years, had successfully run businesses under pre-Internet conditions. Such individuals often had little understanding of e-commerce, and had difficulty envisioning any positive impact of the Internet on their thriving businesses.

Implications for HRM

Employee-employer relationships are constantly changing as companies are forced to cut costs and hence often headcount in achieving revolutionary change. Organizational commitment and loyalty is being undermined, yet we have already seen the importance of developing trust-based relationships within the workplace if a company is to survive in the new economy. This is proving a major challenge for HR departments, resulting in a need for change management activities to be very carefully planned, implemented, and monitored to ensure as smooth as possible transition from a traditional brick-and-mortar culture to a new e-business environment.

Balogun and Hope Hailey (2004) in their book exploring strategic change emphasize the importance of having an understanding of the organization climate and culture, and the current attitude of employees and management in order to assess the best way to tackle revolutionary change. Employee surveys are an appropriate means of looking at issues such as the clarity of corporate strategy and sharing of common values, communication and feedback processes, levels of trust and perceived organizational justice, employee commitment, and organizational readiness and flexibility for change. Appropriate HRM practices can then be implemented to encourage desired behavior and performance in the new e-business environment, based on the enablers and constraints to change identified in the current culture.

In this revolutionary situation, maximizing human resources will, however, not only depend on the effectiveness of organizational change programs. It will also depend on individuals being able to capitalize upon the major opportunities that such a revolutionary situation can bring for management and individual development, and hence the company's HR assets.

Managers learn most, not from any classroom-based course, but rather from their own practical experience, particularly in new situations. Learning experiences can include such activities as cross-boundary movement, being involved in task forces or special projects, managing a downsizing operation, or switching from a series of staff jobs to being a line manager. As long as the situation is important and is new, then learning will be optimal (McCall, 1988). The process and outcomes of the business model redefinition process described above will be a totally novel situation for most of the managers involved. It is clear that this process can have major potential for individual development. Therefore, the choice of who is to take part in such an exercise is extremely

Box 4. Four roles of HR in the knowledge economy (Lengnick-Hall & Lengnick-Hall, 2002)

Human Capital Steward

HR can act as a facilitator in partnership with employees with the aim of achieving the highest return possible on the company's human capital investments. Human capital goes beyond task-related knowledge, skills, and abilities to include general life experiences, social skills, values, beliefs, and attitudes. As such, individuals need to be guided and facilitated rather than controlled and dominated. The HR department needs to lose the policing or paternalistic role to encourage individual voluntary contribution. Given human capital's value to the organization, and that it is both unique and perishable, appropriate strategies for hiring, training, retaining, and removing need to be adopted, including the encouragement of innovation and flexibility.

Knowledge Facilitator

The HR department has a role to play in facilitating both knowledge capital (held in explicit and implicit sources) and knowledge flows. This can be achieved by promoting an understanding and value of knowledge management, creating knowledge sharing and usage expectations. Other strategies include schemes for continuous learning and brokering knowledge exchange. An overhaul of existing appraisal and compensation practices may be required to support the desired knowledge management behaviors. Furthermore, the HR department needs to encourage the organization to change its behavior in light of what it learns.

Relationship Builder

The focus here lies on managing relationships between individuals and groups both internal and external to the organization to enhance social capital across the total value chain. However, relationships are complex, requiring multiple dimensions to be considered, including: rapport (trust, respect, empathy), bonding (collaboration), breadth (scope, range of transactions), and affinity (interest, attraction). Appropriate HRM strategies for building such relationships include cross-functional teamwork, intra- and inter-organizational communication, inter-unit resource exchange, and inter-firm learning.

Rapid Deployment Specialist

As firm competitiveness is increasingly dependent on speed, the HR department needs to take responsibility for the development of flexible human capital resources with an emphasis on adaptability, tolerance, and capacity to learn. This means creating human capital configurations that can rapidly be assembled, deployed, and disassembled to meet the needs of fluid work assignments. This entails the encouragement of appropriate employee attitudes, team behavior, and values that support flexibility, adaptability, and creativity. Employees must be encouraged to self-organize, and be capable of working in situations of crisis, stress, and uncertainty. A culture of widespread sharing of organizational information and team-working is essential to achieve these aims.

important, not just from a business point of view, but also from a human resource development perspective. So what are the implications for HR professionals of this revolutionary change process?

Implications for the HR Department

A major implication for the HR function in a business model redefinition situation is probably the sea of change of the department's own function. Traditionally, the HR function has focused on delivering almost perfect quality HR systems and services to the organization (Wright & Dyer, 2000). To do so has required that they spend considerable amounts of time gathering and analyzing information, garnering political support, and soliciting input from multiple sources at each stage in the development process.

To reach such perfection takes a long time and a great deal of labor. It is hardly surprising therefore that Wright and colleagues (1999) found that the design and implementation of HR systems takes on average between 18 and 20 months. Given the rapid pace of the almost permanent change involved in any organization revolution situation, firms can no longer afford to wait this long, nor to pay the cost of such an elaborate development and implementation process.

HR has to deliver solutions as close to real time as possible, otherwise the firm risks losing its advantage to competitors that are more agile. The outcome is a focus on simpler but satisfactory rather than comprehensive and optimal HR solutions (Wright & Dyer, 2000) — a significant change in culture.

Perhaps it is in this revolutionary situation that we can thus best start to see how Web organizing is impacting on the function of HR as a whole. Lengnick-Hall and Lengnick-Hall (2002) introduce four new roles for HR based on what they describe as the knowledge economy in which many organizations are now working: (a) human capital steward, (b) knowledge facilitator, (c) relationship builder, and (d) rapid deployment specialist (see Box 4).

Parallels can easily be drawn between the new economy that Lengnick-Hall and Lengnick-Hall (2002) describe and the Web-organized structures of brick-and-mortar companies that this chapter has explored. Lengnick-Hall and Lengnick-Hall's roles are all elements of the HR role and HRM practices discussed so far in this chapter as part of company responses to the Internet economy. These responses and implications are now summarized in the following section, drawing out the broader implications of Web organizing in brick-and-mortar companies.

Conclusions

In this brief overview, we have suggested that there are three main ways in which old-economy companies are attempting to integrate the new economy as extensions of their current businesses. These business models are summarized in turn below, considering the implications for HRM practices and the HR department. It is emphasized here that this is a new and interesting field in the HRM literature that has not yet been fully explored empirically. We encourage others to take up the challenge in this dynamic world to explore further the tentative conclusions we are reaching here.

The first e-business model treats the Internet as an extension of the normal marketplace. Companies use it primarily to sell more products or services and to buy cheaper. This will involve many organizations operating primarily through business-to-business exchanges. The transparency and global reach of these exchanges will put major pressure on suppliers' costs and speed and flexibility of response.

We have suggested that the major accepted way for Western companies to achieve necessary cost savings and performance increases is to adopt an agile management approach combined with a flexible, high performance organization to gain the maximum advantage from the globalization of the economy. This implies a clear *human capital steward* role for the HR function to be highly cost-efficient in the way in which it operates. In addition to broadening their portfolio of expertise to cover the implementation of flexible working practices, high performance work systems, and international HRM practices, HR professionals need to rethink how they deliver their service to their clients. E-HRM has been discussed here as a tool for streamlining and improving the scope and depth of service delivery, hence delivering the required cost savings and quality improvements demanded of the department.

The second way in which old-economy companies are attempting to integrate the new economy is by using the Internet to expand and improve collaborative relationships among their key suppliers. We envisage many business-to-business suppliers becoming members of fully integrated virtual supply chains, with a need to develop trusting relationships between all partners in the network, combined with the necessity of constant improvement in performance and innovation.

In such a situation, what is needed is a combination of the rationality and order of high performance work systems along with a willingness to constantly consider change and, where necessary, to implement innovation quickly. This balance between strong routines on the one hand, and the freedom to experiment and innovate on the other, is difficult for any organization to achieve. It requires the development and maintenance of a climate of trust both internally in the firm and externally between network partners. In addition, learning both at individual and at organizational levels will have to be of a high order in order to facilitate the necessary continuous improvement and innovation.

So again the role of the HR department is clear. Not only must they ensure development and maintenance of a high performing, flexible organization, but they must also assist in the development of trusting relationships and learning and innovation. This involves a re-evaluation of the employer-employee relationship that the company advocates, monitoring employee attitudes and encouraging and rewarding participation, knowledge sharing, and risk taking to the benefit of the company. The focus is on the *relationship builder* and *knowledge facilitator* roles of HR professionals in developing a climate of trust, innovation, and learning.

Finally, as we have suggested, there is also a third way that may be a temporary state, but is much more fundamental. This approach requires old-economy organizations to rethink totally their business models before deciding on their e-commerce strategy. They must re-examine why customers buy from them, look at all stages in the processes involved, and consider how the Internet could impact each stage in the processes, and then, if necessary, develop new business models for the required reorganization.

Here, the *rapid deployment specialist* role for HR is clear, alongside the *knowledge facilitator* role. HR professionals must assist in managing the multiple change processes involved and also help those involved in the process to gather whatever learning is available as effectively as possible. And satisfying rather than striving for perfection in daily operations will be the order of the day.

As our overview has pointed out, the uncertainties, problems, and complexities for many organizations of moving business-to-business transactions onto the Internet will mean that the pace for many will be slow even if it is steady. To start with, both Internet-based and non-Internet-based systems are likely to be kept running in parallel. For example, business-to-business selling in many companies will exist side-by-side with a more traditional approach. Selling through the Internet may have major cost advantages, but it does not give much opportunity for developing personal contacts, nor for the flexibility sometimes needed to clinch the sale. For example, it is hard to enquire about a customer's family during an ordering process on the Internet. Moreover, the Internet is often inflexible in quoting a delivery date, whereas a good salesman knows how to twist the system so that the customer gets the goods within his desired timeframe. And so the HR function will also have to move in the directions we have suggested, while at the same time continuing to fulfill its more traditional roles.

Final Remarks

Web-based organizing is a complex issue. Few companies can easily be slotted into the three models we have just described. Sub-units of many companies may well be spread across different models, and some may be moving from one model to another. The speed of change will also vary across business sectors. In addition, there are many and varied problems alongside HRM issues involved in the transfer of business-to-business transactions onto the Internet that we have not discussed here. The move does however appear to be inevitable. There is, therefore, a need to act quickly in order to be ready.

HRM is arguably becoming more important in this changing economy: the relative unique value of fixed assets such as property and factories is declining, while the unique value ascribed to intangible assets is increasing. Intangible assets involve people: people's ideas, people's contacts, people's ability to manage in the midst of chaos, people's vision and experience, people's intuition or understanding of markets, and so on. However, people are free agents; they can, and do, change employers frequently. Therefore, HRM should concentrate on the systems that underpin people's successful behavior, that is to say the systems that stimulate and support the new desired behaviors we have been discussing. These systems are what HR managers need to identify as appropriate for their own company, so that they can then guide management in adapting and improving these systems to realize organizational potential. These internal improvements, necessary for successful transference of business to the Internet, may at last enable the HR function to justify its existence in financial terms.

A fitting end to this chapter is perhaps provided by Braunschvig's (1998, p. 178) conclusion that both American and especially European old-economy firms must leverage their human and technological resources simultaneously to achieve higher productivity growth:

"This could well be the opportunity of last resort for mature economies challenged by companies from younger, hungrier cultures and countries."

References

Atkinson, J., & Meager, N. (1986). *Changing working patterns: How companies achieve flexibility*. London: NEDO.

Balogun, J., & Hope-Hailey, V. (2004). *Exploring strategic change*. Harlow: FT/Prentice-Hall.

Baumard, P. (1999). *Tacit knowledge in organizations*. Thousand Oaks, CA: Sage Publications.

Blois, K. (1999). Trust in business-to-business relationships: An evaluation of its status. *Journal of Management Studies, 36*(2), 197-215.

Boselie, P., & Dietz, G. (2003). Commonalities and contradictions in research on human resource management and performance. Paper presented at the *Academy of Management Meeting*, Seattle, Washington, August.

Bovet, D., & Martha, J. (2000). *Value nets*. New York: John Wiley & Sons.

Braunschvig, D. (1998). Work remade. In D. Leebaert (Ed.), *The future of the electronic marketplace*. Boston, MA: MIT Press.

Brewster, C., Communal, C., Farndale, E., Hegewisch, A., Johnson, G., & Van Ommeren, J. (2001). *The HR Healthcheck. Benchmarking HRM practice across the UK and Europe*. London: Financial Times/Prentice-Hall.

Bunnell, C. (2000). *Making the Cisco connection*. New York: John Wiley & Sons.

Child, J., & Faulkner, D. (1998). *Strategies of cooperation, managing alliances, networks and joint ventures*. Oxford: Oxford University Press.

Cohen, W.M., & Levinthal, D.A. (1990). Absorptive capacity: A new perspective on learning and innovation. *Administrative Science Quarterly, 35*(1), 128-152.

Cool, K. (1997). *The competitiveness of European industry*. Inauguration address for the BP Chair in European Competitiveness, INSEAD, June 3.

Cusumano, M.A. (1994). The limits of lean. *Sloan Management Review, 35*(4), 27-32.

Evans, P.B., & Wurster, T.S. (1997). Strategy and the new economics of information. *Harvard Business Review, 75*(5), 71-83.

Floyd, P. (2002). *Organizational change*. Oxford: Capstone.

Fujimoto, T. (1999). *The evolution of a manufacturing system at Toyota*. New York: Oxford University Press.

Greenspan, A. (2000). Global economic integration: Opportunities and challenges. Retrieved from *www.federalreserve.gov* (symposium speech, August 25).

Grimshaw, D., Breu, K., & Myers, A. (2002). *Releasing the value of knowledge: A Cranfield School of Management and Microsoft survey of UK industry*. London: Financial Times/Prentice-Hall.

Handy, C. (1995). Trust and the virtual organization. *Harvard Business Review, 73*(3), 40-50.

Hansen, M.T., & Deimler, M.S. (2001). Cutting costs while improving morale with B2E management. *Sloan Management Review, 43*(1), 96-100.

Harris, H., Brewster, C., & Sparrow, P. (2003). *International human resource management*. London: CIPD.

Hartman, A., & Sifonis, J. (2000). *Net ready*. New York: McGraw Hill.

Lengnick-Hall, M.L., & Lengnick-Hall, C.A. (2002). *Human resource management in the knowledge economy: New challenges, new roles, new capabilities*. San Francisco, CA: Berrett-Koehler.

McAllister, D.J. (1995). Affect and cognition-based trust as foundations for interpersonal cooperation in organizations. *Academy of Management Journal, 38*(1), 24-59.

McCall, M.W. (1988). Developing executives through work experiences. *Human Resource Planning, 2*(1), 1-12.

McCurry, L., & McIvor, R. (2002). Agile manufacturing: 21st century strategy for manufacturing on the periphery? *Irish Journal of Management, 23*(2), 75-93.

Nooteboom, B. (1996). Trust, opportunism and governance: A process and control model. *Organizational Studies, 17*(6), 985-1010.

Nooteboom, B. (2000). Trust as a governance device. In M. Casson & A. Godley (Eds.), *Cultural factors in economic growth* (Chapter 1). Berlin: Springer-Verlag.

Paauwe, J. (2004). Changing HRM roles: Towards a real balanced HRM scorecard. In J. Paauwe (Ed.), *HRM and performance: Unique approaches for achieving long-term viability* (Chapter 9, pp. 217-251). Oxford: Oxford University Press.

Rayport, J.F., & Sviolka, J.J. (1995). Exploiting the virtual value chain. *Harvard Business Review, 73*(6), 75-85.

Ruël, H., Bondarouk, T., & Looise, J.K. (2003). E-HRM, innovation or irritation? An exploration of Web-based human resource management in large companies. Paper presented at the *7th Conference on International Human Resource Management*, University of Limerick, Ireland, June.

Schwartz, E. (1997). *Webonomics*. New York: Broadway Books.

Seely Brown, J., & Duguid, P. (2000). *The social life of information.* Boston, MA: Harvard Business School.

Shapiro, C., & Varian, H.R. (1999). *Information rules.* Boston, MA: Harvard Business School Press.

Sharp, J.M., Irani, Z., & Desai, S. (1999). Working towards agile manufacturing in the UK industry. *International Journal of Production Economics, 62*(1/2), 155-69.

Shockley-Zalabak, P., Ellis, K., & Winograd, G. (2000). Organizational trust: What it means, why it matters. *Organization Development Journal, 18*(4), 35-48.

Siebel, T. (2001). How Siebel systems found its groove. Retrieved December 19, 2001, from *knowledge.wharton.upenn.edu/*

Stabell, C.B., & Fjeldstad, O.J. (1998). Configuring value for competitive advantage: On chains, shops, and networks. *Strategic Management Journal, 19*(5), 420-431.

Tapscott, D. (1999). *Creating value in the network economy.* Boston, MA: Harvard Business School Press.

Tapscott, D., Ticoll, D., & Lowy, A. (2000). *Digital capital.* London: Brealey.

Timmers, P. (1999). *Electronic commerce.* New York: John Wiley & Sons.

Ulrich, D. (1997). *Human resource champions*. Cambridge, MA: Harvard Business School Press.

Useem, J., & Watson, N. (2001). It's all yours Jeff. Now what? *Fortune, 144*(5), 64-68.

Van Alstyne, M. (1997). The state of network organization: A survey in three frameworks. *Journal of Organizational Computing, 7*(2/3), 83-151.

Van den Bos, M., & Methorst, W. (2004). E-HRM: HRM ondersteund door ICT. In J. Paauwe & J. Van Breukelen (Eds.), *Personeelsmanagement in bedrijf: Een bijdrage aan het beter presteren van individu en organisatie*. Alphen a/d Rijn: Kluwer.

Venkatraman, N. (2000). Five steps to a dot-com strategy: How to find your footing on the Web. *Sloan Management Review, 41*(3), 15-28.

Whitener, E.M. (1997). The impact of human resource activities on employee trust. *Human Resource Management Review, 7*(4), 389-404.

Wood, S. (1999). Human resource management and performance. *International Journal of Management Reviews, 1*(4), 367-414.

Wright, P.M., & Dyer, L. (2000). *People in the e-business. New challenges and new solutions*. Working Paper 00-11, Center for Advanced Human Resource Studies, Cornell University, Ithaca, New York.

Wright, P.M., Dyer, L., & Takla, M. (1999). *Execution: The critical what's next in strategic human resource management. The 1999 Human Resource Planning Society State of the Art and Practice Council report*. New York: Human Resource Planning Society.

Wyckoff, A. (1997). Imagine the impact of electronic commerce. *The OECD Observer*, 208(October-November).

Chapter II

Integrating Handheld Computer Technology into HR Research and Practice

Scott A. Davies, Hogan Assessment Systems, USA

Robert F. Calderón, Caliber Associates, Inc., USA

Abstract

Current theory, applications, and future opportunities for the utilization of handheld computer technology in HR research and practice are presented in this chapter. Empirical research findings on the use of handheld computers for passive collection of workplace data and as a platform for electronic diaries are presented. Potential applications of handheld computers for HR practice are also presented. Finally, current issues and opportunities concerning integration of handheld computer technology into HR research and practice are discussed.

Introduction

The integration of handheld computer technology with human resource (HR) research and application is an area that has not received a great deal of attention from HR researchers or practitioners. However, as the efficiencies and economies associated with handheld computers have continued to increase over the past five years, with meaningful advancements in hardware (e.g., 400 MHz processor speeds, transflective color screens), storage (e.g., 1GB+ memory cards), software (e.g., MS Pocket PC 2003), and wireless connectivity options (e.g., Bluetooth, Wi-Fi, Sprint PCS 153 Kbps service), their utility to human resource research and practice is greater than ever. Based on our research, we believe that full utilization of handheld computers in HR will be most fully realized through the collaborative efforts of HR researchers, practitioners, and IT specialists.

In this chapter we bring together empirical research and practical knowledge on the integration of handheld computer technology with strategic human resource planning, management, and research theory into a working model that may serve as a foundation for future work in this area. We begin with an overview of how handheld computer technology fits into a model with HR research, HR practice, and IT infrastructure. We then review the role of handheld computers in strategic human resource practice and research, including the use of handheld computers to: (a) gather data for business process engineering, workflow mapping, and job analysis; (b) conduct organizational needs assessments; (c) gather and manage performance data, and provide employee feedback in performance management systems; (d) provide training to employees and gather training evaluation data; (e) conduct organizational surveying; and (f) enhance administrative tasks, such as scheduling, messaging, and provision of HR forms. Finally, we present our view of future research opportunities and challenges associated with the integration of handheld computer technology into strategic human resource planning, management, and research.

We hope readers find what we present in this chapter useful to their own HR research and practice. As in all applications of technology, the field is bursting with activity and constantly changing, but we believe that the material presented here will remain a relevant foundation for work in this area for the foreseeable future. It is our goal not only to inform the reader, but to increase interest in pursuing additional research in this area.

A Model of Handheld Computer Technology Integrated into HR

Currently, handheld computers are often used as stand-alone devices in the workplace to supplement individuals' computing resources. This situation neglects the potential for use of the technology in a systematic manner. In our conceptual model (Figure 1), the boxes represent what we see are the three key elements in the relationship between handheld computer technology and HR. As shown by the arrows, this is not a linear relationship, but one of conver-

Figure 1. Working model of handheld computer technology integrated into HR practice, research, and IT infrastructure

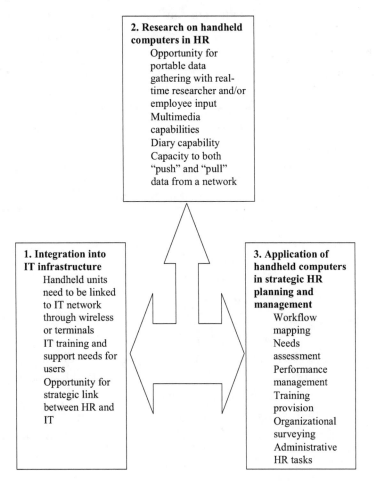

gence, with each element both contributing to and drawing from the other elements. The key to optimizing the use of the handheld in HR research and practice is attendance to all three factors in the model simultaneously.

Factor #1: Integration into IT Infrastructure

As with any organizational technology solution, handheld computers need to be a part of the larger IT system. According to our model, IT integration is linked to both the HR research and HR application factors. Some aspects of these linkages are supported by empirical work in this area. For example, we have found that optimal use of handheld technology in HR research requires integration into the organization's IT system as an enterprise solution (Davies, Rodbard, Brandes, & Poropatich, 2004; Lyons, Davies, Rodbard, Brandes, & Poropatich, 2004; Rodbard, Brandes, Davies, & Lyons, 2002). Furthermore, our research has shown that a lack of integration will be an insurmountable roadblock to successful handheld use. We have also found that successful integration of handhelds as research or applied HR tools is dependent on strategic links to the organizational IT infrastructure through HotSynching terminals or wireless methods. Successful applications also require adequate, ongoing IT-related training and support to handheld users. Finally, collaboration between HR and IT staff is a critical factor in making integration of handheld technology a part of an organization's strategic business plan.

Factor #2: Research on Handheld Computers in HR

While integration into the IT system will make handheld technology available to HR, it is up to the HR researchers to identify opportunities for a wide variety of data-collection activities in the workplace, such as diary studies, multimedia interventions, survey work, and real-time assessments/evaluations. Organizational researchers have begun to utilize handhelds in their research to a limited extent, but the full potential of having entire organizations of respondents voluntarily carrying computers around with them every day has not yet been capitalized on for research purposes. We have identified four research functions in our model that would be accentuated through handheld use, but the published work in this area is scarce. As a notable exception, Miner, Glomb, and Hulin (2001) gathered employee mood data in an experience sampling design using the diary feature of handheld computers. From feedback we received from others in the field, other programs of HR research using handhelds exist, but are being conducted by organizations internally; as is too often the case in applied settings, the results are not available for publication. In our research, we utilized the real-time evaluation and diary function of the handheld, but have not had the opportunity to explore multimedia and wireless capabilities (Lyons et al., 2004; Rodbard et al., 2002). These conceptual factors in our model provide an impetus for future empirical research.

Factor #3: Application of Handheld Computers in Strategic HR Planning and Management

In our research, we have found that introducing handheld technology as a platform for HR applications provides a means of conducting HR-related research on a variety of issues (Lyons et al., 2004; Rodbard et al., 2002). This is the basis for the relationship in our model between Factor #1, HR Research, and Factor #2, HR Application. Our findings support the concept that the research capacity of handhelds can be captured as a byproduct of the implementation of HR functions on the same device. For example, in occupations that rely heavily on forms to complete work activities (e.g., nurses use forms to chart patients, lawyers use forms to bill time, teachers use forms to track students, warehouse workers use forms to maintain inventory), by placing the forms on handhelds and passively gathering form use data from the devices, research on workflow mapping, job analysis, and job design can be conducted with little to no extra data collection. We expand on these findings in the following sections on handheld applications and research.

Overall, we propose that the research and application of handheld technology to HR functions would be well served to follow a conceptual model, not occur in an unsystematic manner with post hoc evaluation, as is often the case. Evidence that this may already be the state of the science in this area is the lack of published research on handheld technology and HR (Cascio, 2003). There is much to be gained in this potentially fruitful area of HR practice and research by working from a common understanding and publishing results both supportive and unsupportive of that understanding.

In our model, we acknowledge the importance of relating IT infrastructure to HR practice and research on handhelds, but we do not further develop the IT issue in this chapter. We urge the reader to examine resources and to collaborate with IT experts in this area. In the following sections, we expand on the research supporting Factors #2 and #3 of our model (Figure 1).

HR Applications on Handhelds

HR-related applications on handhelds are being developed at an ever-increasing pace. The most popular of these falls into the realm of personal information management (PIM) functions, such as a calendar, contact list, to-do list, and e-mail. In our model, these functions on individual employee's handhelds become important parts of a strategic HR practice and, if managed properly, become a system of organizational information management (OIM) functions.

Applications are available for time management, for example, that have advanced capabilities for applying complex work rules (e.g., managing overtime accruals and employee leave periods), processing time billing, providing sophisticated scheduling, and allocation capabilities; they further include the ability to equalize overtime in schedules, match skills to jobs, and provide a platform for resource substitution and alternatives. Physicians in some medical facilities are using a handheld device to manage a variety of workflow functions, including accessing real-time patient scheduling information, capturing charges, and dictating point-of-care patient notes. These professionals use their handheld devices to review medical reference libraries, current diagnostic and procedure coding, and coding compliance rules. These applications are applicable to other occupations as well.

Organizational-level contact management can be accomplished by enabling multiple handheld users to synchronize with a master list of contacts, update the contact list, then resynchronize the changes to the master database. For example, using a .NET Compact Framework solution on Pocket PCs provides a SQL Server CE database on each device that contains a replica of the master database. The handheld database is synchronized with the master database programmatically to build the organizational contact list.

Most directly related to HR practice are applications that make various organizational forms and documents available to employees on the handheld—either downloadable from a PC or via distance connection through land-based or wireless connection. Forms may be "pushed" out to employees as required, or "pulled" as needed, completed, and returned electronically. Other applications enhance record keeping for traveling employees, including programs for time management, project management, sales tracking, and expense accounts.

Handhelds are also capable of holding quick reference material that can be accessed immediately in a non-cumbersome fashion. In some organizations, individuals are able to reference journals/databases with the push of a button and provide critical information in real time. For example, Hayes (2003) examined the benefits of using handheld computers for a population of psychiatrists and found that these devices were extremely useful in storing and retrieving information and applications that could be accessed anyplace at anytime. Basically, the handheld computers can provide the same basic benefits that are available via an individual's personal computer (e.g., reference materials, Web searches), with the added bonus of being with the individual at all times.

There are also many handheld applications with implications for potential HR use. For example, organizations with workers in the field are finding rugged-use handhelds useful for land surveying, mapping, civil engineering and construction, forestry, utility, facilities and asset management, machine control, law enforcement, and military applications. The technology is also being used to assist employment of people with disabilities. For example, networked job training and coaching applications can be provided on handhelds with audio- or graphics-based step-by-step instruction on how to complete a job, check progress to completion, and as a means for family and coach to communicate with workers (MobileVillage, 2003).

In summary, handheld technology is being utilized as a means to provide a wide range of HR-related applications. In many cases, the opportunity exists for provision of the HR function to be improved through the use of the handheld. In our model, we conceptualize the relationship of HR functions on the handheld to the IT infrastructure and increasing capacity for HR research. In the next section, we describe how HR research and handheld research can be accomplished as a byproduct of handheld use.

Researching HR Functions on Handhelds

In preparing this chapter, we discovered that the dearth of published research on integration of HR functions and handheld technology continues. When we first started work in this area in 2001, the lack of existing research was not entirely surprising given the age of the technology. However, now — three years later — the technology has matured and the body of research appears to have grown very little. Much of the work that *has been* accomplished in this area appears to be proprietary and therefore not available for our review. In this section we present reviews of the few published studies we have identified, along with a description of our own research program in this area.

A group of researchers at Carnegie-Mellon have conducted handheld research since 1997 in the PEBBLES project (PDAs for Entry of Both Bytes and Locations from External Sources). Although not explicitly focused on HR functions, the work of the team is of importance to this area. For example, the PEBBLES team has researched multi-machine user interfaces (MMUIs), which are of importance in our conceptualization of handheld integration with the larger IT system. In their research, the PEBBLES team has examined how handhelds and PCs can be used together (Myers, 2001; Myers, Steil, & Gargiulo, 1998).

In one study, the team found that in a meeting setting, handhelds could be used to make a PC-based slide presentation more effective by providing additional details of the presentation to handheld meeting attendees wirelessly, on demand. The details included additional data, graphs, and other information that were not included on the more macro slide presentation, but were of interest to some of the attendees during the slide show (Myers, Steil, & Gargiulo, 1998).

In another study, the team found that real-time classroom assessment via handhelds linked wirelessly to the instructor's PC was more effective from both the student and instructor perspectives. Finally, the PEBBLES team is examining the effectiveness of handheld use by multiple meeting participants when annotating large, shared electronic displays, such as military maps (Myers, 2001).

The bulk of the research on the use of handheld computers in organizational settings has been conducted in medical facilities. Many resources have been devoted to developing medical programs for handhelds, and evaluating both their use and effectiveness in the work of medical professionals. For example, Rosenbloom (2003) reported on the use of handhelds to reduce medical errors in a number of ways across the medical professions. Primarily, Rosenbloom identifies the need for medical providers to have the correct information in a usable format at *the point of care* and recognizes the handheld as the best portable platform for fulfilling this need.

Lanway and Graham (2003) reported a study on handheld implementation in a medical facility, with results that generalize beyond the medical field. The study involved nurses who performed primarily administrative functions in evaluating quality of patient care. This role required a great deal of documentation, usually at the site of patient service. The nurses were using a paper-based system to meet the portability requirements and then transcribing the handwritten notes onto their desktop computers as the opportunity arose. This situation resulted in an unmanageable amount of lag time between evaluation and feedback to the medical providers, and unnecessary costs for double documentation. Finding that laptop computers were too bulky for the job, the organization moved the nurses to wireless handheld computers. The nurses could document the evaluations once and transmit the information immediately to the organization's mainframe for use. The use of handhelds saved the nurses two to three hours each — per day — in the double documentation process. Also, the immediate delivery of information back to the medical facility often results in patient discharge a day earlier than under the old system — an outcome that has shown in the decreasing average length of stay since the handhelds were put into use. Finally, the researchers report that the nurses' job satisfaction has increased since the handheld technology has been implemented. It is unlikely that these results would be specific to the medical field; they would more likely generalize to administrative applications in other professions.

The impact of handheld use in the medical profession has been noticed not only by medical professions, but by corporations paying for healthcare as well. In order to reduce healthcare costs due to prescription inaccuracies, insurance billing errors, and other problems created by poor penmanship, General Motors Corporation has distributed handhelds to over 5,000 physicians who attend to the company's employees (Konrad, 2001). Generalizing this technology effort to the corporate HR program would probably have similar effects.

In our own research program (e.g., Rodbard et al., 2002), we are exploring the use of handheld computers in both laboratory and field settings. Current laboratory research is focusing on the human factors of the user-machine interface and how those factors are impacted by various software solutions. This basic research is primarily of importance to the IT domain for effective hardware and software design; therefore, we do not describe that line of research in this chapter. We will instead focus on the research we have conducted on handheld computers in the field and present findings primarily of importance to HR researchers and practitioners.

Description of the Rodbard Study

The goal of the Rodbard et al. (2002) study was to provide medical professionals with handheld computers, train the professionals to use the handhelds in their work, and then gather data regarding when, how, and why the handhelds were used. This study was unique in its inductive, "bottom-up" approach to understanding how professionals would use handhelds in their work, how work-related functions could be provided on the handhelds, and how handhelds would perform as data-gathering devices for organizational research.

Overall, the study employed both qualitative and quantitative methods, with measurement of actual use from objective data captured from the handheld computers, measurement of user preparation through survey methodology, measurement of real-time user reactions through the use of an electronic diary on the handhelds, and qualitative user input through focus groups and Delphi methods. Use of multiple methods provided more valid measurement of the complex phenomenon of interest in the workplace.

Participants

A total of 84 medical personnel from two military medical facilities participated in our study of handhelds in the workplace. Specifically, the sample distribution by occupation was as follows: 30 physicians, 26 nurses, 15 pharmacists, and 13 combat medics. The overall gender distribution was fairly even: 45 males and 39 females. Ethnic origin was representative of the U.S. military population and the area labor force.

Procedure

The concept of the study was to provide training and experience with handhelds that were equipped with a variety of applications (i.e., 10 medical applications and 14 personal information management applications) to incumbents in the two medical facilities, and subsequently gather: (a) objective data on application usage, (b) feedback through a diary style logbook on the handheld, (c) qualitative information through focus groups, and (d) priorities regarding the information gathered from this group of "experienced" users in a final Delphi-oriented focus group session. In addition to these primary data, secondary analyses were conducted to examine the utility of monitoring handheld use in the workplace as a potential source of workflow mapping and rudimentary job analysis data.

Readiness to Participate

In order to assess readiness to participate in the study and to plan training, we administered a 20-item survey during the initial session with the participants, measuring past experience with handhelds, computers in general, and software use. Figure 2 shows the distribution of survey scores. It is important to note the wide range of scores, indicating that participants came into this study with relevant experiences ranging from none (i.e., "1") to high expertise (i.e., "19"). This is important to note in light of the findings in this study that regardless of previous relevant experience, the majority of participants were willing and eager to use the handheld computers with adequate training and support.

Training

Participants were provided training in three two-hour sessions, one week apart. Training was conducted by an expert in medical informatics with several years of experience with handheld computers, who was assisted by two PhD psychologists. The design of the sessions was interactive, with hands-on experiential learning as the primary focus. After each of the sessions, the participants completed questionnaires to assess increases in relevant knowledge and attitudes towards the handheld devices. Additionally, a 15-minute 'mini' focus group was conducted after each session in order to elicit the major strengths and weaknesses of using the handheld computers in the work environment.

The training sessions were a critical factor in the success of this study. From the results of the knowledge questionnaires, focus group findings, and the observations of the training teams, the trainings effectively prepared even the least experienced participant to use the handheld computer in his/her work. In most cases, attitudes toward the devices (as elicited in the focus groups) moved from negative to positive and fear to trust. Any initial resistance to the use of handhelds by this group of medical professionals was found to diminish across the span of the three training sessions. From our observations, this change was

Figure 2. Histogram of previous relevant experience survey scores by percent of participants at each score point, 1-20

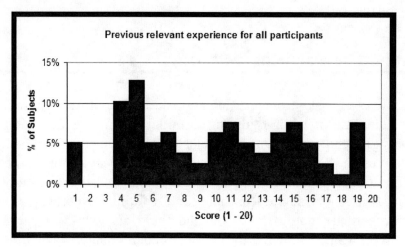

due to an increased understanding of the benefits of the handheld computers to the work through personal experiences and anecdotal learning from fellow professionals (i.e., "I was able to access a necessary medical reference book on my PDA during a critical diagnosis at bedside and this made me more confident in my decision").

Focus Groups

The mini focus group results provided focus for subsequent trainings and support follow-up with individual participants, as well as a basis for the Delphi portion of the study. The primary findings from these early group sessions included:

- Caregivers are enthusiastic about using the handheld computers.
- Caregivers readily adopt both personal information management (PIM) and selected medical applications into their daily practices.
- The handheld computers were easily configured and deployed to the physicians, nurses, medics, and pharmacists.
- Skills sufficient to use the handhelds are easily acquired with limited training and "buddy" support.

- Caregivers request additional functionalities for the handhelds: access to patient records, lab data, x-rays, patient instructional materials, CME credits, and the Internet.

Support

Participants also received ongoing support in their use of the handheld computers through a buddy system. We actively promoted less well-prepared participants to team with better prepared participants within their work environment. This was also a critical success factor in conducting the study and for implementing the technology. Through this system, individuals were able to access support specific to the problem encountered, both at the point in time most needed and from a recognized coworker. Participants were also provided support from the research team via e-mail, telephone contact, site visits, and from the base IT staff on an ongoing basis.

Research Methods

Throughout the course of the study (i.e., eight weeks), we utilized application use tracking software on the handheld computers to track the use of various handheld applications. We employed "App Usage Hack, Version 1.1" from Benc Software for this purpose (Benc, 2002). In addition, we requested the developer of App Usage Hack to create a version that would also record the date, time, and duration of each use of each application. The latter version, designated App Usage Hack Version 1.2, was employed for our studies. In this manner, we were able to examine patterns of use by participant, day, time of day, and day of week.

Use of this advanced version resulted in a decreased need for frequent HotSyncing (i.e., linking the handheld computer to a desktop computer through a cradle to synchronize the data on shared programs) on the part of participants. Even if the participant HotSynced only once — at the end of the study — we could still identify the pattern of use, day-by-day and week-by-week (provided that data were not lost or corrupted due to battery failure or inappropriate use of Backup and Restore functions).

Our analysis of the use-tracking data resulted in profiles of application usage at the person and group level, and provided a basis for describing differences in handheld application usage across medical professions. In order to better understand the usage data, we employed focus groups and logbook software on the handheld devices for gathering reaction data from participants.

The logbook, a form of electronic diary, was designed as a standardized survey form. It was well received by participants and would be useful for gathering a variety of input from employees. The participants were instructed to access the logbook at least once a day, and each time they had a critical experience with the handheld computer. Also, the participants received automatic alarms on their handheld every week reminding them to HotSync, as well as reminders every second day to make a recording in their logbooks. The logbook asked five questions with a five-point response scale for each:

1.   If a specific application was the subject of the report, which application was it?

2.   How many times was the application used today, or if not a specific application, how many times the handheld was used?

3.   Did the application or handheld save time, and if so, how much?

4.   Did the application or handheld make your job easier?

5.   Comments.

The participants had the option to change answers, which were then stored in a HanDBase file for downloading at HotSynch and collection by the research team.

Focus groups were conducted at the end of each training session and followed appropriate protocol for qualitative data gathering (Berg, 2001). The participant discussion was guided by two or three primary points provided at the beginning of the focus group by a trained facilitator. Participants were given the opportunity to speak to the points, with the goal of eliciting the most information possible from the group. The groups were recorded in both audio and video format for content analysis. The audio recordings were transcribed and content analyzed using the Qualrus (2002) software program.

A special type of focus group was conducted at the end of the eight-week study. Ten to 15 participants were assigned to each of five Delphi focus groups. The Delphi method uses a conventional facilitated focus group format, but adds structured lists of issues within a topic of interest. Each member of the group independently reads and rates the importance of the issues on the list, and then the facilitator provides the mean ratings for the group back to the individuals. The differences between any one member and the group mean are then used as a lever to elicit discussion from the group in defense of each individual's ratings. After two iterations of ratings and discussion, a final rating for the list is agreed upon through group consensus. This method provides an optimum amount of group discussion concerning a specific set of issues.

Results

The initial training and focus group sessions were attended by all 84 participants in the study. However, due mainly to work-related reasons (e.g., base transfer, shift change), only 80% completed the training sessions and remained active in the study. To reduce the probability of attrition, the requirements for the study were clearly stated in the materials for recruitment of subjects, in the informed consent, in the initial questionnaire, and in the announcements at the initial session. Conceivably, some or many of these individuals may have been motivated to obtain a handheld computer for their own use, but did not wish to participate actively in the study. This behavior persisted despite the fact that (a) announcements of meetings were made at staff meetings, (b) e-mail reminders were sent prior to each of the focus groups and Delphi sessions, (c) frequent reminders were sent urging participants to enter observations into their logbooks and to HotSync, and (d) the participants received automatic alarms on their handheld reminding them to HotSync and to make recordings in their logbooks.

From the logbook results, we found that across the eight weeks of the study, 47 of the 84 participants made 826 logbook entries for an average of 18 entries per participant who used the logbook and 103 entries per week of the study. It was apparent that many of the participants who did not make logbook entries were also the participants who did not complete training. The participants provided comments on 34 different applications and stated that the handheld saved time in 81% of entries and saved effort in 73% of entries. Overall, the logbook was well accepted and, according to the focus group findings, was unanimously preferred to paper records or e-mail-based data collection.

According to analysis of the application usage data, the total study population of 84 individuals used the PDA 20,250 times during the two-month study. Physicians accounted for 8,751 uses, nurses — 4,839, pharmacists — 2,853, and medics — 3,807. The total number of uses cannot be compared directly because the number of subjects in each occupational group was not identical. Table 1 presents the results relative to the number of individuals in each group, that is, showing number of uses per individual for the total study period.

From our analysis of results such as those presented in Table 1, we found that usage monitoring was useful for examining occupational differences in overall handheld use. Physicians and medics had the highest usage, followed by pharmacists, then nurses. In order to better understand these differences, we analyzed differences in the applications used by each group as well. As expected, we found meaningful differences across medical professions in the types of applications most used by each group. For example, the physicians used medical references and diagnostic applications much more frequently than did the medics, while the medics more frequently used PIM applications for administrative functions. Both groups used the address book, calendar, memo pad, and calculator the most of any non-medically related applications, but we found differences in how these applications were used in participant focus groups. This was a critical component of the study—qualitative input from the participants to help us understand the application usage results collected from the handhelds.

From the usage data, we were also able to chart handheld use patterns over time. Figure 3 shows the aggregate use of the handheld by an average

Table 1. Total uses of handheld applications by medical profession

	USES	
	TOTAL	AVERAGE
Physicians	8,751	292 (n = 30)
Nurses	4,839	186 (n = 26)
Pharmacists	2,853	190 (n = 15)
Medics	3,807	293 (n = 13)
Total	20,250	241 (n = 84)

participant by day over two months of use. The number of applications used daily rose through the period of the training sessions, then dropped off to the number that the participant used on a regular basis.

Figure 4 shows the overall use across participants by time of day. These data were useful for examining differences in handheld use across work shifts. Alone, these results can show differences in overall usage by occupational group and provide insights for training and IT support. When analyzed in relationship to application usage by day of the week, these daily use patterns provided important information concerning the manner in which the handhelds were being used in work-related tasks.

Results obtained at the Delphi sessions at the close of the study corresponded closely to the actual level of usage throughout the study. The final ratings across participants for each topic in the Delphi study are presented in Tables 2, 3, and 4. The participants in each Delphi group individually rank ordered a list within each of the three topic areas, then through an iterative process of group discussion and reranking came to a final consensus set of rankings. The mean rankings provided in each table are the mean consensus rankings for all Delphi groups.

In Table 2 are the mean rankings made by the groups for the most important medical application types on the handhelds. The rankings largely supported the results from the application usage data and from the logbook results.

Figure 3. Daily use of handheld for one participant, based on application usage data

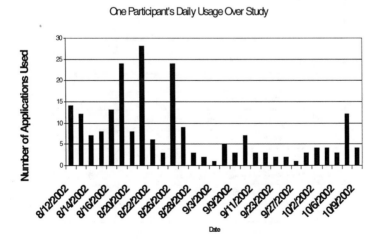

Figure 4. Application usage by time of day for all participants, based on application usage data

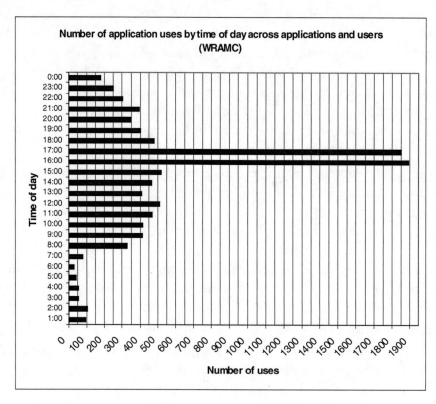

Table 2. Final ranking of the priorities for 10 medical applications

PDA Medical Applications (All Participants)		
Rank of Mean	**Application**	**Mean Rank**
1	Drug formularies (e.g., ePocrates, Tarascon, LexiDrug)	2.1
2	Reference materials, textbooks, manuals (e.g., Harrison's, Merck Manual, Wash U., Harriet Lane)	3.2
3	Medical calculations (e.g., MedCalc)	4.3
4	Patient data retrieval, H&P, lab, x-ray	4.4
5	Patient data entry (e.g., PatientKeeper, Patient Tracker)	4.8
6	Treatment guidelines (e.g., ATP III, Shots)	5.5
7	Decision support (e.g., 5 Min Clinical Consult)	6.0
8	Administrative (e.g., ICD coding, visit coding)	8.0
9	CME☐ multiple topics	8.2
10	Prescription writing	8.5

In Figures 5, 6, and 7 are the mean across Delphi groups of the final set of rankings by occupational group before the consensus round. As shown in Figure 5, the overall ranking trend across occupation groups was similar across applications, but there were group differences. The differences were largest for the applications that were found to be of great importance to one occupational group and of low importance to another group (i.e., patient data entry to medics and pharmacists).

Figure 5. Final round mean ratings by occupation: medical functions

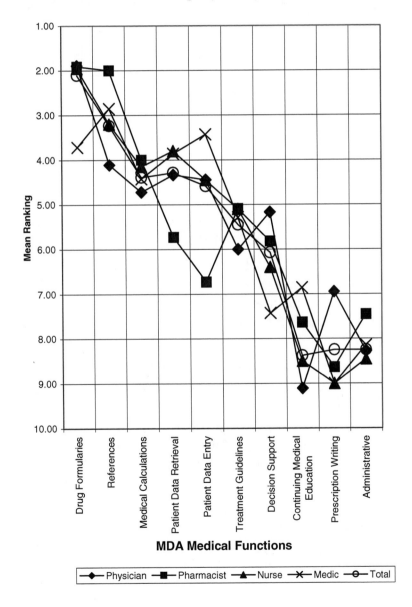

Table 3. Final ranking of the priorities for 10 personal information management (PIM) applications

Personal Information Management Functions (All Participants)		
Rank of Mean	Application	Mean Rank
1	Calendar/storing appointments	2.5
2	Storing addresses/phone numbers	2.8
3	Number calculation	4.9
4	Writing notes/data	5.0
5	Keeping a "to do" list	5.2
6	Reading/writing e-mail	6.1
7	Alarm function	6.2
8	Accessing notes/data	6.4
9	Storing voice recordings	7.7
10	Entertainment	9.2

In Table 3 are the mean rankings made by the groups for the most important PIM application types on the handhelds. The rankings also supported the results from the application usage data and from the logbook results.

There were also differences evident across occupational groups in the Delphi rankings for the most important PIM applications, as shown in Figure 6. The differences in group ratings were similar to those found for the medical applications.

In Table 4 are the mean rankings for the most important areas for change on the handhelds. This information was not collected in the application usage data, but it does mirror what was found in the earlier focus groups.

The differences in mean occupational group ratings for "Most Important Areas for Change" topics are shown in Figure 7. Compared to the two topics presented in Figures 5 and 6, the differences in mean ratings for "Most Important Areas for Change" were less clearly defined for all groups.

The transcripts of the Delphi sessions provided a rich source of data. From our content analysis of these data, the *main* theme expressed from all five Delphi sessions was the need for integration between the PDA applications and clinical work systems. In addition, three *sub-themes* arose from the main theme: (1)

Figure 6. Final round mean ratings by occupation: PIM functions

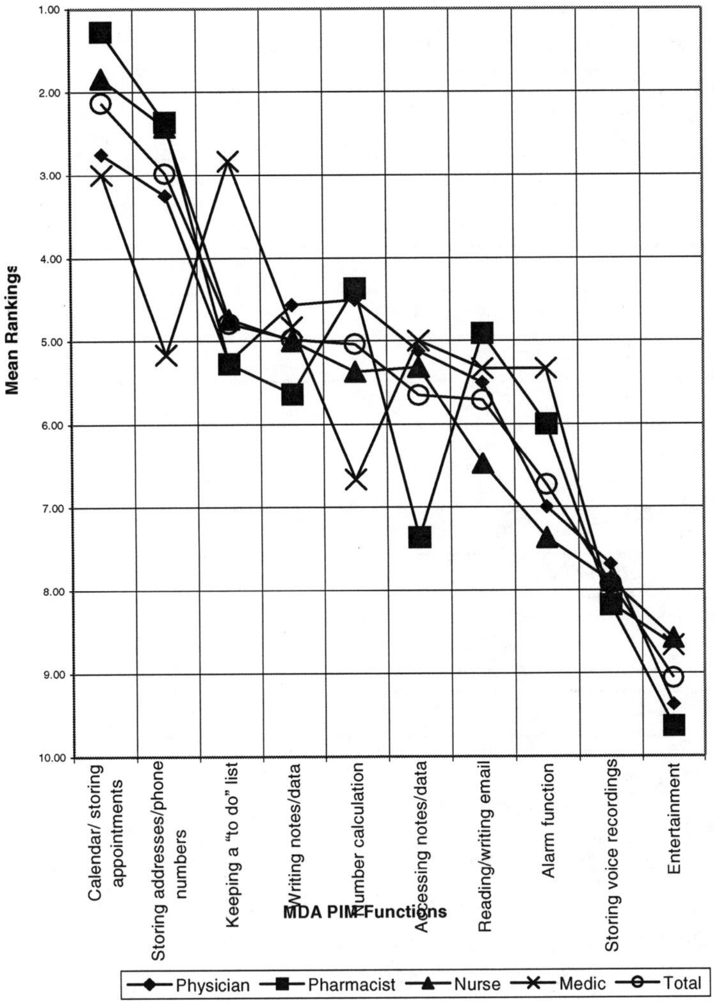

PDA integration with workflow, (2) PDA customization, and (3) PDA standardization.

Several suggestions were offered to improve the use of the PDA by integrating it with the daily workflow. Specifically, several comments focused on automating the workload management (WLM) reporting process for nurses by using PDA HotSync data. Similarly, participants also believed that the opportunity to download patient and staff schedules to their PDA calendars would provide significant time savings to their daily workload. Participants suggested that an

Table 4. Ranking of the priorities for 12 "Most Important Areas for Change in the PDA"

Most Important Areas for Change (All Participants)		
Rank of Mean	Application	Mean Rank
1	Interface with hospital information systems	2.0
2	Memory size and type	5.5
3	Downloading applications to PDA	5.7
4	Drug formulary/drug database	5.9
5	Monochrome display	5.9
6	Readability	6.4
7	Accuracy/reliability of medical decision support applications	6.4
8	Pen (handwriting recognition) versus keyboard data input	7.5
9	Organization of reader applications (i.e., index)	7.5
10	Application familiarity (e.g., look and feel, content)	7.8
11	General navigation in applications	8.0
12	Calculator	9.7

interface between their PDAs and hospital patient information management system would allow them to input and extract patient data at the point of care. By integrating the PDA and hospital patient information management, participants also envisioned the ability to receive wireless notification of laboratory results to their PDA, resulting in savings of a considerable amount of time.

Participants expressed the need for their PDA applications to be specific to their professional specialty. Several participants suggested that the ability to annotate references and to customize provider-specific applications would be useful. Similarly, participants expressed the need to customize each PDA's applications to the individual, professional group, and medical specialty area (e.g., gastroenterology or pediatrics reference materials for nurses). Participants also desired facility-specific applications (e.g., facility-specific drug formulary and staff telephone/address book) adaptable to their PDA. Finally, some participants suggested that the use of multilingual translations (Spanish,

Figure 7. Final round mean ratings by occupation: "Most Important Areas for Change"

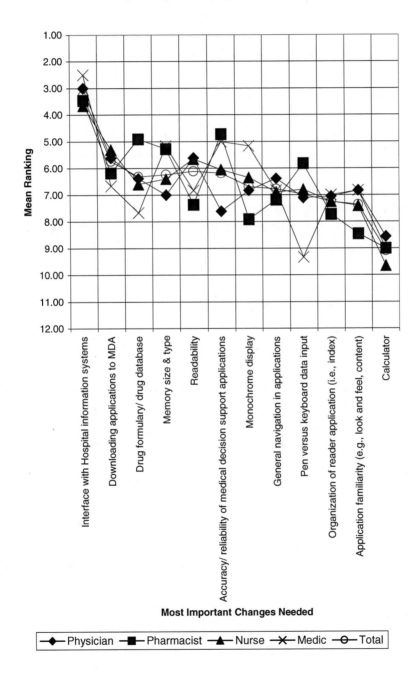

Mean First Round Delphi Rankings By Occupational Group Across Sites (Most Important Changes Needed in PDA)

Chinese, etc.) in each application would be helpful when they are on duty in foreign countries, and when providing care to non-English-speaking patients.

The third sub-theme that arose during the five sessions, standardization, primarily focused on the reliability of the PDA when utilizing it in the clinical workplace (e.g., checking drug dosages, writing prescriptions). Participants wanted each application standardized and reliable across locations to help meet medical certification guidelines. To ease the transition to a PDA-based process, participants also suggested that the forms-based data input screens on their PDA be similar to the current paper-based forms. Finally, participants wanted to incorporate medical error reporting features into the PDA application.

Discussion

Although there was a fairly high attrition rate among the participants, we judged the overall study design and implementation a success. We were able to show that regardless of previous experience, participants were able to use the handheld computers with little training. Also, we were able to show that the handheld computers were useful for providing HR-practice-related applications and for the collection of research data for a variety of HR-related needs. Finally, we found that as a byproduct of handheld use, rudimentary job analysis data could be collected passively from the participants.

That the participants were able to use the handhelds effectively with little training and even less organizational support was an important finding. With only three training sessions provided and minimal follow-up support, most participants were able to successfully utilize the handheld hardware and applications to enhance their work. However, we found one primary support dimension lacking for the participants — integration of the handhelds with the organizational IT system. This lack of support from the IT system resulted in most of the reported usage problems in the study and was the foundation for including this factor in our model (Figure 1).

Our results did show that the handheld could be used successfully to deliver applications and collect data such as that needed for HR practice and research. The logbook application was well received and did show that standardized questionnaires could be administered over a handheld platform. The basic PIM applications were utilized in a work-related fashion and would be beneficial to capturing schedules and contacts across an organization. Finally, with access to a wireless network, the participants reported that they would have utilized forms-based reporting of many administrative work functions. From these results, the second factor in our model in Figure 1 was supported.

Our last claim in the first paragraph of this discussion section, that rudimentary job analysis data can be collected passively from the handheld use, was a primary finding of this study and was supported through the logbook, application usage, and focus group data. The logbook data did show that the handheld computer is useful for collecting job-related information in a standardized format in real time. The application usage data did show that patterns of work-related behaviors, specific to occupation, can be inferred from the applications used by an individual. This is the linchpin in the model presented in Figure 1, that the handheld can be used to provide useful applications in the workplace (i.e., for conducting work and administering strategic HR functions), and through this use, valuable HR-related research data can be collected and utilized.

Handheld technology must be introduced with careful attention to existing workflow processes and possibly combined with process reengineering to take advantage of the mobile and wireless functions. As depicted in the Delphi sessions, there were requests for a single "system" rather than a myriad of disconnected, stand-alone applications. In general, the results from this study should be utilized as a framework for future assessments of handhelds in the workplace.

Our plans for continuing this line of research involves "process reengineering" to permit and facilitate the integration of handheld technology into the clinical and administrative processes utilized by healthcare providers. We plan to examine clinical business practices to evaluate how workflows can be modified to take maximum advantage of handheld technologies. By identifying locations in workflow processes to insert and implement handheld technologies, as well as performance measurement indicators, we will be able to evaluate the impact of handhelds on work performance.

Beyond the Current Research: HR Functions on Handhelds

Beyond the current organizational research that is utilizing handheld technology, there are additional HR functions that could be streamlined via handheld computers. These include areas within performance appraisal/management, selection, and training.

Performance Appraisal

A key concern within the performance appraisal framework, for example, has been the accuracy of the ratings provided by raters. Two proposed solutions to this concern have been frame-of-reference (FOR) training (Murphy & Cleveland, 1991) and behavioral diaries (Sulsky & Day, 1994; Maurer, Palmer, & Ashe, 1993). With frame-of-reference training, a set of raters will typically view vignettes that contain critical incidents of job performance. Each of these is designed to contain examples of outstanding, average, and unsatisfactory performance, and raters are asked to rate the behaviors within the vignettes and provide justification for their ratings. Trainers then inform the raters about what the intended ratings were supposed to be; a discussion follows to determine where there are discrepancies between the "true" ratings and the ratings the individuals provided (Keown-Gerrard & Sulsky, 2001). This calibration task then serves to provide a consistent "frame-of-reference" that is used to evaluate actual performance as it is observed and subsequently rated. In other words, a common framework is established that has been shown to increase 'interrater' agreement on performance ratings. Subsequently, this increase in interrater agreement has been shown to positively impact the accuracy of the performance ratings (McIntyre, Smith, & Hassett, 1984).

With behavioral diaries, raters keep a diary of each ratee's behavior throughout the performance appraisal cycle (Murphy & Cleveland, 1995). These do not need to include lengthy entries on a daily basis, but rather should be meaningful entries of critical incidents that can serve as retrieval cues when it is time to appraise. The rationale is that the rater will then be able to access the behaviors within the journal instead of relying strictly on memory, which can affect accuracy. Furthermore, the diaries will allow raters to establish more accurate descriptions of "typical" performance. Often times a rater can recall extreme performance (either good or bad), but often struggles to describe average performance. The diaries will allow raters to document the full range of each ratee's performance. Lastly, the diaries may help raters organize information into meaningful performance categories (DeNisi, Robbins, & Cafferty, 1989).

Unfortunately, very little technology has been utilized within the performance appraisal framework. However, the opportunities available for technology to address certain issues that can directly affect rating accuracy are limitless. For example, in frame-of-reference training, raters typically work through the initial exercise that is used to calibrate the various raters. However, over time, the raters may become forgetful of what was meant by the different levels of performance. This could lead to a decrease in the accuracy of the ratings, which is a key concern within the literature (Murphy & Cleveland, 1991). A quick reference of the different critical incidents that define outstanding, average, and unsatisfactory performance on something like a handheld computer would be both easy for the rater and would ensure the frame-of-reference training is not lost over time. Furthermore, there may be different sets of criteria for different jobs, and all of this could be centrally located and easily accessible via a handheld computer.

A handheld computer would also be a logical choice for keeping track of a ratee's performance over the period of performance (i.e., an electronic diary). Often times, raters do not take the time to fill in their diaries, or they do not have their diaries handy when certain critical incidents occur during the period of performance. With the handheld computer, the rater would always be able to track performance; this would help in providing accurate examples during the performance review. The handheld computer would also make the categorization of critical incidents into performance dimensions a more manageable task. For example, the handheld computer would allow individuals to search, reconfigure, and crunch data quickly from anywhere (Greene, 2001). This would enable individuals to determine where more data is needed (e.g., certain performance dimensions that do not have any behavioral indicators) as well as sort the data that has already been gathered.

Specifically, a handheld computer would be valuable in both storing and retrieving information on employees which are the areas that often times impact the accuracy of the ratings (i.e., raters have difficulty retaining critical incidents on employees — and often they are responsible for multiple employees — and subsequently retrieving representative behavioral examples of performance over a set period of time). The use of a handheld computer to directly enter performance data would also eliminate the need for later manual data entry of responses written on paper forms (Fletcher, Erickson, Toomey, & Wagenaar, 2003).

Furthermore, by tracking critical incidents of ratee performance as they occur, this will also help in the development (or revising) of the performance appraisal system. The typical method for creating a performance appraisal rating form is to gather a large number of critical incidents that are then sorted into unique performance dimensions. Information contained within each critical incident is then used to define what is meant by good, average, and poor performance via specific behavioral examples (Murphy & Cleveland, 1991; Sanchez & De La Torre, 1996; Smith & Kendall, 1963). A typical problem with this type of development of performance dimensions is that it takes several hundred (at a minimum) critical incidents to complete the process. If the critical incidents were gathered via each rater's handheld computer, as was mentioned above, a large number of critical incidents would be available that could then be leveraged in creating a group's performance dimensions. For example, each rater would be informed of how to generate critical incidents. They would then be asked to provide ratings of each incident. All critical incidents gathered from the various raters could then be grouped together to assist in the process of developing performance dimensions. This use of handheld computers would specifically assist in the gathering of examples of average performance. Often times, individuals do not have any difficulty in describing exceptionally good or exceptionally poor performance. However, as was mentioned above, it can be difficult to describe average performance. The raters who are creating the behavioral diaries should be able to document numerous instances of average performance. Furthermore, all critical incidents would be recent, which is a key element in ensuring that the performance dimensions that are created are relevant to the existing job(s).

Lastly, once the performance dimensions have been created, this information could easily be made available to each rater via a handheld computer. Each rater could make their ratings electronically, and this information could then be linked up to a central database within HR immediately. The transportability of the rating process would also benefit individuals who often find it difficult to find time to complete their ratings (which definitely influences the negative attitude that typically exists with respect to the performance appraisal process). That is, they would be able to carry their ratings around with them, reference the critical incidents as they relate to each individual's performance, and complete their ratings when it is most convenient. Lastly, the interface provided by most handheld computers is very natural (i.e., much like filling out a paper-and-pencil form) which should decrease the time needed to complete the ratings (Tseng, Tiplady, Macleod, & Wright, 1998). The various ways in which handheld computer technology can improve the current performance appraisal framework is truly limitless!

Selection

In addition to the examples with the performance appraisal domain, there are also many facets within the selection framework that could be improved by utilizing a handheld computer. From the applicant side, the application form itself could be posted on a handheld computer. More and more companies are moving in the direction of posting application forms on a computer (Sinar, Reynolds, & Paquet, 2003), so the use of a handheld computer may be an option (especially for jobs where the use of handheld computers will be required). Furthermore, selection tests, as well as real-life scenarios contained within an assessment center or an in-basket task, could be developed and administered via a handheld device. This would contain all the benefits associated with selection tests that may already be in electronic format (e.g., automated scoring, immediate data storage, applicant profile development) as well as allow for better transportability within the selection environment (Burke, 1993). The one facet of using handheld computers in selection that would need to be further examined, though, is an individual's familiarity and comfort level with these devices. A fair amount of research has been conducted recently examining individuals' reactions to computerized testing within the selection context (Heil & Agnew, 2000; Wiechmann & Ryan, 2003), which may transfer directly to handheld computers (i.e., will individuals who are not as familiar with handheld computers be less comfortable and subsequently perform less well than those who are familiar with them?).

From the supervisor side, ratings about different applicants' performances can be made directly into a handheld computer, and analyses can be generated immediately. For example, structured interview questions (complete with rating scales) can be posted on handheld computers. Raters can then take notes directly into the handheld computer and generate ratings in real time. Furthermore, handheld computers can be used by raters to provide ratings in real time for work samples. Lastly, handheld devices allow for greater flexibility in the selection procedure than typical paper-and-pencil formats (e.g., pulling items from larger databases). This would allow supervisors the ability to pull different questions (albeit in a semi-structured format) when evaluating an applicant. Of course the issues of familiarity and comfort level are again facets that may impact the use of handheld computers by supervisors within the selection process. Furthermore, the ability to simultaneously manipulate the PDA while tracking performance (especially within a simulation) has the potential to increase the supervisor's workload rather than reduce it (Johnston, Rushby, & Maclean, 2000). Specifically, there may be certain jobs/situations where the data needs to be collected at a rate that will not make the PDA a viable option. In these instances, however, the use of a handheld computer to enter/ summarize the data immediately upon completion of the exercise may still provide for richer data than are currently available.

Training

Lastly, training is an area within the personnel assessment framework that can be assisted via technology. For example, certain training courses can be offered online complete with certification exams at the conclusion of each module. More and more companies are moving to this concept of distance learning (Burgess & Russell, 2003; Kosarzycki, Salas, DeRouin & Fiore, 2003) that allows for individuals (via larger structured classrooms) to complete required training at the learner's pace. Within the online learning framework, the training can be broken down into manageable modules that are self-contained and allow individuals to complete smaller sections of training at their leisure. These self-contained modules will also provide the individual with easily accessible reference guides that they can access while on the job or in the field (i.e., examine a small section of the content that is relevant to the employee's current situation).

Technology can also play a role in providing a trainee with immediate feedback when the training is online (Goldstein & Ford, 2002). Information about a trainee's performance within a training module can be summarized in real time, and the trainee will be able to understand where follow-up training is needed (and potentially be directed to specific locations that can provide the trainee with detailed information in their weak areas). For example, the trainee would be able to complete a module of training and an online assessment that measures their knowledge based upon the training. The trainee would then be provided with feedback that demonstrates their strengths and weaknesses on the subject matter, and be provided with references that would allow them to review areas where they are deficient. Again, with the use of handheld computers, all of this information could be directly at their fingertips.

Discussion

In this chapter, we have provided a conceptual model of integrating handheld computer technology into HR research and practice, with ties to IT infrastructure. We have presented research supporting our model and described topics for additional empirical work and application in this area. It was not our goal to present only positive aspects of handheld computer technology as related to

HR, although many of our results have been positive and we find the potential for research is exciting. In order to provide a balanced view, we put forward in this Discussion section the most salient negative aspects of utilizing handhelds in HR research and practice.

One of the primary issues regarding new technology is cost. As is true of all current technology solutions, costs are ever changing and, for the most part, diminishing. At the time of publication of this chapter, handheld computer hardware with sufficient capacity to handle the tasks we describe were available for less than US$200 each. The necessary software for performing HR activities on handheld computers varies in scope/price and is often custom built by an organization's MIS department. Also, much of the software infrastructure necessary for implementing handheld computers already exists in an organization's IT system. However, cost will continue to be a major consideration for using handhelds in HR research and practice.

A related issue to new technology implementation is the potential for using "technology for technology's sake." One of the main findings from our research was that in a high-stakes, fast-paced profession that relies heavily on forms, such as the U.S. medical field, handheld computer technology provided several benefits over paper-based solutions and was not viewed by our participants as "technology for technology's sake," but rather technology for the sake of improved patient care. The benefits identified by our focus groups included time savings in critical situations (e.g., emergency room situations) and increased accuracy of job performance.

However, it will be important to revisit this issue in other settings, for the factors identified as benefits in our research setting (i.e., U.S. medical field) may not outweigh the perceived costs in other settings (e.g., other cultures, other professions), where personal interaction is the most important process variable and the handheld computer is perceived as an impediment to this interaction. While our findings replicate those from other U.S. medical settings, such as at Baptist Health (Extended Systems, 2004), St. Vincent's Hospitals, and the University of Miami School of Medicine (Clarinet Systems, 2004, 2004a), little empirical work is currently available from other professions or cultures.

A final issue related to technology in general and specifically the use of handhelds by professionals as a means of accomplishing their work is that of resistance to technology by the professionals themselves. According to research in the U.S. medical field, this does not appear to be a problem. For example, Manhattan Research (Miller, 2004) has found that approximately two-thirds of practicing physicians are currently using a handheld computer in their work and they expect that number to increase drastically as hospitals increase supporting IT infrastructure. These professionals find the handhelds to be one answer to problems created by ever-increasing needs for services often accompanied by decreases in available staff resources. However, differences in reaction to and adoption of handheld technology will be found at the individual, organizational, occupational, and cultural level, requiring additional research on these moderating variables and their impact on the potential value of handhelds as an HR research and practice tool.

Future Opportunities for Handheld Computers in e-HRM

As we pointed out in an earlier section, opportunities abound in this area for both research and application. As the technology continues to improve and expand, the limits to new research on handheld computers in HR will be bounded only by a lack of ideas and resources. Few researchers outside the IT community are currently examining the impact of handheld computers on work at any level, and we propose that this situation leaves us (i.e., HR practitioners and researchers) as spectators in a game we know much about and that would benefit from our direct participation.

As is the case for many organizational research topics, access to data will be an issue, as will security risks and personal privacy issues (particularly with increased use of wireless access). On the other side of the security coin, handhelds are becoming increasingly popular as security enhancements. For example, HP's wireless iPAQ Pocket PC 5500 currently has thermal biometric fingerprint authentication technology capability. It is reasonable to assume that for some organizations, handhelds will become wireless security badges that identify the carrier of the device to the organization's network. The 21st century has brought a heightened awareness of security in organizations around the globe, the impact of which on individuals has not yet received sufficient attention from researchers. The handheld computer provides a platform for gathering diary and behavioral data for forwarding this research.

We anticipate major improvements and widespread implementation of wireless networks within the near future, with resulting implications for worker mobility, availability, and communication. These factors will impact the way we plan work schedules, conduct meetings, share organizational data, and balance work with life. There are a multitude of research questions — both basic and applied — that will be generated from this single facet of implementing mobile handheld computer technology.

We predict that handheld technology in some form, be it PDA, tablet computer, cell phone, or a platform yet to be released, will become a standard component of organizational IT systems — with or without input from HR practitioners and researchers. If we provide our input as the systems and applications are being developed, we stand to gain an excellent opportunity to integrate research opportunities into a system of HR-related applications. As we found in our research, handheld computer use provides both a platform for research and a rich data source.

We hope that this chapter has provided a basis for moving HR practice and research on handheld computers ahead in a focused manner, possibly using the conceptual model presented in Figure 1 as a basis. We also hope that our empirical work will be an impetus to others in the field to conduct additional laboratory and applied research to provide empirical tests of our model. The need for basic human factors research continues to exist as new handheld programs are written and applied in new ways. And the potential for applied research for handheld computer technology within organizations is immense.

References

Benc. (2002). Accessed November 20 from *www.benc.hr/appusage.htm*

Berg, B. (2001). *Qualitative research methods for the social sciences.* Needham Heights, MA: Allyn & Bacon.

Burgess, J.R., & Russell, J.E.A. (2003). The effectiveness of distance learning initiatives in organizations. *Journal of Vocational Behavior, 63*(2), 289-303.

Burke, M.J. (1993). Computerized psychological testing: Impacts on measuring predictor constructs and future job behaviors. In N. Schmitt & W.C. Borman (Eds.), *Personnel selection in organizations.* San Francisco, CA: Jossey-Bass.

Cascio, W. (2003). Personal communication, October 23.

Clarinet Systems. (2004). Putting vital information in physicians' hands: St. Vincent Hospitals and Health Services provides physician access to patient data quickly and securely via PDA. Retrieved December 15 from *http://www.clarinetsys.com/site/downloads-page/St-Vincent-Application-Study.pdf*

Clarinet Systems. (2004a). Wireless, low-cost link to hospital networks: University of Miami School of Medicine uses infrared technology to improve efficiency and satisfaction levels. Retrieved December 15 from *http://www.clarinetsys.com/site/downloads-page/Miami-Application-Story.pdf*

Davies, S., Rodbard, D., Brandes, W., & Poropatich, R. (2004). Human resources in the palm of your hand: Science and practice. *Proceedings of the Society for Industrial and Organizational Psychologists Annual Convention,* April 2, Chicago, Illinois.

DeNisi, A.S., Robbins, T., & Cafferty, T.P. (1989). Organization of information used for performance appraisals: Role of diary keeping. *Journal of Applied Psychology, 74,* 124-129.

Extended Systems. (2004). Baptist Health: Arkansas' largest healthcare provider improves patient care with mobile IT strategy. Retrieved January 5 from *http://software.symbol.com/files/BaptistHealth.pdf*

Fletcher, L.A., Erickson, D.J., Toomey, T.L., & Wagenaar, A.C. (2003). Handheld computers: A feasible alternative to paper forms for field data collection. *Evaluation Review, 27*(2), 165-178.

Goldstein, I.L., & Ford, J.K. (2002). *Training in organizations: Needs assessment, development, and evaluation* (4th ed.). Belmont, CA: Wadsworth.

Greene, P.D. (2001). Handheld computers as tools for writing and managing field data. *Field Methods, 13*(2), 181-197.

Hayes, D. (2003). Personal digital assistants (PDAs) for psychiatrists. *Psychiatric Bulletin, 27,* 161-163.

Heil, M.C., & Agnew, B.O. (2000). *The effects of previous computer experience on Air Traffic-Selection and Training (AT-SAT) test performance.* (DOT/FAA/AM-00/12). Washington, DC: Federal Aviation Administration Office of Aviation Medicine.

Johnston, A.N., Rushby, N., & Maclean, I. (2000). An assistant for crew performance assessment. *The International Journal of Aviation Psychology, 10*(1), 99-108.

Keown-Gerrard, J.L., & Sulsky, L.M. (2001). The effects of task information training and frame-of-reference training with situational constraints on rating accuracy. *Human Performance, 14*(4), 305-320.

Konrad, R. (2001). GM to put more handhelds into doctors' black bags. *CNet News.com,* (January 25).

Kosarzycki, M.P., Salas, E., DeRouin, R., & Fiore, S.M. (2003). Distance learning in organizations: A review and assessment of future needs. In D. Stone (Ed.), *Advances in human performance and cognitive engineering research* (Volume 3). City: Elsevier Science/JAI Press.

Lanway, C., & Graham, P. (2003). Mobile documentation. *Healthcare Infomatics Online,* (October).

Lyons, B., Davies, S., Rodbard, D., Brandes, W., & Poropatich, R. (2004). Needs assessment of PDAs in clinical practice in U.S. Army medical environments. *Proceedings of the Society for Industrial and Organizational Psychologists Annual Convention,* Chicago, Illinois, April.

Maurer, T.J., Palmer, J.K., & Ashe, D.K. (1993). Diaries, checklists, evaluations, and contrast effects in measurement of behavior. *Journal of Applied Psychology, 78,* 226-231.

McIntyre, R.M., Smith, D.E., & Hassett, C.E. (1984). Accuracy of performance ratings as affected by rater training and perceived purpose of rating. *Journal of Applied Psychology, 69,* 147-156.

Miller, J. (2002). PDAs key emerging technology for physicians. Retrieved January 20, 2004, from *http://www.pocketpccity.com/articles/2002/12/2002-12-11-PDAs-Key-Emerging.html*

Miner, A.G., Glomb, T.M., & Hulin, C.L. (2001). Correlates of mood at work: An experience sampling study. *Proceedings of the Meeting of the Society for Industrial and Organizational Psychology,* San Diego, California, April.

MobileVillage. (2003). Pocket PCs can help people with disabilities. Retrieved October 30 from *http://www.mobilevillage.com/news/2003.10.27/disabilities.htm*

Murphy, K.R., & Cleveland, J.N. (1991). *Performance appraisal: An organizational perspective.* Needham Heights, MA: Allyn & Bacon.

Murphy, K.R., & Cleveland, J.N. (1995). *Understanding performance appraisal: Social, organizational, and goal-based perspectives.* Thousand Oaks, CA: Sage Publications.

Myers, B.A. (2001). Using handhelds and PCs together. *Communications of the ACM, 44*(11), 34-41.

Myers, B.A., Stiel, H., & Gargiulo R. (1998). Collaboration using multiple PDAs connected to a PC. Retrieved August 13, 2003, from *http://www.cs.cmu.edu/~pebbles*

Qualrus Software. (2002). Columbia, MO: Idea Works, Inc.

Rodbard, D., Brandes, W., Davies, S., & Lyons, B. (2002). *Clinical needs assessment of medical digital assistants in clinical practice in U.S. Army medical environments.* Technical report.

Rosenbloom, M. (2003). Medical error reduction and PDAs. *International Pediatrics, 18*, 69-77.

Sanchez, J.I., & De La Torre, P. (1996). A second look at the relationship between rating and behavioral accuracy in performance appraisal. *Journal of Applied Psychology, 81*, 3-10.

Sinar, E.F., Reynolds, D.H., & Paquet, S.L. (2003). Nothing but 'net? Corporate image and Web-based testing. *International Journal of Selection & Assessment, 11*(2-3), 150-157.

Smith, P.C., & Kendall, L.M. (1963). Retranslation of expectations: An approach to the construction of unambiguous anchors for rating scales. *Journal of Applied Psychology, 47*, 149-155.

Sulsky, L.M., & Day, D.V. (1994). Effects of frame-of-reference training and cognitive categorization: An empirical investigation of rater memory issues. *Journal of Applied Psychology, 77*, 501-510.

Tseng, H.M., Tiplady, B, Macleod, H.A., & Wright, P. (1998). Computer anxiety: A comparison of pen-based personal digital assistants, conventional computer and paper assessments of mood and performance. *British Journal of Psychology, 89*(4), 599-610.

Wiechmann, D., & Ryan, A.M. (2003). Reactions to computerized testing in selection contexts. *International Journal of Selection & Assessment, 11*(2-3), 215-229.

Endnotes

1   The generic "handheld computer" refers to Personal Digital Assistants of all types, including the currently popular Pocket PC and Palm Pilot models.

2   This study was conducted by the American Institutes for Research (AIR) in Washington, DC, with: David Rodbard, MD, Project Director; Scott Davies, PhD, Deputy Project Director; and Brian Lyons, MA, Research Analyst. The project was funded by Telemedicine and Advanced Technology Research Center (TATRC), U.S., Army Medical Research and Material Command, Ft. Detrick, Maryland, and was conceived by the late Dr. G. Rufus Sessions, Project Officer, TATRC. COL. Ronald K. Poropatich, MD MC, Chief, Telemedicine Directorate, North Atlantic Regional Medical Command, U.S. Army, served as the clinical Principal Investigator. Invaluable research and logistic support was provided to the project by Michael Keeney, PhD (AIR), Jessica Kenyon (TATRC), and Damien Michaels (TATRC).

Chapter III

Social Network Mapping Software:
New Frontiers in HRM

Mousumi Bhattacharya, Fairfield University, USA

Christopher Huntley, Fairfield University, USA

Abstract

Recent developments in social network mapping software have opened up new opportunities for human resource management (HRM). In this chapter we discuss how social network mapping information may provide critical inputs to managers for increasing the effectiveness of their HRM programs.

Introduction

In a knowledge-driven economy, returns on effective management of human capital are likely to exceed those available from more efficient management of financial and physical assets. In order to realize these returns, however, companies must go beyond notions of productivity and cost effectiveness, and develop new approaches and management techniques to tap the knowledge, intellect, and creativity used to achieve these outcomes. Mapping and understanding social networks within an organization is an approach to understand how social relationships may affect business processes. Network perspectives build on the general notion that economic actions are influenced by the social context in which they are embedded and by the position of actors in social networks (Granovetter, 1985). Research on social networks indicates that network structure and activities influence employees and affect individual and organizational outcomes (Sparrowe, Liden, Wayne, & Kraimer, 2001), and provides motivation to explore this rich field for possible inputs in human resource management (HRM) activities. In this chapter we suggest ways in which social networks can be analyzed using network mapping software and how some the information derived can be used meaningfully for HRM.

What do networks within organizations look like? How do we efficiently construct and analyze maps of these networks? What effect do these networks have on HRM activities? What opportunities exist to use social network mapping information to improve HRM activities? These questions are significant for organizations that want to manage their social and human capital efficiently and effectively. Given that vigorous network activities usually take place within organizations, and that social capital may have a direct bearing on human capital management, it becomes important to examine how these social processes affect HRM activities. Recent developments in social network mapping software help organizations to discover and analyze network structures. While such software has been available for quite some time, only recently have high-quality tools become readily accessible to mainstream business users. Partly this is because of improvements in computing power (i.e., modern computers are more capable), but there has also been significant improvements in the functionality and usability of the software. Our discussion highlights the capabilities of some of these software applications, as well as their implications for various HRM functions.

What are Social Networks?

The social network theory (Uzzi, 1996; Ibarra, 1993; Granovetter, 1973, 1985) emphasizes that human decisions are, to a large extent, functions of the ties between people (Burt, 1992). Individuals obtain support, information, and power from the network structure around them and from their position in the network. Factors that determine the influence of a social network on decision making include accessibility to network, network structure, the actors involved, and the location of the decision maker in the network (Burt, 1992).

While the influence of social networks within organizations has long been acknowledged, it is only recently that one could quantify and visualize social networks of substantial size. To understand the complexity of the task, let us consider the various structural measures that can be applied to social networks. Network structures refer to a definable set of relationships, which hold together a number of objects (or people) in juxtaposition with one another (Burt, 1992). These structures are characterized by relationships, entities, context, configurations, and temporal stability. Some of the indices and dimensions that express outcomes of network are:

- *frequency of interaction* among the contacts;
- *structural holes* or non-connectivity between contacts;
- *centrality*, which refers to the extent to which an individual could reach others in the network through a minimum number of links;
- *criticality*, which reveals the degree to which an individual's position was crucial to the flow of materials in the workflow network;
- *transaction alternatives*, which refers to whether or not redundancy was built into the system in terms of inputs to particular individuals and their output to others;
- *reachability*, which focuses on how many links a communication must flow through to get from one node to another;
- *connectiveness*, which refers to whether or not all of the possible linkages in an aggregate are being utilized;
- *inclusiveness,* which refers to the number of points that are included within the various connected parts of the network; and
- *density* of a network, which is defined as the number of relationships expressed as a proportion of the maximum possible number of relationships.

Clearly, with such a rich vocabulary of quantitative terms used to describe just the structure of a network, there is much more to network mapping and analysis than constructing a few diagrams. Calculating even one measure manually would be quite tedious and error-prone. Thus, network analyses are almost always performed using specialized software, the subject of our next section.

Social Network Mapping Software

Figure 1 summarizes the common features of network mapping software. Most social network analysis software supports at least one of three functions: data collection, descriptive modeling, and decision support. Data collection is the most fundamental requirement. Generally, the input data takes on one of two forms, depending on the focus of the analysis. For perceptual or egocentric data, the traditional method is to survey individuals about themselves (age, gender, etc.) and their relationships to others in the organization. If the objective is to provide a onetime or occasional snapshot of the network, such methods can work very well. However, for more frequent analyses, an alternative method is to collect interaction data (e.g., adjacency matrices) based on some measure of activity between people in the organization. The data is then input to the software through some sort of import utility. In some cases, the import utility can be used to collect activity data from e-mail servers, instant messaging gateways, and other "watering holes" in cyberspace.

Descriptive modeling, the second function, is used to "map" the structure of the network. Quantitative models use descriptive statistics (e.g., centrality, criticality, etc.) to measure global or local properties of the network. For example, IKNOW (2003) can calculate measures of centrality and prestige for demographic groups within a larger network. Similarly, UCINET (2003) provides dozens of analytical models, ranging from measures of criticality, cohesion, inclusiveness, and similar quantities, to more advanced procedures like correspondence analysis and multiple regressions. Visualization models are also useful, particularly when looking for useful patterns (e.g., centers of control) in the network structure. Two of the most common visual models are network "graphs" (NetVis, 2003) that look like stick and ball models used in chemistry classes and clustering diagrams (UCINET, 2003) that use tree shapes called "dendrograms" or colored scatter plots to group individuals within the network.

The last and most advanced function of social network software is to provide

Figure 1. Social network mapping software classification

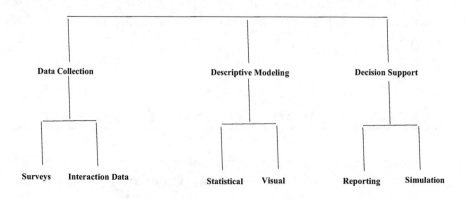

decision support to those who seek to alter or manage the social network itself. Providing that the data collection process is sufficiently automated, customized reports can be used to detect trends or unusual activity in the network. They may also be used in so-called what-if analyses, where the network is analyzed under various scenarios. Since in principle any descriptive model can be used as the basis for the report, virtually any package will support this functionality to some degree. A somewhat more sophisticated use of such longitudinal data is simulation (SIENA, 2003), which tries to predict the evolution and long-term behavior of the network given certain network parameters. Typically, these parameters are estimated from several snapshots of the interaction matrices.

A representative sample of the available software packages taken from the INSNA Web site (INSNA, 2003) is presented in Table 1. IKNOW (2003) is a Web-based package that uses surveys to elicit network data. It is free for noncommercial use, but you must contact the developer for a commercial license. InFlow (2003) and NetForm (2003) are offered as part of consulting services by the developers and include a formal methodology for conducting network analysis. NetVis (2003) and SIENA (2003) are free packages targeted at researchers that support advanced statistical features like simulation. UCINET (2003) is similarly advanced, but requires a commercial license.

As even this small sample demonstrates, social network software is quite a diverse lot, ranging from relatively simple network mappers to comprehensive methodologies to cutting-edge research tools. Further, each tool has its strengths and weaknesses, making the choice of which to use somewhat

Table 1. A sample of social network software

	IKNOW	InFlow	NetVis	NetForm	SIENA	UCINET
Data Collection						
Surveys	X	X	X	X		
Import Utility		X	X		X	X
Descriptive Modeling						
Statistics	X	X	X	X	X	X
Graphs	X	X	X	X		X
Decision Support						
Custom Reports	X	X		X		
Simulation			X		X	
Software						
Vendor	Univ. Illinois	Orgnet.com	Netvis.org	NetForm	Tom Snijders	Analytic Technologies
Platform	Web	PC	Web	PC	PC	PC
Free Download	Yes	No	Yes	No	Yes	Evaluation
Licenses	Free Commercial	Commercial	Free	Commercial	Free	Commercial
Paid Support Available	Yes	Yes	No	Yes	No	Yes

dependent on individual needs and resources. If your needs are extensive and you have the budget to afford it, then you may want to consider software like InFlow or NetForm that are backed by consulting organizations. Similarly, if you can't afford consulting services and do not want to scale the learning curve of the more advanced tools like SIENA or UCINET, then you may want to opt for the simplicity of a tool like IKNOW or NetVis which, once installed, requires very little maintenance or training.

HRM and Social Network Mapping

Social network theorists have discussed how networks provide access to information and knowledge (Burt, 1992). Flow of information, power, and status are the three major outcomes from social networks and the network position of an individual or a group facilitates this flow (Sparrowe et al., 2001). From the HRM perspective, information on knowledge, power, and status flow can be input for effective management of people. HRM activities like recruitment and selection, performance management, training and development, communication, employee relation, and compensation can use this information for better decision making. Flow of knowledge tells us how human, social, and intellectual capital are generated within an organization (Ibarra, 1993). Power and status flows help HR managers to identify sources of motivation and greater productivity. Thus, visualization of social networks and measurements of network properties within an organization reveal information that may lead to new frontiers in HRM functions.

Before the advent of network mapping software, subjective assessments of social processes were made by supervisors and managers. However, recent research reveals that supervisors' assessments do not correlate with either the perceptions of the actual incumbent, or with critical work outcome measures (Marchese & Delprino, 1998). Network mapping provides visual as well as statistical representation of network structures and the actual flow of information, providing a much-needed quantitative tool for this type of information. Depending on the type of software used, this information can be collected over time for several different occupants of a position so that a generic picture of the 'social' requirements of the position emerges. Equipped with this information, the manager can make a better-informed decision about how to manage people within an organization. While we certainly do not wish to imply that objective data is better than subjective assessment, there is a case for numbers and pictures from actual data supplementing qualitative judgments for greater accuracy in decision making.

Table 2 shows the type of information relevant to HRM from social networks mapping and how they can be possible inputs in HRM processes. Social networks within an organization can reveal information related to a *job*, an *employee*, a *group* (team, department, unit, etc.), or the whole *organization*. We discuss input from social network mapping to each of these levels within the organization and the impact of this information on HRM functions. In doing so, we follow our classification of social network software (Table 1) and discuss data collection methods and the descriptive statistics that are relevant for the HRM functions and are inputs to decision-making processes.

Information Relevant to the Job

Social network mapping can be a valuable source of information for social interaction activities associated with a job or position. Recent research has highlighted that even for a 'technical' position like webmaster, organizational and management skills are critical and can make a difference in performance (Wade & Parent, 2002). Social interaction is a major requirement in organiza-

Table 2. HRM and social network mapping

HRM practice	Input from social network mapping		Use in HRM				
	Data collection	Descriptive modeling	Decision support	Job related	Employee related	Group related	Organization related
Recruitment and selection	Temporal and snapshot, periodical, infrequent	Frequency, structural holes, centrality	Identify patterns, detect outliers, detect abnormal patterns, prediction of skill requirements, forecasting models	Identify interpersonal/organizational skill requirements, cross-functional skill requirements, leadership skill requirements	Match social profile for internal selection	Skill demand analysis, select group members	Organizational skill demand analysis
Training and development	Temporal, periodical, frequent	Centrality, criticality, connectiveness, structural holes	Prediction of skill requirements, forecasting models	Identify current and future training requirements, succession planning	Identify training candidates, career planning	Culture building, consensus building	Organizational communication
Performance management	Temporal, ongoing	Frequency, structural holes, centrality, criticality, transaction alternatives, reachability, inclusiveness, density, social profile	Normative models	Set normative targets for organizational skills, identify or build redundancies	Evaluate against targets, identify high performers	Optimize reachability and inclusiveness, facilitate goal-sharing and team work, maximize efficiency	Set organizational targets, balance efficiency and flexibility among inter-unit work
Employee relations	Snapshot, based on requirement	Frequency, centrality, criticality	Negotiation models	Identify critical positions for maintaining harmonious relations	Identify critical/central candidates for negotiation/consensus building	Identify critical/central groups for negotiation/consensus building	Monitor overall employee relations patterns
Compensation and benefits	Temporal, ongoing	Structural holes, centrality, criticality, connectiveness, inclusiveness	Identify patterns in information flow	Measure the social component of a job for determining compensation	Identify motivating factors for an individual	Identify groups for similar compensation patterns	Architecture for compensation and benefit management

tional skills. Therefore mapping of the 'social' interaction requirements of a job helps managers learn more about it and may provide critical information that constitutes the job description of a position, either formal or informal. Data collection for such information may be periodical, although temporal data is needed to get a stable pattern for the social aspect of the job.

Job-related information provided by social network mapping can be of several types. What is the level of interaction requirement of the job in relation to other jobs/positions at the same or different organizational levels (frequency of interaction)? Complex interaction patterns would reveal a higher requirement of people-related skills, while sparse interaction may indicate either technical/specialized skills or lower skill requirements. Structural holes — that is, the distance between the network contacts — is also relevant for describing a position. Are the network contacts far apart or close together? Far-flung networks may indicate cross-functional interaction requirements, sometimes across hierarchical levels, while tightly knit networks indicate homogeneous work groups. Centrality of the position is yet another critical dimension that indicates requirement for leadership abilities because the incumbent may need to exercise more decision-making capabilities if most of the contacts in the network are referring back to this position often. All this information provides critical input for recruitment and selection processes, and helps in choosing the 'right' candidate for a job.

Job-related information provided by social network mapping can be used for training and development purposes as well — to identify current and future training requirements for a job. For example, central and critical jobs have greater requirement for interpersonal training. Effective succession planning, an emerging critical HRM activity (Burke, 1997), can also benefit from network information on jobs. Jobs that are more central and critical in a network would require more planning for succession in case of turnover/retirement of the current incumbents. Network-based decision support tools may help to set normative targets for a job used in performance management processes. For example, transaction alternatives, a dimension of networks, show redundancies in the system in terms of input to particular individuals and their output to others. Redundancies need to be optimized because of the trade-off between efficiency (low redundancy) and flexibility (high redundancy). Performance management processes need to incorporate these trade-offs in their normative targets for job performance. In yet another function of HRM, employee relations, identification of central and critical jobs would help in determining better negotiation strategies, as well as assist in maintaining a harmonious relationship. Management can focus their efforts on these jobs, and achieve greater efficiency in employee relations. Finally, network information related to job can also be an input for compensation and benefit management processes. By measuring the social component of a job, managers get an opportunity to reliably incorporate the social components in their compensation design.

Information about the Person

Who does an individual interact with? Are they strong or weak ties? Are they static or dynamic ties? What types of information flow through these ties? Are there power and status flow through these ties? How can the network determine performance outcomes? These are some of the questions that can be answered by social network mapping at the individual level. This information can be an input for several HRM functions that aim to motivate people to give their best and to improve productivity and creativity.

For example, different network positions represent different opportunities for an individual to access new knowledge. An employee's network position reveals his/her ability to access external information and knowledge. By occupying a central position in the intra-organization network, an employee is likely to access desired strategic resources. Such resources will fuel the individual's innovative activities by providing the external information necessary to generate new ideas. If an organization can identify the individuals who occupy central positions in networks through social network mapping, then more targeted efforts can be directed towards these individuals in developing them for greater creativity and productivity.

At the same time, the innovative work of the organization will benefit from direct access to the knowledge residing in the individual. Knowledge is usually distributed unevenly within an organization (Ibarra, 1993) because it is difficult to spread it across different individuals where preexisting relationships among people are absent. Indeed, innovative ideas are often the result of interaction among groups and team members. To foster innovation, information and knowledge should be deliberately distributed. A network of people provides channels for distributing information and knowledge that as to stimulate and support innovative activities. Therefore a central network position is associated with innovation outcomes within an organization (Tsai & Ghoshal, 1998). An individual occupying a more central position in the network is likely to produce more innovations.

Network information that profiles the social capabilities of individuals may be used for effective selection, for training and development, for matching them with positions, as well as to grow them within an organization. Effective utilization of social skills would enable the firm to achieve better productivity. Fulfillment of social needs of individuals will increase the probability of retention of the individual. For performance management processes, individuals can be assessed reliably against normative targets set through established patterns of interaction. This would be a significant improvement over subjective assessments of organizational and social skills, and may help reduce costs associated with alternative evaluation processes like 360-degree feedback. In employee relations activities, identification of central and critical individuals helps management to focus efforts towards negotiation and harmony. Networks of these individuals can be reached quickly and effectively through them. Exercise of control in difficult situations can also be accomplished using their network leverage. For compensation and benefit management processes, the social profile of an individual helps managers to identify some of the factors that would motivate him/her. Therefore, customized compensation and benefits may be designed to match each individual's preferences.

Information about Groups

Social network mapping information is most relevant for management of groups or units within an organization. Although there is an increasing recognition that groups and teamwork are essential for organizational success, to date we know little about how to best manage social activities within a group. Network mapping helps by providing some answers to questions like:

- Is the group formal or informal (compare mapped interactions with organizational design)?
- Do members of the group change?
- How does the group operate?
- Are interactions frequent or sparse?
- Who occupies the central position, the group leader or somebody else who is socially more powerful?
- Do most of the interactions within the group occur during projects or do the social interactions continue in between projects too?

Structural holes, which are non-connected distances between contacts in a network; connectiveness, which refers to whether or not all possible linkages in an aggregate are being utilized; density, which is the number of relationships expressed as a proportion of all possible linkages — are some of the main parameters of network information that are useful for management of groups. A network showing large structural holes indicates either a less cohesive group or a diverse group in terms of functional or cultural background. This will impact the skill demand analysis of the group, selection of members for the group, as well as culture and consensus-building exercises that can be applied to the group. Connectiveness is a relative concept, and the optimal level of connectiveness is different for different groups. Centrality of a group and its connectiveness, both within the group and with other groups, can provide significant input for training of the group members. For example, cross-training is expected to increase connectivity. Similarly, density of interaction may indicate the homogeneity/heterogeneity of the group culture, which is an important input for group intervention processes.

Performance management implications of network information of groups are the most significant. Mapped patterns allow managers the scope to optimize reachability (how many links a communication must flow through to get from one node to another) and inclusiveness (number of points that are included within the various connected parts of the network) for greater efficiency in communication within groups. This facilitates management of performance by effective sharing of goals, and by fostering efficient team work. Employee relations efforts are also aided by improvement of communication channels for reaching out to groups. Moreover, network information helps management to identify critical and central groups for negotiation and consensus building. For compensation management, network mapping helps the management identify groups, either formal or informal, for whom compensation and benefit packages should be homogeneous. Research indicates that employee dissatisfaction arises most from perceptions of inequitable compensation (Mowday, 1991), compared to referent others in the organization. Network mapping provides information on who these referent others are so that the cause of dissatisfaction may be addressed.

Information about Organization

At the organizational level, network mapping provides an overall picture of network patterns within the organization. Although it may get extremely complex and difficult to interpret these networks, there is quite some usefulness for this information. Apart from showing the social culture of the organization, network mapping identifies the communication pattern within the organization. Does the CEO communicate with the managers and the employees? If so, what is the frequency? What is the pattern of interaction of managers with employees? Can employees, in general, cross hierarchical, functional boundaries to get the work done? Is knowledge shared among employees? These are some of the challenging but critical organizational questions that network mapping can shed some light on.

Research has already highlighted the significance of intra-unit network ties in spreading knowledge and best practices (Tsai & Ghoshal, 1998). Organizational units differ in their internal knowledge, practices, and capabilities. Networks of inter-unit links allow organizational units to access new knowledge from each other and may increase their cost efficiency through dissemination of "best practices" within organizations. The centrality and criticality of a unit in the intraorganizational network may determine the unit's access to different knowledge, thus affecting its ability to recognize and respond to new market opportunities.

The HRM outputs that can be derived from network mapping information at the organizational level are organizational skill demand analysis for recruitment and selection, organizational communication patterns for training need analysis, organizational target setting for performance management processes, balance between efficiency and flexibility among inter-unit workflow, monitoring of overall employee relation patterns, and ascertainment of an overall architecture for compensation and benefit management.

Complementary Network Information at Difference Levels

Although social network maps can be constructed and analyzed at different levels within the organization, and the information is useful for individual HRM processes, the best usage of network data are complementary and symbiotic. Consistent with the 'configurational' approach to HRM (Delery & Doty, 1996), this view is represented diagrammatically in Figure 2. The configurational view proposes that HRM activities are most effective when applied in

Figure 2. Use of social network mapping information at different levels

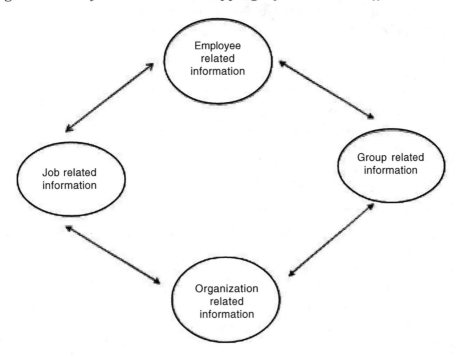

'bundles' where practices are synergistic with each other. We assert that information from social network mapping can also be applied in 'bundles'. Information at the job-, employee-, group-, and organization-level can be used interactively in HRM decision processes.

Discussion

In this chapter we have discussed a new use of information technology in management of people: the use of social network mapping software for making better-informed decisions in HRM. The advent of user-friendly, yet advanced network mapping software has prompted us to enquire how this software can provide meaningful information for HRM processes. We have classified the functionality offered by the software into data collection, descriptive modeling, and decision support, and have discussed how each of these functions can provide information relevant to HRM functions. We have identified four levels of information usage in HRM related to a job, to a person, to a group or unit, and to the organization as a whole. For each of these levels, we have explored how the information obtained from social network mapping can translate into HRM input and assist in more informed decision making.

The contribution of this chapter lies in opening up a whole new way of looking at HRM decision making. Traditionally, the informational content for social processes within an organization is assessed subjectively, through perceptions of individual managers or supervisors. Social network mapping software permits a radical change in assessing the social interaction within organizations. Through visual mapping as well as statistical modeling, the software can provide precise, relevant quantitative data for the network interactions. We have explored the intersection of this technology and HRM activities to inquire how it can assist decision making in HRM.

We feel that such application of social network mapping software would be especially beneficial for managers at all levels. For the supervisor or HR manager looking to fill a given position, studying the network interactions of current or previous holders of that position can greatly aid in selecting candidates with the "intangibles" desired for success. Similarly, for a manager investigating the behavior or performance of a particular employee, taking a snapshot of activity around the employee can greatly aid understanding. At the group or department level, network models may help to identify synergies or other strong linkages between the groups. Finally, at the enterprise or organizational level, a survey of the social network may help to explain certain phenomena discovered through benchmarking studies of other firms. For example, if a firm is an early adopter of advanced communication technology, one might expect it to have fewer layers of communication between decision makers (i.e., improved reachability) which could permit the firm to have a "flatter" organizational structure.

However, technology is not an end by itself, it is an enabler. By no means do we imply that technology can replace the human judgment element in decision making. The applicability of social network mapping software is limited by the capability of the decision maker. Nonetheless, tools like visualization and descriptive modeling do make the task easier. The learning curve for using the software and interpreting the results is relatively low compared to other extensive database management or knowledge management packages. We can conclude, therefore, that social network software has the potential to be a convenient and effective input for HRM processes.

References

Burke, W.W. (1997). What human resource practitioners need to know for the 21st century. *Human Resource Management, 36*(1), 71-79.

Burt, R.S. (1992). *Structural holes: The social structure of competition.* Cambridge, MA: Harvard University Press.

Delery, J.E., & Doty, D.H. (1996). Modes of theorizing in strategic human resource management: Tests of universalistic, contingency, and configurational performance predictions. *Academy of Management Journal, 39*, 802-835.

Granovetter, M. (1973). The strength of weak ties. *American Journal of Sociology, 78,* 1360-1380.

Granovetter, M. (1985). Economic action and social structure: The problem of embeddedness. *American Journal of Sociology, 91*(3), 481-510.

Ibarra, H. (1993). Personal networks of women and minorities in management: A conceptual framework. *Academy of Management Review, 18,* 56-87.

IKNOW. (2003). Retrieved from *iknow.spcomm.uiuc.edu*

InFlow. (2003). Retrieved from *www.orgnet.com*

INSNA. (2003). Retrieved from *www.sfu.ca/~insna*

Marchese, M.C., & Delprino, R.P. (1998). Do supervisors and subordinates see eye-to-eye on job enrichment? *Industrial and Labor Relations Review, 51*(4), 179-191.

Mowday, R.T. (1991). Equity theory predictions of behavior in organizations. In R.M. Steers & L.W. Porter (Eds.), *Motivation and work behavior* (5th edition) (pp. 111-131). New York: McGraw Hill.

NetForm. (2003). Retrieved from *www.netform.com*

NetVis. (2003). Retrieved from *www.netvis.org*

SIENA. (2003). Retrieved from *stat.gamma.rug.nl/snijders/siena.html*

Sparrowe, R.T., Liden, R.C., Wayne, S.J., & Kraimer, M.L. (2001). Social networks and the performance of individuals and groups. *Academy of Management Journal, 44*(20), 316-325.

Tsai, W., & Ghoshal, S. (1998). Social capital and value creation: The role of intrafirm networks. *Academy of Management Journal, 41*(4), 464-476.

UCINET. (2003). Retrieved from *www.analytictech.com/ucinet_5_description.htm*

Uzzi, B. (1996). The sources and consequences of embeddedness for the economic performance of organizations: The network effect. *American Sociological Review, 61,* 674-698.

Wade, M.R., & Parent, M. (2002). Relationships between job skills and performance: A study of webmasters. *Journal of Management Information Systems, 18*(3), 71-96.

Section II

Redesigning
HR Administrative
Processes

Chapter IV

E-Recruiting:
Categories and Analysis of Fortune 100 Career Web Sites

In Lee, Western Illinois University, USA

Abstract

Since the mid-1990s, a number of e-recruiting methods such as job boards, corporate career Web sites, and e-recruiting consortia have been introduced into the labor market. Recruiting through the corporate career Web site has been touted as the most efficient and cost-effective recruiting method among them. While most large and medium-sized organizations have deployed corporate career Web sites, many of them have failed to achieve the maximum benefits because they do not have the appropriate e-recruiting practice in place. After identifying six categories of e-recruiting sources, this study analyzes the corporate career Web sites of the Fortune 100 companies. Thirty-three attributes that characterize the corporate career Web sites were identified, named, and analyzed around four major categories: recruiting methods, job search tools, job application tools, and information on organizational attributes.

Introduction

Currently, e-recruiting is one of the most successful e-commerce applications as a method for quickly reaching a large pool of the potential job seekers. The capability of advanced e-recruiting tools has enabled recruiters to quickly identify and hire qualified candidates, and to build ongoing relationships with prospective employees. According to Forrester Research (www.forrester.com), the average cost of hiring an employee via the Internet is US$183, whereas the average cost of hiring an employee via the traditional methods (i.e., newspapers or magazines) is $1,383. Forrester Research predicted that corporate recruiters would increase the e-recruiting budget by 52% by 2004, while cutting the budget for traditional recruitment by 31%.

Major advantages cited for the successful adoption of e-recruiting methods include cost savings, efficiency, and convenience for both recruiters and job seekers (Tomlinson, 2002; Miller, 2001; Gale, 2001). In a 2001 poll of 400 recruiters by Recruiters Network (www.recruitersnetwork.com), 46% indicated that e-recruiting was the most effective way to get the most hires and best résumés, followed by referrals (35%) and newspaper classifieds (11%).

There has been a fundamental shift in the way companies use the e-recruiting methods since their inception in the mid-1990s. While most companies utilize at least one of the third-party job boards, more and more companies are creating their own corporate career Web sites. According to iLogos' research (http://www.ilogos.com), 29% of Global 500 companies had corporate career Web sites and 57% subscribed to the third-party job boards in 1998. In 2002, the figure had changed to 91% and 9%, respectively.

The main purposes of this chapter are to classify the various e-recruiting sources and to analyze the content of Fortune 100 companies' career Web sites. This chapter is organized as follows: The first section compares the traditional recruiting and e-recruiting processes. Six major categories of the e-recruiting sources are then discussed, followed by a content analysis of the Fortune 100 companies' career Web sites. The chapter concludes with future e-recruiting trends.

Background: Traditional Recruiting vs. E-Recruiting Processes

The traditional recruiting process consists of the following iterative phases: identification of hiring needs; submission of job requisition and approval; job posting, submission of job applications; screening of résumé/application; interviewing; pre-employment screening; and job offer and employment contract. Both hiring managers and recruiters rely on hard-copy documents and conventional delivery mechanisms to complete the recruiting process.

The traditional recruiting process is typically a step-by-step sequential process whereby the subsequent phase starts the required tasks only after the previous phase completes its tasks. Labor-intensive hiring tools like face-to-face interviews, paper and pencil tests, and job previews are widely used in traditional recruiting. The traditional process has been fraught with task delays and miscommunications, which result in the long hiring process and high hiring cost.

Computers had been used in the traditional recruiting process even before the introduction of e-recruiting. However, computer applications were limited to the automation of internal processes rather than the rationalization of the process. Software packages could not communicate with each other, and the quantity and quality of the job applications remained the same. Even with automation, most recruiting processes were still batch processes. The advent of e-recruiting moved the computer application of the recruiting process to a higher level. The e-recruiting system is a Web-enabled, "anytime-anyplace," ubiquitous system for both job seekers and recruiters.

We define the e-recruiting as *practices and activities carried on by the organization that utilizes a variety of electronic means to fill open positions effectively and efficiently*. The e-recruiting process consists of the following iterative steps: identification of hiring needs; submission of job requisition; approval of the job requisition via a job database; job posting on the Internet; online search of the job database by job seekers, online pre-screening/online self-assessment; submission of applications by applicants directly into an applicant database; online search of the applicant database for candidate selection; online evaluation of résumé/application; interviewing by recruiters/hiring managers; online pre-employment screening; and job offer and employment contract.

While traditional recruiting is characterized as a sequential batch process, e-recruiting is characterized as a continuous and online process in which some of the recruiting activities may be performed concurrently. The benefits of e-recruiting are accomplished with the extensive use of a centralized job database and an array of Web-enabled integrated applications. For example, when there is a need for a new employee, hiring managers may prepare the job requisition by entering the predefined job code into the job analysis database and retrieving a detailed list of the job requirements. The submission of the retrieved job requisition to division managers is electronically processed. Once the job requisition is approved, the job requisition data are used for the job posting at the career Web site. The job requisition data are also used to search résumés based on specific criteria/keywords. The qualified candidates are further narrowed down with an additional screening process that utilizes various online

Table 1. Summary of six categories of the e-recruiting sources: Recruiters' perspectives

E-Recruiting Source	Advantages	Disadvantages	Sample Participants
General-Purpose Job Board	Brand recognition; E-recruiting experience; High traffic; Industry best tools; Large candidate base; Large recruiter base	Relatively high job posting cost; Potentially low quality applications; Limited content control; Stickiness of the job board; Limited candidate relationship	Monster.com; HotJobs.com; CareerBuilder.com
Niche Job Board	Gathering of passive job seekers; Focused search; Community of professionals	Low brand recognition; Possibility of identity theft	Dice.com; Erexchange.com; Taon-line.com; JournalismJobs.com; MarketingJobs.com; TexasJobs.com
E-Recruiting Application Service Provider	Low application development cost for recruiters; Quick application development	Integration issues with existing systems; Possibility of closeout due to competition; Possibility of lock-in; Low traffic	Recruitsoft; Brassring; RecruitUSA; PeopleClick; TalentFusion; Lawson
Hybrid Recruiting Service Providers	Expertise in advertising industry; Portfolio of recruiting media; Price bundling with conventional media	Strong image as a conventional media; Low traffic; Low technology	*New York Times, Wall Street Journal; Chronicle of Higher Education*
E-Recruiting Consortium	Low service cost; Direct and immediate link to corporate career site	Potential conflicts among members; Low exposure; Low technology	DirectEmployers.com; NACElink
Corporate Career Web Site	Candidate relationship management; High interest in jobs by job applicants; Integration with exiting systems	Needs for IT specialists; High up-front development cost	94% of Fortune 100 companies; 81% of Fortune 500 companies

and off-line interview and test tools, and then the company conducts an online pre-employment background check and makes a job offer to the best candidate.

Categories of E-Recruiting Sources

Corporate recruiters tend to be interested in such factors as whether certain recruiting sources are more likely to yield a higher percentage of new hires, whether certain sources are likely to generate minority applicants, and whether the quality of job applicants is higher for certain recruiting sources (Barber, 1998). While numerous e-recruiting sources have been introduced to improve the recruiting effectiveness since the mid-1990s, no formal classification system for e-recruiting sources has been developed yet.

In order to give recruiters and job seekers a better understanding of the e-recruiting methods, we surveyed a wide range of recruiting sources. Based on this analysis, we identify six basic categories of the e-recruiting sources: (1) general purpose job board, (2) niche job board, (3) e-recruiting application service provider, (4) hybrid (online and off-line) recruiting service provider, (5) e-recruiting consortium, and (6) corporate career Web site. Table 1 summarizes the six categories of the e-recruiting sources.

The *general-purpose job board* provides a comprehensive online recruiting solution to both employers and job seekers across different industries. Monster, HotJobs, and Careerbuilder are leaders in this category. Job seekers can search for jobs by category, experience, education, location, or any combination of these job attributes. Most of the leading general-purpose job boards employ an agent technology to increase utility for the job seekers and recruiters. Personalized job agents match job seekers' profiles with the latest job postings and e-mail the list of the matched jobs to the job seekers.

The recruiters can search the job boards' database based on the skill, experience level, job preference, salary, education, and any combination of keywords to find qualified candidates. To address job seekers' and recruiters' rising dissatisfaction with services and costs, the general-purpose job board has evolved into an array of comprehensive career services, offering customized placement services, applicant assessment, and candidate relationship management.

The *niche job board* serves highly specialized job markets such as a particular profession, industry, education, location, or any combination of these specialties. Sample profession-oriented niche job boards include JournalismJobs.com, MarketingJobs.com, AllRetailJobs.com, and JobsInLogistics.com. Location-oriented niche job boards include NJ.com, TexasJobs.com, and ArizonaJobs.com. The advantage of the niche job board is a focused search with which recruiters can reach a large pool of qualified candidates most effectively. Most niche job boards operate specialized online communities or newsgroups that draw professionals, such as engineers, programmers, and journalists who share specific interests, skills, experience, and knowledge.

Both the general-purpose and niche job boards generate revenue by providing recruiters with applicant tracking service, hiring tools, job posting, Web site hosting, pre-screening tools, and advertisements. As the success of the job boards depends on the critical mass of job applicants, the job boards typically provide job seekers with free access to the services. Advanced services such as résumé writing and interview guidance may be accessible to the job seekers for a fee. The advantages of using the job boards include access to a large pool of recruiters and job seekers, and availability of state-of-the-art e-recruiting tools. Medium- and small-sized recruiters with low name recognition can access a large pool of qualified job applicants at a reasonable cost.

Because of the relative ease of entry into the e-recruiting market, the general-purpose and niche job boards overcrowded the e-recruiting industry in the late 1990s, and went through a series of mergers and acquisitions in the early 2000s. For example, TMP, the parent company of Monster, acquired FlipDog in 2001 to gain competitive advantage in the general-purpose job board market. Careerbuilder acquired CareerPath in 2000 and Headhunter.net in 2001. Yahoo! acquired HotJobs, which became a wholly owned subsidiary of Yahoo!

The *e-recruiting application service provider (ASP)* develops and markets to recruiters and job boards a combination of specialized services in recruitment software, recruitment process management, education and training, and management expertise. Specialized recruitment software for the in-house development of larger-scale e-recruiting Web sites is available for recruiters who want to quickly develop career Web sites on their own servers. Some service providers also support the hosting of the corporate career Web sites. Widely known e-recruiting application service providers include Recruitsoft, BrassRing, RecruitUSA, PeopleClick, TalentFusion, Lawson, and Development Dimensions International Inc. These e-recruiting application service providers are competing with larger enterprise system developers such as Oracle, PeopleSoft, and SAP, which have been developing recruiting software as a part of their enterprise-wide systems.

The *hybrid (online and off-line) recruiting service provider* is the traditional media or recruiting firm that provides e-recruiting services to both recruiters and job seekers. Employment advertising in newspapers has suffered significant percentage declines as recruiters switch to the more efficient and cost-effective recruiting methods. The Help Wanted Index, a measurement of how many help wanted ads run in newspapers, has registered a continuous decline in the past few years. In the face of losing significant revenue sources, media organizations such as the publishers of the *New York Times*, *Chronicle of Higher Education*, and the *Wall Street Journal* now provide e-recruiting services as well as paper-based job advertisement services in order to compensate for the loss of job ad revenue.

The traditional media companies have reduced job ad prices and introduced new recruiting services to differentiate themselves from the job boards and corporate career Web sites. The *New York Times* now offers a variety of e-recruiting services including résumé builders, search engines, and job market research reports to both employers and job seekers. CareerJournal.com, developed by the *Wall Street Journal*, focuses exclusively on the career needs of executives, managers, and professionals, leveraging the *Wall Street Journal* brand. CareerJournal.com provides recruiters and job seekers with a database of job openings and résumés, as well as salary information, career news, and industry trends. The advantage of the hybrid recruiting service provider comes from the leveraging of existing resources and expertise developed in the traditional job ad industry. The premier content of CareerJournal.com comes from the editorial resources of the *Wall Street Journal* as well as from the CareerJournal.com editorial team.

An *e-recruiting consortium* is a cost-effective alternative to the services provided by the job boards. DirectEmployers.com, the first cooperative, employer-owned e-recruiting consortium, was formed by DirectEmployers Association, a non-profit organization created by executives from leading U.S. companies. According to a 2003 press release by Recruiters Network (www.recruitersnetwork.com), DirectEmployers Association achieved a 500% increase in membership within just one year after its launch in February 2002. While the job boards place much importance on the "stickiness" of their Web sites (because job seekers who stay longer will be more likely to read the employment opportunities), DirectEmployers' search engine merely drives traffic directly to members' corporate career Web sites. A vast majority of members reported that DirectEmployers.com is driving more traffic to their Web sites than any other job board.

NACElink is another e-recruiting consortium that was created as a result of an alliance between the DirectEmployers Association and the National Association of Colleges and Employers (NACE) (http://www.naceweb.org). NACElink — a national, integrated, Web-based college recruiting system — was designed to better meet the placement and recruiting needs of colleges, students, and employers. In the fall of 2003, 137 colleges were using the NACElink system, and more colleges are joining daily. Cost saving was the greatest incentive for forming NACElink. For example, depending on company size, the members of DirectEmployers Association pay annual dues of $6,000 to $60,000, which is only a fraction of the job ad costs paid to the job boards.

The *corporate career Web site* is the hiring source most widely used by Fortune 500 companies (2002 iLogos Research study). While the majority of the companies (64%) used a combination of the job boards and their career Web sites to advertise job openings, they posted more jobs on their career Web sites than on the job boards. On average, the corporate career Web sites listed 184 jobs, compared with 118 on CareerBuilder, 99 on Monster, and 37 on HotJobs. The deployment of the corporate career Web site is a natural extension of the e-commerce applications when companies have already established high-traffic e-commerce Web sites. The exposure of the corporate career Web site to visitors is almost as great as the exposure of the existing e-commerce Web site as long as the e-commerce Web site has a hyperlink to the career Web page.

The cost of posting an additional job opening on the corporate career Web site is marginally increased, whereas the fee for posting the additional job opening is considerably higher on the job boards. The career Web site also has a cost advantage and flexibility compared with the job boards in publishing other corporate information — such as university recruiting, workplace, diversity, benefit, career, and culture — with which the applicants can make an informed decision about the job applications. In view of the significant impact of the corporate career Web site on the corporate recruiting strategy, the following section discusses the evolution of the corporate career Web site.

Table 2: Composition of industries by Fortune 100 companies

Industry	Number of Companies
Retail/Distribution	19
Manufacturing	20
Finance (Banking, Insurance)	24
Telecommunication	6
Chemical (Oil, Pharmaceutical)	12
IT (Computer Manufacturing, Consulting)	8
Food	7
Others (Broadcasting, Entertainment, Healthcare)	4

A Content Analysis of Fortune 100 Career Web Sites

In this section, we analyze e-recruiting practices of the Fortune 100 companies. Data were collected from the career Web sites of the Fortune 100 companies listed by the 2003 *Fortune* magazine (http://www.fortune.com/fortune/fortune500). All attributes analyzed were derived and developed from the reviews of the Fortune 100 companies' career Web sites. Thirty-three attributes were selected, named, and organized around four major categories: recruiting methods, job search tools, job application tools, and information on organizational attributes. We divided the statistics of the Fortune 100 companies into two groups (Fortune 1 to 50 company group and Fortune 51 to 100 company group) to investigate the relationships between the company size and the characteristics of the career Web sites. Each of the Fortune 100 companies' Web sites was visited to determine the content of the corporate career Web sites. Table 2 shows the composition of the industries in the Fortune 100 companies.

Findings

We searched each company's homepage for information on career opportunities (or jobs). If information on the career opportunities was not found, search engines were used to identify the existence of the career-related Web pages. Once the career Web pages were accessed, the contents were analyzed and

Table 3: Summary of the content analysis of Fortune 100 companies'

Category	Attribute		Fortune 1-50	Fortune 51-100	Total (%)
E-recruiting methods	Corporate career Web site		46	48	94
	No corporate career Web site*		4	2	6
	Homepage's hyperlink to career Web site		37	35	72
	Use of third-party job boards	Hotjobs	38	38	76
		Monster	39	32	71
		Careerbuilder	31	27	58
Job search tools	Job search engine	Category	40	38	78
		Location	38	36	74
		Type (part/full time)	17	8	25
		Experience level	10	7	17
	Posting of featured (hot) jobs		11	2	13
	Job posting☐ No job search engine provided		5	5	10
Job application tools	Online résumé submission		42	41	83
	Profile update		25	26	51
	Job basket		21	15	36
	Job agent		17	14	31
	E-mail application		8	13	21
	Regular mailing application		2	8	10
	Fax application		1	5	6
	Prescreen/online interview		3	2	5
Corporate information	Benefit		41	35	76
	Privacy/security policy		39	26	65
	Work environment		28	27	55
	Diversity		34	20	54
	Core value/vision		27	22	49
	Career development		20	18	38
	FAQ		13	16	29
	Culture		15	14	29
	Employee testimonials		13	11	24
	Training		14	9	23
	Interview tips		7	9	16

recorded with respect to all 33 attributes. In order to analyze the use of the three major job boards (i.e., HotJobs, Monster, and Careerbuilder), we searched each job board and identified the job postings placed by each of the Fortune 100 companies. Table 3 summarizes the result of the content analysis.

The first category is the e-recruiting methods adopted by the Fortune 100 companies. The results show that all the Fortune 100 companies use at least one of the e-recruiting methods. The most widely used method is the corporate career Web site: 94% of the companies have corporate career Web sites. The remaining six companies subscribe to the third-party job boards. Overall, the findings are similar to those of iLogos' 2002 research, which reported that 90% of the Global 500 companies had corporate career Web sites. Of these 94 companies, 72 post employment opportunities on their homepages and have hyperlinks to the career Web sites to provide job seekers with detailed job information. The other 22 companies have a hyperlink to the career Web sites through the "About our Company" or "Corporate Overview" Web page. For example, ChevronTexaco has a hyperlink to the career Web page through the "About ChevronTexaco" Web page.

While some job seekers prefer the corporate career Web site when looking for job openings, others prefer the third-party job boards. One of the advantages of the third-party job boards is that job seekers can apply for multiple jobs with only one submission of the résumé. The third-party job boards maintain a list of prospective employers and hyperlinks. While most companies use corporate career Web sites, they also supplement with the third-party job board: 96 of the Fortune 100 companies subscribe to at least one of the three general-purpose job boards we studied. On average, each company subscribes to two out of the three job boards.

Our analysis indicates that the Fortune 100 companies are more actively utilizing the job boards than the Global 500 companies surveyed by iLogos in 2002. Our study also found that HotJobs.com, a subsidiary of Yahoo.com, has the largest number of Fortune 100 companies as customers (76 Fortune 100 companies), followed by Monster.com (71 companies) and Careerbuilder.com (58 companies). This result is consistent with the recent poll conducted by Recruiters Network in November 2002, in which HotJobs.com is ranked as the most popular job board among job seekers (45%), followed by Monster.com (37%) and Careerbuilder.com (8%). Overall, we found no significant difference in terms of the use of the recruiting methods between Fortune 1-50 and 51-100 companies.

The second category is the search capability of the corporate career Web sites. Eighty-four out of the 94 companies employ a search engine. Category and Location are the most widely supported job attributes by the search engine (78 and 74 Web sites, respectively). Searches for Job Type and Experience are the least supported (25 and 17 Web sites, respectively). Thirteen Web sites provide a list of featured ("hot") jobs. Ten companies provided a list of jobs without the support of search engines. Overall, the Fortune 1-50 companies provide more sophisticated search engines than the Fortune 51-100 companies.

The third category is the job application tools. Eighty-three companies allow online résumé submissions via online forms and résumé builders. The résumé is transmitted to an internal database to be used for automated candidate management. Fifty-one companies provide profile updating. Thirty-six companies utilize job baskets, and 31 companies employ job agents. Several companies such as Merck and Washington Mutual explicitly indicate that they do not accept job applications via fax and regular mail due to the cost and difficulty in transferring data from hard copy into the résumé database. Other companies such as State Farm, MassMutual Financial Group, and Dell allow job seekers to use a variety of application tools such as fax, mail, e-mail, or online résumé builders.

It is surprising that only five companies utilize pre-screen/online interview tools to screen out candidates. The corporate career Web sites are quite often flooded with job applications, due to the fact that applicants can apply for as many jobs as possible to different companies at the same time. The pre-screening/self-assessment tools can quickly separate qualified job applicants from unqualified ones by accurately matching applicants' skills and experience to the job requirements. In a 2000 survey of more than 1,500 visitors to the career Web sites of four Fortune 500 companies, iLogos Research found that a large majority (88%) of job seekers are willing to answer questions and provide information about their skills. Job seekers wanted to utilize the self-service to expedite the process of matching themselves with the appropriate job opportunity. The pre-screening/self-assessment tools give the job seekers a more accurate picture of what a job will entail and better insight into their own capabilities. As the e-recruiting technologies and management practices improve, we expect that leading companies will deploy pre-screening/self-assessment tools more extensively in the near future. It is noted that a larger number of the Fortune 51-100 companies accept the traditional submission methods, such as fax, e-mail attachments, and regular mail, than the Fortune 1-50 companies.

The fourth category is the information on organizational attributes. During the job search, job seekers frequently lack information on organizational attributes (Breaugh & Starke, 2000). Barber and Roehling (1993) reported that job seekers who had more information about the job and/or organization were more attracted to the organization. The information provided most frequently is about benefits (76 Fortune 100 companies). While privacy and security is the most important concern to job seekers who use the e-recruiting services, 39 companies from the Fortune 1-50 and 26 companies from the Fortune 51-100 include their privacy and job security statements on their career Web sites. Most of the companies share the same privacy/security statements across different purposes (e.g., customers, suppliers, and job seekers). Work environment, diversity, and core value/vision follow next. While job seekers typically are interested in training, information on training is provided by only 23% of the companies.

Overall, companies can improve this category significantly. The employee-organizational fit is important for long-term retention and job satisfaction. Barber and Roehling (1993) found that job applicants pay more attention to specific than to general information. Other research also suggested that specific information and more information have positive effects on job seekers (Yuce & Highhouse, 1998; Mason & Belt, 1986). The Fortune 1-50 companies provide more information on their organizations than the Fortune 51-100 companies.

Conclusions

The purposes of this chapter were to classify e-recruiting sources and to analyze the content of the Fortune 100 companies' corporate career Web sites. We classified e-recruiting methods into six categories: (1) general purpose job board, (2) niche job board, (3) e-recruiting application service provider, (4) hybrid (online and off-line) recruiting service provider, (5) e-recruiting consortium, and (6) corporate career Web site. Among them, the corporate career Web site is the most popular recruiting method used by the Fortune 100 companies. We expect that with the growth of Internet users and advances in e-recruiting technologies, the deployment of the corporate career Web site will increase. The career Web site has a cost advantage and flexibility compared with the job board in publishing corporate information such as university recruiting, workplace, diversity, benefits, career, and culture with which applicants can make an informed decision about their job applications.

In recognition of the significant impact of the corporate career Web site on the corporate recruiting strategy, our chapter conducted the content analysis of the Fortune 100 companies' career Web sites All the Fortune 100 companies practice e-recruiting. However, the content analysis indicates that most of them need to develop better e-recruiting systems to improve their recruiting performance. Specific areas of improvement include deployment of advanced e-recruiting technologies such as job agent and job basket. In addition, companies need to provide as much specific information about the job and organization as possible on their career Web sites to attract better-qualified applicants.

Hiring the most qualified employees is one of the most critical organizational decisions in the knowledge-based economy. Moving one step ahead of competitors in recruiting is a source of strategic advantage. The technology advances very quickly, and with it, the recruitment practices should change accordingly. As more people search and apply for jobs through the corporate career Web site, the timely development and management of the corporate career Web site becomes more important. As each organization may have different e-recruiting needs, the best fit between the technological options and the organization should be identified.

One of the disadvantages of the e-recruiting methods is a lack of the human touch, such as face-to-face meetings or conference calls. Even though embracing the most current e-recruiting technology is crucial to companies competing for the best candidates, the human touch is still indispensable (Cappelli, 2001). Giving applicants a feeling that they have an ongoing relationship with the company through a *"virtual human touch"* will enhance the chance of the job acceptance and post-recruitment performance.

While there are numerous opportunities in e-recruiting, there are also a number of drawbacks to an electronic recruiting system, not the least of which is legal defensibility. The problems with discouraged job applicants, differential access to e-recruiting technologies across ethnic groups, and the differences in access by other demographic features have not been well understood yet. Research in the perception of the job seekers on the different e-recruiting methods and job attributes can give recruiters valuable design guidelines. The longitudinal study of e-recruiting methods and job performance may provide important information that can be used to optimize the mix of recruiting methods and budget allocations.

Acknowledgment

The author gratefully acknowledges helpful comments from the anonymous reviewers, which resulted in this improved version.

References

Barber, A.E. (1998). *Recruiting employees*. Thousand Oaks, CA: Sage Publications.

Barber, A.E., & Roehling, M.V. (1993). Job posting and the decision to interview: A verbal protocol analysis. *Journal of Applied Psychology, 78*(5), 845-856.

Breaugh, J.A., & Starke, M. (2000). Research on employment: So many studies, so many remaining questions. *Journal of Management, 26*(3), 405-434.

Cappelli, P. (2001). Making the most of on-line recruiting. *Harvard Business Review, 79*(3), 5-12.

Gale, S.F. (2001). Internet recruiting: Better, cheaper, faster. *Workforce, 80*(12), 74-77.

Gill, J. (2001). Now hiring apply on-line. *Businessweek,* (July 18).

Mason, N.A., & Belt, J.A. (1986). The effectiveness of specificity in recruitment advertising. *Journal of Management, 12*(3), 425-432.

Miller, S.M. (2001). Help wanted: Is the on-line job market working for your business? *Office Solutions, 18*(4), 27-29.

Tomlinson, A. (2002). Energy firm sharpens recruiting, saves money with in-house job board. *Canadian HR Reporter, 15*(20), 7-8.

Yuce, P., & Highhouse, S. (1998). Effects of attribute set size and pay ambiguity on reactions to "Help Wanted" advertisements. *Journal of Organizational Behavior, 19*(4), 337-352.

Chapter V

Employee Self-Service HR Portal Case Study:
Access, Content, & Application

Andrew Stein, Victoria University, Australia

Paul Hawking, Victoria University, Australia

Abstract

A number of Australian companies have realized the relative quick gains with low associated risks that can be achieved through the business-to-employee (B2E) model. Employee Self Service (ESS) is a solution based on the B2E model and it enables employee access to the corporate human resource information system. This chapter looks at the development of a human resources (HR) ESS portal and presents the findings of a case study of three Australian organizations that have implemented an ESS portal. A model depicting portal maturity is presented and analysis shows that ESS portals can be categorized as first generation with an "Access Rich" focus, second generation with a "Collaboration Rich" focus, or third generation with an "Application Rich" focus. The information and process focus of the ESS portal of three organizations will be presented and will be used to place the organization into the portal development model proposed by Brosche (2002).

Introduction

Approximately 320 of Australia's top companies have implemented SAP's ERP system (SAP R/3), and of these approximately 150 have implemented the human resources (HR) module, with 33 implementing the ESS component. These companies include Toyota, Westpac, RMIT, National Australia Bank, Siemens, Telstra, and Linfox (Hawking & Stein, 2002). In recent times there has been a plethora of research associated with the impact and implications of e-commerce. Much of this research has focused on the various business models, such as business-to-business (B2B) and business-to-consumer (B2C), with the importance of developing customer and partner relationships being espoused. There has been little attention paid to the potential of B2E systems and the role that B2E systems can play in improving business-to-employee relationships. Many organizations have realized the relative quick gains with low associated risks that can be achieved through the B2E model.

The B2E human resources Employee Self Service (ESS) system is claimed to incorporate "best business practice" and therefore the significant growth in ESS systems (Webster Buchanan, 2002) is understandable when you consider the potential return on investment of ESS applications. Lehman (2000) saw ESS transforming labor-intensive, paper-based HR forms to digital-enabled forms, allowing a 50% reduction of transaction costs, 40% reduction in administrative staffing, 80% reduction in management HR duties, and a 10-fold speed-up of HR processes (Workforce, 2001). Many of Australia's larger companies and public sector organizations are implementing ESS functionality as an adjunct to their enterprise resource planning (ERP) human resources systems, and this chapter looks at case studies of three major Australian organizations, the pre-eminent Australian telecommunications company and two state government departments.

From Traditional HR to ESS Portals

The function of Human Resource Management has changed dramatically over time. It has evolved from an administrative function, primarily responsible for payroll, to a strategic role that can add value to an organization. Organizations have now realized the importance of this function and are investing resources into supporting Human Resource Management Information Systems (HRMIS). Hamerman (2002) describes a model of how Internet technology can be applied to HR functions. His Employee Relationship Management (ERM) landscape presents corporate, personal, and employee elements (Figure 1). Hamerman (2002) views ERM suites as being platforms for information delivery, process execution, and collaboration in the organization. He sees the ERM suite being focused on organization-wide issues including recruitment, development, retention, progression, and succession. Within the ERM suite sits ESS functionality. The ESS allows for greater operational efficiency and the elevation of the HR function from a reacting function to a more creative strategic function. The Human Capital Management (HCM) component signifies that the human resource is a very important resource for modern organizations. Hamerman proposes the advantages in empowering employees through an ERM suite include:

- multiple value propositions,
- consistent portal GUIs,
- all employee 24x7,
- real-time dynamic information delivery, and
- A comprehensive collaborative work environment.

The evolution of traditional HR to ESS portals has been accelerated by the convergence of several organizational forces. The internal process of HR is changing its role from support to a more strategic focus in the organization. The role has developed from being primarily administrative, to support, then to the role of a business partner. At the same time HR is a stable, reliable business process; has high recognition within the organization; and touches every employee. This high recognition gives HR a rapid acceptance when being given the "e" treatment. Another force acting on HR is the "adding value" imperative.

Figure 1. Employee Relationship Management landscape (Hamerman, 2002)

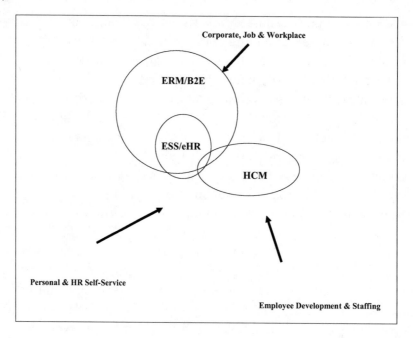

Organizations are involved in a "war on talent" (Link, 2001), and organizations see e-HR as an important technological tool in winning the war. HR has seized this change in organizational focus and adopted the B2E model to further enhance the business partner role.

Internet technology continues to shape the way that HR information is being delivered to employees (Gildner, 2002). There are three main information delivery platforms — Customer Service Representative (CSR), Interactive Voice Response (IVR), and ESS Web applications. CSR and IVR systems are used in 20-30% of employee enquiries, with ESS Web applications used in another 50% of employee enquiries. The Customer Service Representative is still the dominant access method for complex transactions, with ESS access replacing IVR as the preferred self-service method in large organizations.

Many of the world's leading companies are using ERP systems to support their HR information needs. This is partly due to the realization of the integrative role HR has in numerous business processes such as work scheduling, travel management, production planning, and occupational health and safety (Curran & Kellar, 1998). The B2E ESS model involves the provision of databases, knowledge management tools, and employee-related processes online to enable greater accessibility for employees (Deimler & Hansen, 2001).

B2E Employee Self Service (ESS) is an Internet-based solution that provides employees with a browser interface to relevant HR data and transactions. This enables employees' real-time access to their data without leaving their desktop. They can update their personal details, apply for leave, view their pay details and associated benefits, view internal job vacancies, and book training and travel. The benefits of this type of technology have been well documented (Alexander, 2002; McKenna, 2002; Webster Buchanan, 2002; Wiscombe, 2001). They include reduced administrative overheads and the freeing of HR staff for more strategic activities, improved data integrity, and empowerment of employees. One report identified a major benefit as the provision of HR services to employees in a geographically decentralized company (NetKey, 2002). Tangible measures include reductions in administrative staff by 40%, a reduction in transaction costs of 50% (Wiscombe, 2001), and the reduction of processes from two to three days to a few hours (NetKey, 2002). A recent study of the UK's top 500 firms revealed that the majority of B2E ESS solutions were still at a basic level, and have focussed on improved efficiency and electronic document delivery (Dunford, 2002). Ordonez (2002) maintains the theme of information delivery in presenting ESS as allowing employees access to the right information at the right time to carry out and process transactions, and further, ESS allows the ability to create, view, and maintain data through multiple access technologies. Companies such as Toyota Australia are now extending this functionality beyond the desktop by providing access to electronic HR kiosks in common meeting areas.

ESS: State of Play

The Cedar Group (2002, 2001, 2000, 1999) carries out an annual survey of major global organizations in regard to their B2E intentions. The survey covers many facets of ESS including technology, vendors, drivers, costs, and benefits. The average expenditure in 2001 on an ESS implementation was US$1.505 million. This cost is broken down:

- Software – 22%
- Hardware – 18%

- Internal implementation costs – 18%
- External implementation costs – 17%
- Marketing – 10%
- Application Service Providers – 17%

Looking at this cost from an employee perspective, we see the average cost of an ESS implementation ranging from US$32/employee for a large organization (>60,000 employees) to US$155/employee for a medium-size organization (7,500 employees). The funding for the HR ESS comes from the HR function in North American and Australian organizations, whereas the head office funds the solution in European organizations. The study found that the main drivers for ESS are improved service (98%), better information access (90%), reduced costs (85%), streamlined processes (70%), and strategic HR (80%). Employees can utilize a variety of applications in the ESS, and the main ones identified in the Cedar survey are: employee communications (95%), pension services (72%), training (40%), leave requests (25%), and many others.

Manager Self-Service (MSS) is used differently in the three regions of the survey. North American managers use MSS to process travel and expenses (42%), European managers to process purchase orders (48%), and Australian managers to process leave requests (45%). Employee services can be delivered by a variety of methods, and the Web-based self-service (B2E) is undergoing substantial planned growth from 42% in 2001 to 80% planned in 2004.

The trend is for implementing HRMIS applications from major ERP vendors like SAP or PeopleSoft. ESS implementations show overwhelming success measures, with 53% indicating their implementation was successful and 43% somewhat successful. The value proposition for ESS includes:

- Average cost of transaction (down 60%)
- Inquiries (down 10%)
- Cycle time (reduced 60%)
- Headcount (70% reduction)
- Return on investment (100% in 22 months)
- Employee satisfaction (increased 50%)

The culmination of the Cedar Group reports lists the barriers to benefit attainment and critical success factors in ESS applications. North America and Australian organizations both list cost of ownership/lack of budget as the main barriers, while European organizations perceive lack of privacy and security as the main barriers. Other barriers include lack of technical skills, inability to state business case, low HR priority, and HRMS not in place. As with other complex IT application projects, executive commitment, internal collaboration, and availability of technical skills to implement the application are all considered important success factors.

Web Portals

The term "portal" has been an Internet buzzword that has promised great benefits to organizations. Dias (2001) predicted that the corporate portal would become the most important information delivery project of the next decade. The term portal takes a different meaning depending on the viewpoint of the participant in the portal. To the business user, the portal is all about information access and navigation; to the organization, the portal is all about adding value; to the marketplace, the portal is all about new business models; and to the technologist, a portal is all about integration.

The portal was developed to address problems with the large-scale development of corporate intranets. Corporate intranets promised much but had to address multiple problems in the organization (Collins as reported in Brosche,

Table 1. Portal generations (Eckerson, 1998)

Generation	Descriptor	Features
First	Referential	Generic focus Hierarchical catalog of pages Pull flow Decision support
Second	Personalized	Personalized focus Push and pull flow Customized distribution
Third	Interactive	Application focused Collaborative flow
Fourth	Specialized	Role focused Corporate applications Integrated workflow

2002, p. 14). On the user side, employees must make informed and consistent decisions, and are being implored to access multiple information sources on the Web. On the technology side, intranet sites in organizations have proliferated, resulting in an increase in search complexity for corporate users. Early versions of portals were merely Web pages with extensive document linkages, a gateway to the Web. These early versions have been replaced by several generations of portals.

Eckerson (1998) proposed four generations of portals (Table 1) and that portals can be analyzed by the information content, information flow, and the technology focus that make up the portal. Just as the intranet proliferated within organizations, portals are now starting to multiply. The portal management system or the mega portal is being developed to take control of portal proliferation with the aim to enhance business process convergence and integration. Shilakes and Tylman (1998) coined the term "Enterprise Information Portal" (EIP), and this definition encompassed information access, application nature, and Internet gateway that are apparent in the second and third generations of organizational portals.

One area that is being developed via portal technology is employee relationships. We have already looked at ESS as an example of a B2E system; some additional employee applications are M2E (Manager to Employee), E2E (Employee to Employee) and X2E (eXternal to Employee). Taken together, all these relationships are considered part of the ERM strategy (Doerzaph & Udolph, 2002). An ERM strategy is made up of the following components:

- self-service technology,
- collaboration tools,
- communication tools,
- knowledge management techniques,
- personalization focus, and lastly
- access technology.

The access technology can encompass employee interaction centers like hotlines, Helpdesks or enterprise portals.

General Motors is one of the leading HR portals in the world and they have proposed three generations of HR portal (Dessert & Colby, 2002). The three

Table 2. Generations of HR portals (Dessert & Colby, 2002)

Dimensions	1st Generation	2nd Generation	3rd Generation
User Stickiness	Static Web High Usage Search	Dynamic Personalized Robust Search	Anywhere Access Analytics Dashboard
Communications & Collaboration	News Chat Jobs	Unified Messaging Targeted Push vs. Pull Role Based	E-Learning E-Culture Broadcast Media
Information Access	Online Publications Links Launching Pad	Dynamic Publishing Native Web Apps Content Integration b/w Functions	Online Publishing Int Content
Services	Travel Expenses Payroll E-Procurement	Life/Work Events Communities E-Health	Role Based Online Consulting
Technology	Web/App Servers Unsecured Basic Login	Content Management LDAP Int E-Mail, Chat, IM,	Federated Services Wireless Multi-Media Broadband

phases are presented in Table 2 and are presented in five organizational dimensions.

A conceptual model of portal architecture is proposed by Brosche (2002, p. 19) and depicts a portal having core, key elements and specialization components.

The components proposed by Brosche (2002) can be further categorized as having an information focus, technology focus, or a process focus. We can further combine Eckerson generations with the Brosche portal model and analyze an organization's portal by its information focus, process focus, and technology focus, and categorize it as being first, second, or third generation (Figure 3).

Access rich refers to a portal that is a static information dissemination tool where the information is "pushed" to the user. This could be a portal where minutes, memos, and notices are posted and "pushed" to the user. The content rich portal has information that is posted by users in a two-way flow. In this portal information is "pulled" from the portal by the user and the real issues are all concerned with content management. The application-rich portal elevated the portal to be more than an information tool; it becomes a fundamental process tool where business is conducted. Using this proposed categorization of portals, we will analyze ESS portals of three major Australian organizations

Figure 2. Conceptual model of the corporate portal (Broche, 2002)

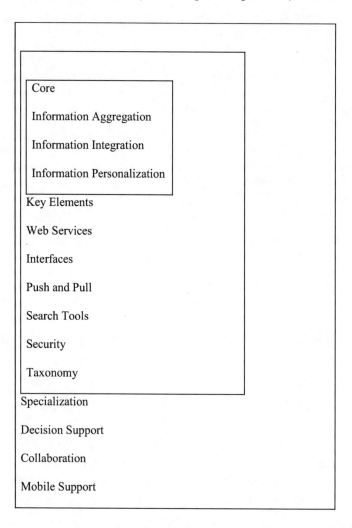

Core

Information Aggregation

Information Integration

Information Personalization

Key Elements

Web Services

Interfaces

Push and Pull

Search Tools

Security

Taxonomy

Specialization

Decision Support

Collaboration

Mobile Support

Figure 3. Portal generations by Brosche categories

Portal Generations	First	Second	Third
Portal Categories	ACCESS RICH	CONTENT RICH	APPLICATION RICH
Information Focus	Static Aggregated	Dynamic Personalized	Integrated Analytics
Process Focus	Single HR Forms	Multi HR Publication	All HR Application
Technology Focus	Unsecured Web Servers	Content Management	Wireless Broadband

by analyzing their information and process focus of their portal. This analysis will then allow us to substantiate the applicability of Broche's categories of portal development.

Research Methodology

The move to B2E ESS portals is detailed through the use of a case study. Case study research methodology was used, as the chapter presents an exploratory look at implications of ESS implementations. Yin (1994, p. 35) emphasizes the importance of asking "what" when analyzing information systems. Yin goes further and emphasizes the need to study contemporary phenomena within real-life contexts. The ethic or outsider approach was used in this case study. This approach emphasizes an analysis based upon an outsider's categorization of the meanings and reading of the reality inside the firm. The analysis is based upon objective methods such as document analysis, surveys, and interviews. Assumptions that were gleaned in the analysis of maturity of portal development were queried and clarified by interview. Walsham (2000, p. 204) supports case study methodology and sees the need for a move away from traditional information systems research methods such as surveys toward more interpretative case studies, ethnographies, and action research projects. Several works have used case studies (Chan & Roseman, 2001; Lee, 1989) in presenting information systems research. Cavaye (1995) used case study research to analyze inter-organizational systems and the complexity of information systems.

A multiple company case study was chosen in an attempt to identify the impact of an ESS implementation and the associated development across both the private and public sector. The case study companies were chosen because they are leading Australian organizations with a long, mature SAP history and had implemented SAP ESS module. Initially information was collected as a result of the company's presentation at the ESS forum in June 2002. Interviews were conducted firstly by e-mail with managers from the organizations. These predetermined questions were then analyzed and enhanced, and formed the basis of the interviews supported by observations through access to the ESS system. Project documentation and policy documents were also supplied. The name of one of the case study organizations has been withheld due to conditions set in the case study interview. The analysis will look at the information, process, and technology aspects as derived from the Broche model and will also look at implementation issues in developing the HR ESS portal.

Case Study

Private Sector Organization (Auscom)

Auscom is one of Australia's leading companies. Auscom's vision is to be a world-class, full-service organization by delivering company-wide process improvement, productivity gains, and cost efficiency (AuscomVision, 2002). It was privatized in 1997 and currently has 40,000 full-time employees, 20,000 contractors, 2,000 information systems, and 50,000 desktops (Greenblat, 2002). In the year ending June 2002, it had AUD$20 billion of sales and a profit of AUD$3 billion. The company operations are divided into several business units: retail, wholesale, infrastructure, and corporate center. This last unit is responsible for the HR processes within the company and had full responsibility for the IT strategy underpinning the ESS implementation initiatives, as well as the end-to-end project management of the implementations. One of the areas that Auscom had analyzed and felt was able to better deliver their vision was HR. The existing HR system was cost bloated, process fragmented, and had poor data access. Auscom wanted to explore the strategic aspects of HR, especially the concept of "employer of choice," and instigated "People Online" in May 2001. Initially the project was to be developed in three phases:

- Phase 1 introduced ESS to provide simple HR employee-based transactions and information search facilities. Phase 1 had two components, MyDetails, the simple employee HR ESS, and PeopleSearch, the information search component.
- Phase 2 would introduce workflow for both HR and non-HR processes.
- Phase 3 would provide access to corporate-wide applications.

Phase 1 was rolled out in May 2002 and Phase 2 was scheduled to be rolled out in November 2002 with Deloitte Consulting the implementation partner.

Details of the benefit metrics were not available due to commercial in confidence. The business case for Phase 1 identified four groups of benefits:

- quantifiable cost savings,
- increased data integrity,
- enabling process re-engineering, and
- e-enabling the workforce.

Four months after the implementation, an external organization carried out a review and analyzed the business requirements, performance, implementation, and project management of PeopleOnline. An analysis of the review is presented with reference to the portal generations in Figure 2.

Government Organization 1

Victorian Department of National Resources & Environment (NRE)

The NRE was formed from six state government organizations and employs approximately 5,000 staff at more than 200 diverse locations across Victoria. The NRE is responsible for preserving and managing Victoria's vast wealth of natural resources, including major oil and natural gas fields, substantial mining and agricultural resources, as well as one of the world's (On Sun, 2000) largest deposits of brown coal. The NRE must balance the need for development and wealth generation with the obligation to protect the land and its resources for sustainability and long-term benefits. On discussing the importance of IT in the strategic plan, Secretary Michael J. Taylor of the department commented:

"The information revolution is inescapable. Managing IT strategically in NRE is the department's response to that revolution." (NRE, 2003)

NRE first implemented SAP R/3 in 1999 to support its HR function (Shone, 2002). Prior to this, NRE was using another HR system with a customized ESS. One of the major benefits the department noticed with the implementation of SAP's ESS was the reduction in payroll processing, which was partly achieved through the introduction of online payslips. There was improved data integrity, not just with the use of ESS but due also to the integrative nature of the ERP system. Data only needed to be entered once and employees could then ensure the accuracy of their own data. Staff were also able to apply for leave and overtime electronically, and apply and receive approval for training courses.

Government Organization 2

NSW Department of Housing (DoH)

The Department of Housing in New South Wales aims to assist people into lower cost housing when their needs cannot be met by private sector housing. The mission statement of the department reflects this focus:

"The purpose of the New South Wales Department of Housing is to work in partnership with the community to supply and sustain safe, decent, and affordable housing for people on low incomes, and to enable people in need to create environments where they live with dignity, find support, and make sustainable futures". (DoH, 2002/2003)

It has approximately 130,000 properties across NSW and employs about 2,300 people. The information technology drivers for the DoH ESS portal include (King, 2003):

- replace technology of unsupported legacy systems;
- enable best-practice HR processes;
- deliver information to support modern people management; and
- empower employees through the provision of ESS, MSS, and workflow process systems.

It is important to consider that the terms *information, processes,* and *technology* are paramount in the statement of DoH's main technology drivers. The ESS project was developed in two phases, with the first phase being rolled out in April 2003 after a project length of 11 months.

Discussion

Information Focus

Information focus or stickiness refers to the ability of the ESS portal to draw and retain the user. In Auscom the Mydetails application did provide enhanced stickiness, but PeopleSearch did not. The review team found that the needs of super/power users in switchboard/reception who use PeopleSearch extensively had not been analyzed enough in the initial business requirements analysis. There was also a problem when cost considerations created a scope and software change, and project requirements of the special power users were not re-visited after this change. There was also an operational problem where service level agreements did not have adequate time/penalty clauses and/or metrics built in, thereby causing performance problems to be neglected. The implementation of the Phase 2 ESS portal led to the reduction from 40 to 16 HR systems and the savings of AUD$5 million per year (Fleming, 2003).

In NRE the ESS portal has six employee information categories: employee details, leave information, payroll, training, recruitment, and résumé information (Shone, 2002). Earlier versions of the software were primarily information browsing applications, whereas this version allows employees to read and amend a multitude of information. Overtime hours, bank details, taxation details, and leave details are all live. One of the major benefits they noticed with the implementation of SAP's ESS was the reduction in payroll processing which was partly achieved through the introduction of online payslips. There was improved data integrity, not just with the use of ESS, but also the integrative nature of the ERP system. Data only needed to be entered once, and employees could then ensure the accuracy of their own data. The leave details instigate a workflow request that is transported via e-mail to supervisors.

In DoH, Phase 1 looked to extend information access and dissemination across the enterprise to allow employees to process payroll information, personnel details, and financial posting and reporting (King, 2003). Both employees and managers were able to access information from the portal, but the information flow was mainly directed to the employee.

Process Focus

This dimension looks at the extent that the portal reaches out to other areas of the organization, and the extent that the portal enables collaboration and cross-integration business process operations, like e-procurement, travel expenses authorization, payroll, time, and HR data management. In Auscom the services provided by the Phase 1 project were limited to HR type data including payroll. The extension into other areas of the organization and across business units was achieved in Phase 2. The Peopleseach component enhanced communications by providing a one-stop search facility in the whole organization. It was important that this communication tool should have been aligned to the corporate intranet look and feel. The process focus of the NRE portal emphasized traditional HR business processes and activities (Shone, 2002). The more strategic HR processes of recruitment and training were present, but there was no employee scheduling. Cross-functional processes were not accommodated greatly except for the ability to enter the SAP R/3 system to do maintenance tasks. Staff were also able to apply for leave and overtime electronically, and apply and receive approval for training courses. The DoH was again focused on the traditional HR processes, with the only cross-functional process being financial posting and reporting (King, 2003). This entailed some degree of collaboration into other functional areas of the organization with resultant problems of lack of integrative business processes.

In analyzing the portals for their information content, all three ESS portals did enhance information stickiness as they provided the full range of typical "pull" ESS features: personal details, pay, leave, bank, and benefit packages. They also provided a range of personalized "push" features. This type of ESS site is somewhere between a first-generation "*access-rich*" site with predominately "pull" features (static Web, high usage) and a second-generation "*content-rich*" site.

In analyzing the portals for their process focus, the information provided to the user was limited to HR- or employee-based information. There was no across-function process information, business transaction information, or product information provided. The process focus of the portal would indicate that the portal was immature and still first generation. All portals demonstrated moderate communications but limited collaboration features, again an example of a first-generation "*access-rich*" HR portal. The DoH portal was somewhat more advanced with the ability to access financial reports, demonstrating cross-process collaboration. As organizations move to more advanced portals like

Auscom Phase 3 and DoH Phase 2, it is expected that more collaboration will be used. The Auscom representative touched upon this collaboration focus when he commented on the difficulty of developing the interface between the corporate and the HR portal. It is almost a necessity to have a line of delineation between the functional areas.

Conclusions

Compared to other e-business solutions, B2E portals have a relatively low impact on the organization, employees, and processes. The risks of a B2E portal are minimal, as it provides a Web interface to an existing system and improves data integrity, as employees are responsible for much of their own data. ESS portals do promise to provide extended functionality into and across the organization. We can analyze the relative positions of Auscom, NRE, and DoH portal maturity by referring to Table 3.

Auscom developed its first-generation portal to be primarily an information pull application, with the main focus on traditional HR forms. Little collaboration or communication applications were developed in the first release. The next version of the portal looked at the online routing of standard HR transactions, online recruitment, talent management, and an enhanced emphasis on training. This development would move the Auscom portal into the "*content-rich*" and partially into the "*application-rich*" phases. Auscom seems to be moving in the right direction. There seems no doubt that the technology exists to move an organization like Auscom from first-generation "*access-rich*" to second-

Table 3. Portal generations by Brosche categories

Portal Generations	*First*	*Second*	*Third*
Portal Categories	*Access Rich*	*Content Rich*	*Application Rich*
Information Focus	Static Aggregated	Dynamic Personalized ***Auscom*** ***NRE*** ***DoH***	Integrated Analytics
Process Focus	Single HR Forms ***Auscom*** ***NRE***	Multi HR Publication ***DoH***	All HR Application

generation "*content-rich*" and onto third-generation "*application-rich*" portals. The DoH portal seems to be located in Broche's "*content-rich*" phase, ready for the implementation of additional applications. The NRE portal still is placed in the "*access-rich*" phase, but is developing the collaboration focus of a Phase 2 portal.

While the technology exists, organizations seem to be slow in moving to the more developed cross-process, integrated functional portal. It is possible that the business processes that would be utilized in an "application-rich" portal do not exist in the organizations. Portal development must follow the business, not lead the business. What is not vague is the understanding that ESS portals are information delivery platforms that have much potential to deliver not only cost-focused savings, but the more important strategic HR benefits being sought by modern organizations. The recent Cedar Report (2002, p. 1) commented on the importance of high performance workforces and the need for enterprise-to-employee solutions.

Major Australian organizations are exploring the use of ESS portals, and these modern e-enabled applications set the stage for other Australian organizations to be aggressive followers. We will watch with great interest the march to ESS and then the advancement to HR/corporate/enterprise portals.

References

Alexander, S. (2002). HR e-power to the people. Retrieved August 2002 from *archive.infoworld.com/articles/ca/xml/01/02/12/010212cahr.xml*

Auscomvision. (2002). Auscom's vision and direction. Retrieved October 2002 from *www.Auscom.com.au/investor/vision.html*

Brosche, C. (2002, May). *Designing the corporate portal.* Masters Thesis, Department of Computer Science, University of Gothenburg, Sweden.

Cavaye, A. (1996). Case study research: A multi-faceted approach for IS. *Information Systems Journal, 63*, 227-242.

Cedar Group. (1999). *Cedar 1999 human resources self service.* Baltimore, MD: Cedar Group.

Cedar Group. (2000). *Cedar 2000 human resources self service.* Baltimore, MD: Cedar Group.

Cedar Group. (2001). *Cedar 2001 human resources self service/portal survey.* Baltimore, MD: Cedar Group.

Cedar Group. (2002). *Cedar 2002 Human resources self service/portal survey.* Baltimore, MD: Cedar Group.

Chan, R., & Roseman, M. (2001). Integrating knowledge into process models – a case study. *Proceedings of the Twelfth Australasian Conference on Information Systems,* Southern Cross University, Australia.

Curran, T., & Kellar, G. (1998). *SAP R/3 business blueprint.* Englewood Cliffs, NJ: Prentice-Hall.

Deimler, M., & Hansen, M. (2001). The online employee. Boston Consulting Group. Retrieved March 2002 from *www.bcg.com/publications/files/ Online_Employee_Aug_01_perpsective.pdf*

Dessert, M., & Colby, E. (2002). General Motor's employee portal – lift-off plus 1 year: The sky's the limit. *Proceedings of the IHRIM2002 Conference,* Boston, USA.

Dias, C. (2001). Corporate portals. *International Journal of Information Management, 21,* 269-287.

Doerzapf, A., & Udolph, S. (2002). Maximising return on employee relationships. *SAP Insider, 4*(1), 20-29.

DoH. (2003). DoH corporate plan 2002/2003. Retrieved August 2003 from *www.housing.nsw.gov.au/*

Dunford, I. (2002). B2E: The future looks rosy. Retrieved March 2002 from *www.computing.co.uk/Analysis/1136393*

Eckerson, W. (1999). Plumtree blossoms: New version fulfils enterprise portal requirements. Patricia Seybold report. Retrieved March 2003 from *www.e-global.es/017/017_eckerson_plumtree.pdf*

Fleming, F. (2003). *mySAP from a customer perspective: Auscom Ltd.* Presentation at *Saphire2003,* Sydney, Australia, May.

Gildner, initial. (2002). Trends in HR service delivery. White paper for Gildner Human Resources Outsourcing Forum. Retrieved March 2003 from *www.gildner.net/White%20Paper%20-%20HR%20Service%20 Delivery%20Trends.pdf*

Greenblat, E. (2002). Auscom hurting on profit of 3.6 billion. Retrieved October 2002 from *www.theage.com.au/articles/2002/08/28/1030508 074093.html*

Hamerman, P. (2002). Extending employee relationships with web applications. Presentation to *SAPPHIRE Conference,* Lisbon, Portugal, July.

Hawking, P., & Stein, A. (2002). Second wave ERP applications: (B2E) employee self- service. *Proceedings of ISONEWORLD Conference* (pp. 555-568), Las Vegas, Nevada, USA, July.

King, B. (2003). mySAP from a customer perspective: NSW Department of Housing. Presentation at *SAPPHIRE Conference*, Sydney, Australia, May.

Lee, A. (1989). Case studies as natural experiments. *Human Relations, 422,* 117-137.

Lehman, J. (2000). HR self-service strategies: Lessons learned. *Gartner Research Note,* (September 26).

Link, D. (2001). How HR can shape corporate portals. *HR Magazine, 46*(9), 131-137.

McKenna, E. (2002). Empowering employees. Retrieved August 2002 from *www.fcw.com/fcw/articles/2002/0107/tec-hr-01-07-02.asp*

Netkey. (2002). Unlocking the power of HR self service. Retrieved September 2002 from *www.netkey.com*

NRE. (2003). Managing IT strategically, State Government of Victoria policy paper. Retrieved June 2003 from *www.resourceweb/corpmgt/its/index.html*

Ordonez, E. (2001). MySAP human resources: Human capital management for your business. Retrieved July 2002 from *www.sap.com*

Shilakes, C., & Tylman, J. (1998). Enterprise information portals. Merrill Lynch Report. Retrieved March 2003 from *emarkets.grm.hia.no/gem/topic7/eip_ind.pdf*

Shone, J. (2002). *Employee Self Service: ESS.* Presentation at the *Australian SAP Users Group Meeting,* Gold Coast, Queensland, Australia, July.

Sun. (2000). Natural selection: Victoria's NRE turns to Sun. Retrieved June 2002 from *www.sun.com.au/news/onsun/2000-07/naturals.html*

Walsham, G. (2000). Globalisation and IT: Agenda for research. In R. Baskerville, J. Stage, & J.I. DeGross (Eds.), *Organizational and social perspectives on information technology* (pp. 195-210). Boston, MA: Kluwer Academic Publishers.

Webster Buchanan. (2002). HR self service – the practitioners' view. Retrieved August 2002 from *www.leadersinHR.org*

Wiscombe, J. (2001). Using technology to cut costs. *Workforce,* (September). Retrieved August 2002 from *www.workforce.com/archive/feature/22/29/82/index.php*

Workforce. (2001). HR statistics. *Workforce, 79*(10), 54-61.

Yin, R. (1994). *Case study research – design & methods* (2nd ed.). Newbury Park, CA: Sage Publications.

Chapter VI

Human Resource Portals and the Protean Career:

A Three-Factor Model

Constant D. Beugré, Delaware State University, USA

Abstract

This chapter discusses the role of human resource portals in the management of the protean career. A protean career is a career that is frequently changing due to both changes in the person's interests, abilities, and values, and changes in the work environment. The chapter develops a three-factor model, which contends that three types of variables (individual attributes, characteristics of the human resource portals, and organizational factors) influence the effective use of Web-based human resource services. The model also argues that the effective use of Web-based human resource services plays an important role in the management of the protean career since employees act as free agents, responsible for their own career advancement opportunities. The three-factor model has implications for research and practice for both employees and employers.

Introduction

Careers have been traditionally conceived as linear trajectories where employees advance hierarchically within a single organization over the course of their working lives (Eby, Butts, & Lockwood, 2003). The traditional career is a linear one, measuring success through upward promotions and salary increases. Recently, however, evolving organizational forms are moving workers away from traditional career patterns that emphasized upward progression within a limited number of traditional, pyramid-type organizations to nontraditional career patterns (Sullivan, Carden, & Martin, 1998). Careers are no longer limited to positions in one organization, but rather are viewed as more diversified professional experiences entailing working in different organizations and in different occupations. Hall (1996) and Mirvis and Hall (1996) used the construct of *protean career* to describe such career patterns. A protean career is a career that is frequently changing due to both changes in the person's interests, abilities, and values, and changes in the work environment (Hall, 1996). No longer do we expect a lifetime career to involve working in a single occupation or for a single employer (Jackson, 1996).

The purpose of this chapter is to shed light on the role of human resource portals in managing the protean career. In so doing, the chapter develops a three-factor model of the impact of human resource portals on the management of the protean career. The chapter is divided into five sections. The first section discusses the reasons leading to the emergence of the protean career. The second section explains the protean career. The third section describes HR portals. The fourth section presents the three-factor model of the protean career, which contends that three types of variables — organizational factors, HR portals system, and individual attributes — influence the effective use of Web-based HR services. Effective use of Web-based HR services plays an important role in the management of the protean career since employees act as free agents, responsible for their own career advancement opportunities. Finally, the fifth section discusses the model's implications for research and practice.

Background

Four reasons at least explain the emergence of the new view of a career. First, downsizing has dramatically transformed the landscape of organizations not only in the United States but also in other industrialized nations, breaking the old psychological contract between employers and employees. A psychological contract refers to expectations about reciprocal obligations between employees and employers (Rousseau, 1989). Whereas under the old psychological contract, employees traded loyalty against job security, the new contract calls for employees to "look out" for themselves. Thus, the new career requires employees to be in the driver's seat, leading both to personal responsibility and accountability in managing their careers. Under the new contract, the company undertakes to:

> "...add labor market value to employees by helping them acquire portable and marketable skills — employability...Self-determination is the underlying principle governing the organization, and in this spirit individuals manage their own careers." (Nicholson, 1996, p. 41)

Second, the emergence of knowledge workers — those workers who have specific rather than general competencies (Higgins & Kram, 2001) — redefines the role of careers. Because knowledge workers have skills and expertise that are in high demand, they tend to define the terms of their employment. For them, career success is defined in terms of knowledge acquisition and personal challenges, rather than in terms of progression in the hierarchy within the same organization. In a knowledge and information-based economy, the skills and knowledge of people with special expertise replace physical and financial capital as the essential assets of the organization (Brousseau, Driver, Eneroth & Larsson, 1996).

Third, the entry of Generation Xers in the workforce also shapes the dynamics of workplace demographics. They entered the workforce between 1985 and 2000, and are generally between 25 and 40 years old. Indeed, members of Generation X have more loyalty toward themselves and their networks of social relations than toward their employers. They are less willing to make personal sacrifices for the sake of their employers. But they are willing to trade off salary increases, titles, security, and promotions for increased leisure time and expanded lifestyle options (Robbins, 2003). This generation has values that do not favor organizational commitment (Brousseau et al., 1996). Generation Xers want to explore and do different kinds of work in order to learn about themselves and express their individual values (Sellers, 1994).

Fourth, the advance of information technology and particularly the Internet and the World Wide Web has dramatically changed how organizations operate. The most far-reaching changes to careers are coming from transformations of work and organization by information technology (Nicholson, 1996). Information technology helps improve employee skills and the ability to acquire, process, and disseminate information. Information technology not only quickly spreads knowledge, but also gives power to those who possess it, challenging old assumptions about organizational hierarchy and leadership. It also helps create new forms of organizations. Such organizations strongly impact careers. Information technology also allows employees to develop networks including other experts and professionals, thereby playing a critical role in the development of the protean career. Information technology facilitates organizational changes, such as delayering, outsourcing, and offshoring (moving a company's operations in a foreign country to benefit from a cheaper labor pool). Such organizational changes make careers less permanent and versatile. By reducing management layers, today's organizations provide very few upward movements. Thus, career success is no longer defined in terms of vertical progression in a hierarchy, but in terms of psychological and personal success.

One of the implications of information technology is the development of human resource portals and Web-based human resource self-service systems. These information technologies have allowed employees to self-manage activities previously handled by human resource professionals. However, the mere development of these tools cannot enhance the self-management of careers unless employees effectively use them. The extent to which some employees are more likely than others to rely on human resource portals and Web-based human resource self-service systems to manage their own careers has received scant attention in the human resource management literature. This is a surprising view of the increasing use of these technologies in modern organizations. A survey of Fortune 500 companies conducted by Towers Perrin found that 39% of the companies provided annual benefit enrollment on the Web in 2000 compared to just 10% in 1999 (HR Focus, 2001).

Despite this increasing investment in human resource portals and Web-based human resource self-service systems, employees often do not use these tools for career management opportunities. A 2000 human resource self-service survey by the Hunter Group found that today's most widely used self-service applications are employee communications (used by more than 60% of respondents) and 401(k) pension plans (more than 50%) (HR Focus, 2001). Although respondents in the same survey plan to greatly expand the use of personal data maintenance, benefit inquiries, open enrollment, family status changes, training registration, and so forth, they did not report using human resource self-service systems as tools for managing their own careers. Thus, understanding the factors influencing the effective use of HR portals is of paramount importance. In addition to providing information related to work benefits, HR portals offer opportunities for continuous learning and self-development.

The emergence of new technologies, competitive pressures from an ever-changing work environment, globalization of the world economy, and organizational changes, such as workforce diversity, delayering, outsourcing, offshoring, teamwork, networks, and the entry of Generation Xers in the workplace, are factors that call for a redefinition of the concept of a career. For instance, information technology makes it possible for employees to learn about the strategic direction of the business, about work opportunities in different areas, about specific position openings, and about upcoming training and development programs (Hall & Moss, 1998). This knowledge may help employees take advantage of new opportunities. Today's work environment, characterized by change and the breach of the psychological contract, requires employees to take control of their own careers. It is no longer the organization that "takes care" of the employee's career. Rather, it is the age of the "do-it-yourself" career. What the organization can do is provide opportunities for employees to manage their own careers. Human resource portals and Web-based human resource self-service represent such opportunities.

Protean Career

Defining the Protean Career

The term protean is derived from the Greek god Proteus, who could change shape at will. Hall (1996) used this construct to describe a career that is constantly changing and mostly driven by the employee himself or herself. The construct of protean career is similar to that of boundaryless career (Arthur &

Rousseau, 1996). Boundaryless means employment and careers unfolding overtime across multiple employment opportunities and employer firms (Rousseau & Arthur, 1999). Most research on the new career has often used the concept of boundaryless career (Arthur & Rousseau, 1996; Arthur, 1994). The boundaryless career is characterized by paths and trajectories that are not fixed lattices within organizations (Bird, 1994). As Sullivan (1999, p. 477) put it, "The term 'boundaryless career' is really a misnomer, as systems need boundaries in order to define themselves and to separate themselves from the environment. Therefore, in a real sense, careers are not boundaryless." What authors using this concept really mean is that barriers across occupations and organizations are permeable. In this chapter, I use the construct of protean career to describe a career that is constantly changing, creates a free-agency relationship between employees and employers, and is self-directed. In discussing the protean career, I rely on the literatures on the protean career and on the boundaryless career. Although these literatures use different constructs, they describe the same reality, which is a career that is dynamic, changing, and self-directed.

Components of the Protean Career

The protean career includes constant change, free-agency relationship between employees and employers, continuous learning, employability, self-direction, and multiple commitments. In a free-agency relationship, employees and employers exercise their right to form new contracts as needed, deploying their resources for their own benefit (Rousseau & Arthur, 1999). The free-agency relationship also implies that employees and employers consider their relationship as more transactional than relational. This contractual relationship is likely to continue as long as it is beneficial to both parties. Boundaryless careers treat both employers and employees as free agents even more explicitly than in traditional conceptualizations of the employment relationship (Van Buren III, 2003).

Another key element of the protean career is continuous learning and personal development. To the extent that employees possess skills that are valued by their employers, they will be likely to remain members of the organization. Therefore, employees have to seek out opportunities to develop and update their skills. Kanter (1989) used the concept of employability to explain the extent to which employees must acquire skills that increase their marketability.

Employability refers to a commitment to enhancing the skills and competencies of the employees so they can protect and continuously improve their options for gainful employment (Van Buren III, 2003). Developing skills is important in the age of the protean career because it helps improve both internal and external marketability. Employees with highly transferable competencies are not organizationally bound, but instead are highly marketable. Their competencies are portable and can be applied to different organizational settings (Sullivan et al., 1998).

A corollary of portable skills is the lack of organizational commitment. This is understandable since possessing a 'repertoire of portable skills' will allow employees to 'travel' from organizations to organizations. Thus, commitment is less directed toward a specific organization. According to Sullivan et al. (1998), the role identification of self-designing careerists comes predominantly from their profession rather than from their organizational membership. Whereas the traditional career separates work and family, the new career blends the two. In the traditional career, success is at the expense of the family and vice versa, leading to a zero-sum game situation. In the new career, however, professional success and family are not necessarily incompatible. This multiplicity of commitment includes the profession, the organization, the family, and social activities that the employee deems important. Diversity of activities in the new career helps the employee broaden his or her horizon, expertise, and knowledge.

Critical Success Factors in the Protean Career

According to Hall (1996), there are three indicators of success under the protean career: (1) psychological success; (2) perceived internal marketability; and (3) perceived external marketability. Psychological success stems from accomplishing goals that the employee considers important. These goals may be career-related or personal goals. Success in the new career stems from fulfilling specific objectives that may not be career related. Since the protean career is not limited to one organization, employees must develop skills that increase their employability (Kanter, 1989). Employability is increased by both internal marketability and external marketability. The former refers to the extent to which employees have skills that are valued by their current employers, whereas the latter refers to skills that are valued by outside employers.

Employees under the protean career should also be able to develop social networks. Such networks are important for success. They may help garner information about job opportunities both inside and outside the employing organization. These social networks should extend beyond one's unit, department, or organization. Eby, Butts, and Lockwood (2003) consider the extensiveness of social networks within and outside the organization a critical success factor in the protean career. An employee may use networks to gather career-relevant rather than employer-relevant information (DeFillippi & Arthur, 1994).

Despite its positive impact, the protean career has some pitfalls. Not all individuals will fare equally well in the protean career. Most employees are in a weaker bargaining position in the employment relationship than employers (Van Buren III, 2003). The path of a protean career is not linear; it can even be chaotic. What then would explain the extent to which some employees strive in the protean career, whereas others fail? Several factors, individual as well as contextual, may help explain success in the protean career. Since the protean career is marked by peaks and valleys, employees should develop the kind of skills and *persona* that will help them navigate such situations. For instance, a layoff can have damaging effects on employees. Those employees who are emotionally strong may use the situation to revamp themselves and start anew. Those who cannot effectively manage this transition may have their professional career threatened. Technology, and especially information technology, can help successfully navigate the protean career. In the following section, I explain human resource management portals before developing a model of their impact on the management of the protean career.

Human Resource Portals

A human resource portal (or HR portal) is a set of applications that provides users with a single gateway to customized and personalized information (Walker, 2001). This portal can be limited to a company intranet or it can extend to the Internet or include both. Using these portals, employees can collect information related to benefits, compensation, training opportunities, knowledge management, and continuous learning, to name a few. Human resource portals allow the development of Web-based human resource self-service.

"Web-based human resource self-service involves the use of interactive technology by employees and managers to obtain information, conduct transactions, and essentially shortcut processes that previously required multiple steps, paperwork, the involvement of human resource staffers, and all the delays such processes are heir to." (Zampetti & Adamson, 2001, p. 15)

With the self-service provided by human resource portals, employees are able to become more self-sufficient with respect to many items previously handled by the human resource staff, such as making changes and additions to their own benefit programs, participating in annual benefit enrollments, selecting training and development plans, investigating job opportunities and postings, handling payroll deductions, participating in retirement planning, changing records such as marital status or address, and having access to company policies and procedures. By putting the responsibility for many information-management tasks, such as filing change-of-address forms and completing benefits enrollment, in the hands of employees, Web-based human resource self-service dramatically reduces the amount of time that human resource staffers spend on administrative tasks and frees them to focus their energy on achieving more strategic goals for the company, such as reducing turnover and developing skills inventories, and helps deliver human resource services with fewer people (Gale, 2003). Thus, the human resource function becomes less administrative and more strategic, aligning itself with the organization's goals and objectives.

Such tools may help employees manage their own careers. What is particularly important in HR portals is the opportunity to collect information about job opportunities inside and outside the organization, and to exploit training and learning opportunities. The Internet can be used as a self-learning tool, thereby helping employees develop new skills. HR portals must offer value to both employees and employers. According to Hansen and Deimler (2001), the benefits of business portals for both employees and companies are obvious:

"Having information tools available on the company portal makes employees' jobs easier and less stressful by reducing interaction time and effort. Because they spend less time searching for information, they are able to accomplish more and productivity rises. From the company's perspective, not only are employees more efficient at getting work done, their efficiency reduces delays in core processes." (p. 98)

Benefits of HR Portals for Employees

Why do employees have to take care of the management of their own career? One of the key reasons is that organizations can no longer do it. Thus, the protean career requires personal initiative and responsibility. In protean careers both employers and employees are free agents (Van Buren III, 2003). Free agency means that people and firms exercise their right to form new contracts as needed, deploying their resources (skills, discretionary time, money, reputation) for their own benefit (Rousseau & Arthur, 1999, p. 9). Therefore, employees should develop skills to increase their level of employability (Kanter, 1989). Employees who will strive in the protean career are those who have specialized knowledge and expertise that make them valuable partners. They can exchange this expertise anywhere. Specifically, knowledge workers may strive in the protean career. For these workers, professional commitment may replace organizational commitment. As Sullivan et al. (1998, p. 168) put it: "Individuals with highly transferable competencies are not organizationally bound, but instead are highly marketable. Their competencies are portable and can be applied to different organizational settings." Employees should develop a *repertoire of portable skills*, which refers to a set of skills that an employee possesses and that can be used in several organizations. The repertoire of portable skills may increase the employee's internal and external marketability.

Benefits of HR Portals for Organizations

HR portals may help reduce costs and improve productivity. Organizations using HR portals can save an average of 60% (HR Focus, 2001). HR portals improve communication, reduce paperwork, and above all increase productivity. Portals in some ways create an organization without boundaries. For example, General Motors, DaimlerCrysler, and the International Union UAW (United Auto Workers) announced a plan in November 2000 to provide human resource functions to U.S. workers through employee portals. This plan connected 200,000 employees at General Motors and 100,000 employees at DaimlerCrysler with HR technology (Workforce, 2001). One of the goals of this plan was to improve efficiency and productivity.

The return on investment (ROI) of HR portals includes reduction in phone calls, the availability of accurate data and information, improved retention and recruitment, and increased satisfaction with the human resources department. It also includes tangible costs, such as reduction in call center staffing, reduction in interactive voice response traffic and cost, and saving in paper and production (Brooks, 1998). HR portals can help locate those employees with particular expertise for new product development. They can also help easily locate suppliers and clients. In the recruiting area, an organization may create a database of prospective employees. Such a database may contain the names of employees from competitors, former employees who have left the company, job applicants who have rejected previous job offers, and friends of current employees. The organization may then manage the relationship established with these prospective employees (Michaels, Handfield-Jones, & Axelrod, 2001).

HR portals also offer opportunities for e-learning. Employees can scan the site for training and development opportunities. By so doing, they may develop new skills that will increase both their internal and external marketability. Employers may also benefit from employees taking care of their own careers. To the extent that employees manage their own careers, organizations would reduce time and costs related to providing career counseling to employees. In the protean career, employers are able to purchase labor on a just-in-time basis, allowing them to gain flexibility (Van Buren III, 2003). Employers may also connect their portals to Internet recruiting sites, allowing them to facilitate the recruitment process. Employees and potential job applicants may directly apply for job vacancies. E-recruiting may lead to an open-labor market (Michaels et al., 2001) in which employees may apply for openings inside or outside their companies. To explain the role of HR portals in managing the protean career, I develop a three-factor model, which is discussed in the next section.

Three-Factor Model

The three-factor model (Figure 1) contends that three types of factors — individual factors, factors related to HR portals, and organizational factors — influence the effective use of HR portals.

Figure 1. A model of the Web-based human resource self-service and the protean career

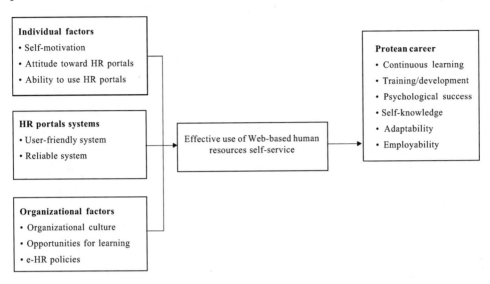

Individual Factors

In this model, individual factors refer to the employee's personal characteristics that may affect the likelihood of using HR portals to manage his/her own career. These individual characteristics include self-motivation, attitude toward HR portals, and ability to use the HR portals. Although this list is not exhaustive, it captures the key individual factors that influence the effective use of Web-based human resources services. Self-motivation is a key determinant not only of the protean career, but also of an employee's growth and personal development in an organization:

"Pursuing the protean career requires a high level of self-awareness and personal responsibility. Many people cherish the autonomy of the protean career, but many others find this freedom terrifying, experiencing it as a lack of external support." (Hall, 1996, p. 10)

To the extent that employees are "masters" of their own careers, they must find the inner drive that will help them pursue a meaningful career. Self-motivation may help employees look for opportunities for continuous improvement and learning. Using Web-based human resource self-service requires self-discipline and self-motivation. Employees who are highly self-motivated would be likely to profit from the technology.

Likewise, employees who harbor a positive attitude toward the technology will be likely to embrace it. Indeed, employees who have a positive attitude toward HR portals would embrace them, whereas those who have a negative attitude would tend not to use the system. Thus, the mere existence of HR portals in an organization is not enough to make it successful. Employees must be willing to use the system. However, self-motivation and positive attitudes are not enough to use the system. Employees should be able to use HR portals. Organizations may help employees develop such abilities through training. Training employees to use the system would enhance the ability and level of comfort in using the system. Employees who are technologically challenged will not reap the benefits offered by such HR portals in managing their own careers.

Factors Related to the HR Portals

These factors include the reliability of the system and the extent to which the system is user friendly. An HR portal is useful only if it is reliable and provides complete and accurate information. To the extent that it offers such information, it can be used as a tool for career information and continuous learning. The system should continuously work and the information it provides must be constantly updated. When the system does not provide accurate and complete information, employees may refrain from using it. In addition to being reliable, an HR portal system should be user friendly. A user-friendly system is less intimidating and likely to spur employee enthusiasm. Using the system should be straightforward and not cumbersome.

The system should also meet employee needs. Thus, before building an HR portal, a company should clearly determine which goals it intends to accomplish, and then select an appropriate team of information technology professionals and a vendor. An HR portal system that is not reliable and user friendly will have little appeal to employees. There are two types of e-learning that impact employee behavior, synchronous e-learning and asynchronous e-learning. In the first one, live instructors engage trainers into online discussions, whereas in the second one the trainer works at his/her own pace. Attendance in asynchronous e-learning requires self-discipline and self-motivation. However, technology is not the key issue when implementing HR portals. It is essentially the organizational culture and employee attitudes toward change that matter.

Organizational Factors

Organizational factors include organizational culture, opportunities for continuous learning, and the existence of e-HR policies. When the organization supports the development and implementation of HR portals and provides opportunities for training and continuous learning, employees would be likely to use the system. An organizational culture that encourages innovation and continuous improvement would motivate employees to use new technologies. However, an organizational culture that cultivates the status quo may not generate the incentives for using new technologies. For instance, the effective use of HR portals entails an environment of continuous learning. Organizations may encourage continuous learning in different ways, including rewarding employees for skills developed (skill-based pay) and providing opportunities to learn new skills. Such opportunities may create an enthusiasm for e-learning. E-learning is an efficient way to re-skill employees. However, employees need self-management skills in order to tap the opportunities HR portals offer. The adoption of HR portals in an organization requires the development, implementation, and enforcement of e-HR policies. E-HR policies refer to rules and regulations guiding the proper use of HR portals. For instance, an organization may require employees not to abuse the system. Such policies must be enforced for an efficient use of the system.

Although the model identified three types of factors, it is worth mentioning that these factors are somehow related. For instance, the ability to use HR portals may influence attitudes toward the system. Indeed, employees who have developed the ability to use the system may view the system positively, whereas those who do not have the ability to effectively use it may view it negatively. Likewise, the reliability of the system may influence an employee's ability to use it. Employees may be more likely to use a system that is reliable than one that is unreliable. It is also possible that e-HR policies may affect the system usage. For instance, if managers train employees to use the portals, they may develop the skills required to effectively use the system.

In helping to manage the protean career, the three-factor model contends that the three types of factors facilitate the effective use of Web-based HR portals.

Specifically, the model contends that managing the protean career requires continuous learning from the employee, seeking out opportunities for training and development, psychological success, self-knowledge, employability, and adaptability. The use of Web-based human resource self-service transforms employees into discretionary investors of their own human capital (Gibbons, 2001). For instance, Allred, Snow, and Miles (1996) note that in today's environment, even in traditional organizations, managers and employees are assuming greater responsibility for planning their career moves and identifying the steps required to achieve them.

Implications of the Three-Factor Model

The three-factor model contends that individual characteristics, factors related to HR portals, and organizational factors influence the effective use of Web-based human resource self-service. The effective use of such self-services dramatically impacts the management of the protean career. This model has implications for both research and practice.

Implications for Research

Several lines of research may be gleaned from the three-factor model. First, researchers in career management and human resource management may test the key assumptions of the three-factor model. For instance, in analyzing the impact of HR portals on the management of the protean career, one may explore the following issues: What factors lead to the effective use of HR portals? Are these factors related to the individual, the technology itself, or the organizational context? Answers to these questions may prove useful since they may help improve our understanding of the impact of HR portals on the effective management of the protean career. Thus, the three-factor model awaits empirical validation.

Second, the protean career requires personal resilience and accountability. The extent to which such employees are likely to favor such career paths, whereas others may reject them, remains unclear. Perhaps individual factors, such as age, intelligence, and need for achievement, may play a role in such endeavors. Research explaining the impact of individual factors on the protean career is very limited, if not nonexistent. The three-factor model identified only three individual factors—self-motivation, attitudes toward the system, and ability to use the system. Although these individual factors may play a key role in the effective use of Web-based HR self-services, other individual factors may also be explored. For instance, Sullivan et al. (1998) speculate that high intelligence may be a stronger predictor of an individual's choice of a self-designing career over a more traditional career. To the extent that self-designing careerists are good problem solvers, they may be likely to take advantage of the opportunities HR portals offer in managing their own careers. Empirical studies may investigate such claims.

Third, researchers should explore the extent to which some organizational factors facilitate or inhibit the use of Web-based HR self-services. The three-factor model postulates that organizational factors, such as culture, the existence of an environment of continuous learning, and e-HR policies may facilitate the effective use of Web-based HR self-services. Research on the effects of such organizational factors may also have practical implications since managers tend to control more organizational factors than individual attributes. For instance, managers may design organizational cultures that are conducive to continuous learning and the use of new technologies.

Finally, researchers may explore the impact of societal culture on the adoption of Web-based HR self-services, and most importantly the emergence of the protean career. In a given country, attitudes toward change may influence workers' readiness toward less traditional career types. For instance, employees in a risk-averse culture may be less likely to embrace the protean career than their counterparts from a risk-prone culture. Indeed, the protean career requires that employees manage their own careers. However, in a culture where employees expect organizational authorities to meet their career needs, they may consider the organization as the ultimate authority that should manage their career. Addressing these issues requires empirical investigations. Although the three-factor model awaits empirical validation, it presents some insights for management practice.

Implications for Practice

The three-factor model contends that individual characteristics, factors related to HR portals, and organizational factors influence the effective use of HR portals. Although managers may not directly control individual factors related to employees, they may impact the remaining two. For instance, managers may develop an organizational culture that facilitates the implementation of changes, and specifically technological changes. To the extent that employees are allowed to experiment with new processes and ideas, they would be likely to use new technologies that help develop such skills. Managers may also help develop HR portals that are user friendly and meet employee needs. They may also develop clear policies guiding the use of Web-based HR self-services.

For organizations, managing the protean career can represent a challenge. How do you provide opportunities for employees if these employees do not have any loyalty and commitment to the organization? How do you tap the productivity of employees who have a free-agency relationship with the organization? Why should employers create organizational environments where employees would become externally marketable and leave the organization? What does such a strategy bring to the bottom line? Indeed, discussing the management of the protean career raises more questions than it provides answers. The implementation of HR portals helps employers streamline operations and processes, reduce costs, and provide employees opportunities for skill development and personal growth. Such gains may help improve productivity. However, changes in both the external and internal environments of organizations require a new definition of the career. Since organizations are becoming leaner, they are fewer positions at the top to which employees can aspire. Therefore, one of the new strategies would consist of developing a free-agency arrangement in which both employers and employees meet their obligations as long as their mutual contract holds.

Managers should consider the effective use of Web-based human resource self-services as stemming from the combination of individual, organizational, and technological factors. For instance, employees would be more likely to use a system that is reliable and user friendly. However, when the system is not reliable or does not provide complete and up-to-date information, employees may see no reason to use it. Similarly, employees should develop the skills to use the system. This requires training opportunities from the organization. Finally, the adoption of an HR portal requires the development and implementation of policies governing the use of the system. The existence of such policies may reduce the likelihood of abusing the system. However, organizations should realize that the system might be a double-edged sword. As HR portals help organizations reduce costs and improve efficiency, they also help employees develop skills and competencies, making them marketable in the open labor market (Michaels, Handfield-Jones, & Axelrod, 2001). Such employees may be likely to leave the organization for better opportunities. However, it is better for an organization to lose an uncommitted employee than to keep such an employee. Lack of commitment and loyalty may prove more damaging to the organization than the loss of an excellent employee.

Despite management efforts to facilitate the effective use of HR portals and thereby the management of the protean career, the bulk of this process lies with individual employees. Employees must assume personal responsibility. The three-factor model takes the view that although organizational programs must support nontraditional careers, individuals must assume responsibility for their own career management (Sullivan et al., 1998). However, managing the protean career can be a daunting task. Although most people are highly optimistic all the time (Lovallo & Kahneman, 2003), employees should avoid over-optimism when it comes to managing their careers. They should objectively assess their own strengths and weaknesses and develop career strategies accordingly. With its emphasis on personal responsibility, accountability, and continuous learning, the protean career is more suitable to knowledge workers.

Conclusions

This chapter has developed a three-factor model that provides an insight in understanding the role of HR portals in managing the protean career. To realize the potential of the new career, the individual must develop competencies related to the management of self and career (Hall, 1996). Technology, and specifically information technology, can provide such an avenue:

"HR is simultaneously positioning firms and workers to respond flexibly to market changes while seeking stability by recruiting, developing, and retaining people whose talents are critical to the firm." (Rousseau & Arthur, 1999, p. 7)

Despite its advantages, the protean career is not necessarily for everyone. The protean career may be beneficial to people with valuable skills, but might prove harmful to employees who do not have such skills. The protean career requires personal responsibility as well as accountability. Employees are responsible for developing their own career trajectories and managing them. In case of success, the glory will be theirs. However, in case of failure, the blame will be theirs too. Employees should therefore avoid being victims of the self-serving bias — that is, taking credit for positive outcomes (e.g., career success) and blaming external factors for negative outcomes (e.g., career failure). An employee embarking on the path of the protean career may reflect on Komisar's (2000) advice:

"Figure out who you are. What do you love to do? How do you want to live? Then, don't let a career drive you, let passion drive you." (p. 174)

References

Allred, B.B., Snow, C.C., & Miles, R.E. (1996). Characteristics of managerial careers in the 21st century. *Academy of Management Executive, 10*(4), 17-27.

Arthur, M.B. (1994). The boundaryless career: A new perspective of organizational inquiry. *Journal of Organizational Behavior, 15,* 295-309.

Arthur, M.B., & Rousseau, D. (1996). A new career lexicon for the 21st century. *Academy of Management Executive, 10*(4), 28-39.

Bird, A. (1994). Careers as repositories of knowledge: A new perspective on boundaryless careers. *Journal of Organizational Behavior, 15,* 325-344.

Brooks, M.K. (1998). HR intranets: An ROI strategy. *HR Focus,* (August), 13-14.

Brousseau, K.R., Driver, M.J., Eneroth, K., & Larsson, R. (1996). Career pandemonium: Realigning organizations and individuals. *Academy of Management Executive, 10*(4), 52-66.

DeFillipi, R.J., & Arthur, M.B. (1996). Boundaryless context and careers: A competency-based perspective. In M.B. Arthur & D.M. Rousseau (Eds.), *The boundaryless career* (pp. 116-131). New York: Oxford University Press.

Eby, L.T., Butts, M., & Lockwood, A. (2003). Predictors of success in the era of the boundaryless career. *Journal of Organizational Behavior, 24,* 689-708.

Gale, S.F. (2003). Three stories of self-service success. *Workforce, 82*(1), 60-62.

Gibbons, J. (2001). Technology and employee development. In A.J. Walker (Ed.), *Web-based human resources* (pp. 96-110). New York: McGraw-Hill.

Hall, D.T. (1996). Protean careers of the 21st century. *Academy of Management Executive, 11*(3), 8-16.

Hall, D.T., & Moss, J.E. (1998). The new protean career contract: Helping organizations and employees adapt. *Organizational Dynamics*, (Winter), 22-37.

Hansen, M.T., & Deimler, M.S. (2001). Cutting cost while improving morale. *MIT Sloan Management Review, 43*(1), 96-100.

Higgins, M.C., & Kram, K.E. (2001). Reconceptualizing mentoring at work: A developmental network perspective. *Academy of Management Review, 28*, 264-288.

HR Focus. (2001). The payoffs of self-service HR are significant. *HR Focus, 78*(1), 10-11.

Jackson, C. (1996). Managing and developing a boundaryless career: Lessons from dance and drama. *European Journal of Work and Organizational Psychology, 3*(4), 617-628.

Kanter, R.M. (1989). *When giants learn to dance: Mastering the changes of strategy, management, and careers in the 1990s*. New York: Basic Books.

Komisar, R. (2000). Goodbye career, hello success. *Harvard Business Review*, (March-April), 160-174.

Lovallo, D., & Kahneman, D. (2003). Delusions of success: How optimism undermines executives' decisions. *Harvard Business Review*, (July), 56-63.

Michaels, E., Handfield-Jones, H., & Axelrod, B. (2001). *The war for talent*. Boston, MA: Harvard Business School Press.

Mirvis, P.H., & Hall, D.T. (1994). Psychological success and the boundaryless career. *Journal of Organizational Behavior, 15*, 365-380.

Nicholson, N. (1996). Career systems in crisis: Change and opportunity in the information age. *Academy of Management Executive, 10*, 40-51.

Robbins, S.P. (2003). *Essentials of organizational behavior* (7th ed.). Upper Saddle River, NJ: Prentice-Hall.

Rousseau, D.M. (1989). Psychological and implied contracts in organizations. *Employee Responsibilities and Rights Journal, 2*, 322-337.

Rousseau, D.M., & Arthur, M.B. (1999). The boundaryless human resource function: Building agency and community in the new economic era. *Organizational Dynamics*, (Spring), 7-17.

Sellers, P. (1994). Don't call me a slacker. *Fortune*, (December 12), 181-196.

Sullivan, S.E. (1999). The changing nature of careers: A review and research agenda. *Journal of Management, 25*, 457-484.

Sullivan, S.E., Carden, W.A., & Martin, D.F. (1998). Careers in the next millennium: Directions for future research. *Human Resource Management Review, 8*, 165-185.

Van Buren III, H.J. (2003). Boundaryless careers and employability obligations. *Business Ethics Quarterly, 13*(2), 131-149.

Walker, A.J. (2001). Best practices in HR Technology. In A.J. Walker (Ed.), *Web-based human resources* (pp. 3-14). New York: McGraw-Hill.

Workforce. (2001). *Making on-line self-service work*, (January), 54-61.

Zampetti, R., & Adamson, L. (2001). Web-based employee self-service: A win-win proposition for organizations and employees. In A.J. Walker (Ed.), *Web-based human resource* (pp. 15-23). New York: McGraw-Hill.

Section III

E-Learning Strategies

Chapter VII

Keeping Up with the Corporate University:
Resources for HRM Faculty and Practitioners

Pamela D. Sherer, Providence College, USA

Timothy Shea, University of Massachusetts Dartmouth, USA

Abstract

The number of corporate universities is increasing by leaps and bounds, and the role of corporate universities is rapidly evolving and becoming more tightly integrated with an organization's strategic planning and assessment. How can HRM faculty and practitioners keep their respective curricula and organizations up to date? The first section of this chapter provides an overview of the current corporate university landscape, discussing the three major factors that influence both their growth and their role in organizations: strategy and human resources, knowledge management, and technology and e-learning. The second section includes an annotated compendium of key resources in each of these areas, especially Internet resources.

Introduction

Corporations have been in the business of training and developing employees for a long time. It was estimated that U.S. companies would spend approximately $56.8 billion (Galvin, 2002) on education and training in 2002 as a means both for keeping employee skills, knowledge, and abilities updated, and to better retain top employees (Van Buren & Erskine, 2002; Dillich, 2000; Koprowski, 2000). The rapid development of corporate universities, especially during the last few years, has proven effective in meeting these educational needs (Vine & Palsule, 1999).

The idea of a corporate university is not new. Meister (1998) describes the General Motors Institute, founded in 1927, as the first. However, the origins of modern corporate universities can be traced to the period of the late 1950s through the 1960s. During that time Disney University, General Electric's Crotonville Management Development Institute, McDonald's Hamburger University, and several others were established. Jarvis (2001) indicates that these in-house training programs were developed in large part to supplement the traditional, off-site education that their staff members were receiving.

Over the past 15 years, the number of corporate universities has increased from 400 to over 2,000; that number is expected to surpass 3,700 by the end of this decade (Anderson, 2001). Corporate universities are found in virtually all industries: consulting, high tech, military, entertainment, financial services, healthcare, automobile, and fast food, to name a few. Examples of domestic and international companies with corporate universities include American Skandia, Black and Decker, Booz Allen Hamilton, Daimler-Chrysler, Defense Acquisition, Dell, Disney, eArmy, General Motors, Harley-Davidson, Infosys Technologies Limited, Intel, Isvor Fiat, McDonald's, Land Rover, Motorola, the North Shore - Long Island Jewish Health System, Oracle, the Tennessee Valley Authority, Schwab, and Unisys.

Of particular interest is the fact that many corporate universities are now extensively involved with their organization's strategic planning processes (Carter, Giber, & Goldsmith, 2001). As a result, leaders of human resource management and development departments in these organizations are rapidly becoming repositioned to the highest levels of organizational influence and decision making, including the introduction of a new position, the Chief Learning Officer (CLO) (Baldwin & Danielson, 2000). Utilizing the rapid advancement of e-learning and e-human resource development technologies, in conjunction with knowledge management concepts, the corporate university of today is quickly becoming the primary vehicle for conceptualizing, implementing, and assessing workplace learning opportunities based upon corporate strategies. However, because we are in the middle of a rapid evolutionary phase in the shape and purpose of corporate universities, the final shapes are unclear. A major issue that is currently being worked out is whether organizational strategic learning objectives are best served by companies that emphasize blended learning solutions or those that are pursuing Web-based virtual corporate universities.

A steady stream of articles, conferences, and on-site workshops on corporate university concepts has emerged over the past few years. Consulting organizations have developed expertise and can guide corporations through the design and implementation of a corporate university. Yet, with all the corporate university developments and accomplishments — in fact, because of the speed of the evolution of corporate universities — HRM practitioners wishing to develop a corporate university and HRM faculty wishing to create or update their courses or conduct research can find it difficult to keep up. For example, our leading graduate and undergraduate management and human resource textbooks currently provide minimal exposure to corporate universities and their impact on workplace learning and their role in organizational change (Jackson & Schuler, 2003; Mathis & Jackson, 2003; Noe, Hollenbeck, Gerhart, & Wright, 2003; Wexley & Latham, 2002). This chapter provides a way to "jump in" to the world of corporate universities and key resources to help in "keeping up" as the number of corporate universities continues to grow and the concept itself continues to evolve.

Based on a year-long funded study of corporate universities that included a number of site visits, a review of the literature, and a review of relevant Web sites, this chapter provides a primer on corporate universities for HRM practitioners, researchers, as well as management and human resource faculty responsible for delivering HRM curriculum to undergraduate and graduate students.

The first section of this chapter provides an overview of the current corporate university landscape by discussing the definition of a corporate university, the different purposes of corporate universities, the three major factors that influence both their growth and their role in organizations (strategy and human resources, knowledge management, and technology and e-learning), examples of corporate universities today, and emerging research models and research opportunities. The second section of the chapter provides HRM practitioners and faculty with a ready means for periodically updating their understanding of these rapidly evolving phenomena. This section includes an annotated compendium of key resources (books, articles, reports, and Web sites) organized by the four subject areas — corporate universities, strategy and human resources, knowledge management, and technology and e-learning.

The Web sites, in particular, offer up-to-date perspectives on corporate universities through information resources (current news, links to related periodicals, white papers, case studies, books, consulting companies, vendors, upcoming conference and event information, and research centers), as well as online communities and interactive forums that textbooks cannot keep pace with. This chapter provides a filter so practitioners and faculty can keep up with the latest changes in this field without having to endure the time needed to sift through the massive amount of resources available on the Internet.

What is a Corporate University?

The definition of a corporate university continues to evolve, and as yet no single universally accepted one has emerged. Some examples:

"A corporate university is the strategic umbrella for developing and educating employees, customers, and suppliers in order to meet an organization's business strategies." (Meister, 1998, p. 267)

"The corporate university concept involves a process — not necessarily a place — by which all levels of employees (and sometimes customers and suppliers) participate in learning experiences necessary to improve job performance and enhance business impact." (American Productivity and Quality Center, 2000, p. 6)

The above two definitions underscore the strategic focus of corporate universities and their emphasis on process and assessment. Critical to the sustainability of an organization's corporate university has been the accountability of its contributions through enhanced metrics (Becker, Huselid, & Ulrich, 2001; Berry, 2000; Fitz-enz, 2000; Kirkpatrick, 1998).

The next two definitions broaden these definitions by addressing corporate universities' critical role in knowledge management, and in leading and supporting a corporate learning system:

"A corporate university is an educational entity that is a strategic tool designed to assist its parent organization in achieving its mission by conducting activities that cultivate individual and organizational learning, knowledge, and wisdom." (Allen, 2002, p. 9)

"A corporate university is a company-run post-secondary educational entity that focuses on enhancing the knowledge and skills of its workforce members by strategically intertwining learning with work. Whether it exists as a physical campus or a virtual one, the focus has shifted from providing a classroom to developing a learning process where networking the entire organization's knowledge becomes the priority." (National Alliance of Business, 2002)

Together these definitions describe the potential breadth of corporate universities today, and highlight some differences in their goals, foci, and emphasis, depending on the organization. In addition, the last definition reminds us again that at this point in the evolution of corporate universities, a key challenge is to closely align the corporate university mission and structure with an organization's strategic objectives. Recent research efforts have begun to develop frameworks that detail the various components of the corporate university (Argote, McEvily, & Reagans, 2003; Prince & Stewart, 2002).

Differing Foci of Corporate Universities

A commonly raised issue is whether corporate universities are simply human resource training departments with a new name. The literature suggests this is not the case. In fact six possible foci have been identified for corporate universities.

These foci are not mutually exclusive. From Table 1, it is apparent that corporate universities differ from each other even though some have elements of all the foci under their corporate university umbrella. Table 2 identifies

Table 1. Corporate university foci

Focus	Description
A training department with a new name	Focus on traditional HR training and development
Competency-based career development	Focus on developing individual skills and providing the tools necessary to meet business challenges, including career development activities, facilitating succession planning, and helping to retain key employees
Change-management	Focus on easing major changes and transformations within the company
Initiative driven	Focus on facilitating the accomplishment of a corporate-wide initiative
Leadership development	Focus on management development and leadership
Customer-supplier relationship management	Focus on educating and managing employees, suppliers, and customers about customer-supplier relationships

Sources: Fulmer (2002), Global Learning Resources (2001)

Table 2: Differing characteristics of traditional HR training and development departments and corporate universities

Traditional HR Training & Development	Corporate Universities
Reactive	Proactive
Short-term focus	Long-term focus
Problem oriented	Strategically aligned
Proprietorship	Partnership
Compartmentalized	Integrated (under one umbrella)
Individual development focus	Corporate growth focus
Limited role for higher education	Expanded role for higher education
Resistance to evaluation	Grounded in evaluation (ROI)
Classroom based	More Web-based delivery
Limited metrics	Effective measures
Open enrollment	Managed enrollment
Learning as an employee benefit	Learning as an employee requirement

Sources: Barley (2001); Meister (1998)

common differences cited in the literature between traditional HR training departments and today's corporate universities, and thus provides characteristics of corporate universities as they continue to emerge.

Major Influences on Corporate University Growth

As previously mentioned, the conceptualization, development, and implementation of today's corporate universities have been significantly influenced by three major trends:

1. Recognition of human resource management as an instrumental player in corporate strategy (Prince & Stewart, 2002; Becker et al., 2001);

2. Emergence of knowledge management concepts and their integration into organizational practices (Argote et al., 2003; Allee, 2002; Alavi & Leidner, 2001); and

3. Availability and continued development of new technologies that support e-learning approaches to human resource development (Allen, 2002; Rossett, 2002).

These trends, taken together, have contributed to the significant growth of corporate universities and ultimately influence their role in the organization. Today's corporate university is actively exploring what was once considered the "holy grail" of training departments — a link between training, job performance, and an organization's goals.

Strategy and Human Resource Management

In recent years, organizations have awakened to the critical need to include human resources as part of their strategic planning processes (Spitzer & Conway, 2002; Becker et al., 2001; Aldelsberg & Trolley, 1999; Rossett, 1999). Many factors have influenced this change; for example, organizations are recognizing that:

- employees and their continued work-related learning are key to organizational goal attainment;

- corporate strategies must link training and development (learning) to key business goals, with an emphasis on measurement, such as return on investment (ROI) and the accompanying new tools for human resource measurement;

- continuous improvement at all levels requires ongoing work-based learning opportunities — that is, organizations need to become "learning organizations";

- partnering with multiple organizations requires learning about, from, and with other organizations and helps each organization meet its own goals;

- the extensive diffusion of enterprise resource planning (ERP) systems has opened up extraordinary opportunities, often bundled under the label of "e-HRM," for communicating with an organization's employees, workflow improvements related to HR activities, and the management of organizational learning initiatives;

- spreading and sustaining organizational culture, especially in today's global organizations, requires new ways to coordinate and deliver consistent information and values about one's organization;

- quality is a strategic goal requiring involvement of employees (at all levels), customers, and suppliers in organizational change efforts;

- developing measurement standards for quality requires organization-wide learning through training (e.g., Six Sigma; ISO 9000+);

- national and international standards of excellence (e.g., Malcolm Baldridge Awards) facilitate the sharing of organizational "best practices";

- lifetime employability, effective recruitment, and retaining best employees have renewed importance; and

- learning is no longer just an employee benefit, but rather a competitive necessity.

Each of these factors points to the need for continuous learning by employees and requires a strategic role for human resources. As an organizational entity, corporate universities have emerged as a means to initiate, coordinate, implement, and evaluate organizational learning to meet organizational goals.

Knowledge Management

Knowledge management is a high priority topic today because companies are struggling to keep up with the ever-increasing rate of change in their environments and the resulting need for analysis of greater variety and complexity (Malhotra, 2001). Organizations need to be able to evaluate and adapt faster than ever. In the short term, they need the ability to bring as much organizational knowledge, wisdom, and experience to bear on business challenges as possible, and faster than ever. In the long term, and this is where corporate universities come in, organizations need to determine gaps in their knowledge competencies and work diligently to close those gaps.

Knowledge management has been prominent in the literature since the 1980s and its definition is still evolving. However, there are some enduring common components. Knowledge management is about maximizing the knowledge assets in a company and recognizing that the combination of information, knowledge, and wisdom that both humans and digital files (e.g., e-mail, Excel spreadsheets, Word documents) possess represent an asset (Barth, 2002). Whereas traditionally the working axiom was "knowledge = power, so hoard it," today the theme has become "knowledge = power, so share it and it will multiply" — quite a different approach (Allee, 2002). In summary, knowledge management is about the creation, retention, and transfer of knowledge within the organization (Argote et al., 2003).

Knowledge management is best understood, not as an end, but as a means or a tool (Malhotra, 2001). That is, knowledge management is the path to better understand a company's mission, competitive environment, and/or performance, and for creating value from knowledge-based assets. Such a process often includes capturing, retaining, and sharing the assets "among employees, departments, and even other companies" (Santosus & Surmacz, 2002), including assets that may exist across many miles.

"With on-demand access to managed knowledge, every situation is addressed with the sum total of everything anyone in the organization has ever learned about a situation of a similar nature" (Bellinger, 2002, p. 6). Knowledge management, therefore, can increase the effectiveness of the organization and result in greater customer value (Barth, 2002).

Over the past few years, the concept of knowledge management (KM) has moved from niche applications limited to certain industries to a generally discussed concept across all types of business. Today, "every business is a knowledge business; every worker is a knowledge worker" (Allee, 2002, p. 1).

Currently KM use has taken two tracks: KM related to information technology and KM related to people (Sveiby, 2001). IT-related KM, that dates back to the late 1980s, focuses on the management of information through sharing information (e.g., via intranets, Web technologies, e-mail, virtual teams, and groupware applications such as Lotus Notes); managing and analyzing large volumes of management-oriented data — past and present (e.g., through databases, data warehousing; data mining; and On-Line Analytic Processing, or OLAP); and tools to create interactive e-commerce applications that can bring the supplier and customer closer to the business than ever before (Allee,

2002). Together, these technologies are being used to create knowledge management systems (KMSs) in order to code and share best practices (especially internal benchmarking), create corporate knowledge directories (mapping internal expertise), and create knowledge networks (bringing experts together) (Alavi & Leidner, 2001).

People-related KM, a much more recent usage, focuses on "assessing, changing, and improving human individual skills and/or behavior" (Sveiby, 2001, p. 1). This type of KM, tied more closely to corporate universities, is far more difficult to employ since it relates to creating a learning organization, improving the corporate culture, and investing in people and recruitment. Thus, KM includes understanding the development and accessing of tacit knowledge —the information and wisdom that only exists in the minds of the organization's employees (Santosus & Surmacz, 2002). Support vehicles include physical structures (learning centers, libraries, meeting rooms, and executive strategy rooms), tools (job aids, knowledge maps, and computer-based performance support), and e-learning (Allee, 2002).

Overall, the benefits of KM fall into six categories (Santosus & Surmacz, 2002; Kaplan, 2002):

1. fostering innovation by encouraging the free flow of ideas;
2. improving customer service by minimizing response time;
3. boosting revenues by getting products and services to market faster;
4. enhancing employee retention rates by recognizing the value of employees and rewarding them for it;
5. streamlining operations and reducing costs by eliminating redundant processes; and
6. reducing training time.

Today's knowledge management is a key component of any corporate university. Knowledge competencies are defined and measured by a company. Over time, employees become familiar with the competencies required for their current job and for achieving promotions, and they can then take more responsibility for their own knowledge competencies development (Allee, 2002).

Technology and E-Learning

The American Society for Training and Development (2002) defines e-learning as:

"...a wide set of applications and processes, such as Web-based learning, computer-based learning, virtual classrooms, and digital collaboration. It includes the delivery of content via Internet, intranet/extranet (LAN/WAN), audio and videotape, satellite broadcast, interactive TV, and CD-ROM."

A few years ago, other than CD-ROM-based Computer Based Training (CBT) and satellite broadcasts, most e-learning had asynchronous delivery and low multimedia content. Today, both asynchronous and synchronous delivery are possible. Asynchronous delivery can include various mixes of recorded audio, video, simulation, and more traditional text and slides. Synchronous communication, even with a 56k phone line, can also include a virtual classroom with PowerPoint slides, multi-person audio, the ability to share applications such as a whiteboard or a spreadsheet, and provide various participation features and several ways for class members to "virtually" participate. When the participants have broadband communications capability, the virtual classroom can also include videoconferencing. Today's delivery options, then, cover a broad spectrum, ranging from asynchronous to synchronous to blended combinations (Rossett, 2002; Schank, 2002).

The benefits of e-learning include cost savings/avoidance; greater flexibility, including 24/7 delivery; and increased productivity, especially where learners are geographically dispersed (Hall, 2002). These benefits have fueled optimism that e-learning will explode and overtake classroom training as the predominant mode of delivery even when e-learning was still primarily asynchronous with low multimedia content. Yet, even in 2001, e-learning represented only 4% of the worldwide corporate training market (Graunke, 2002). However, by 2006, when instructor-led training is only expected to grow by 2%, e-learning is expected to grow by 30% (Bean, 2002). And these percentages are based on a large market. The overall enterprise learning market (where the two largest components are instructor led and e-learning) is expected to grow from $11.2 billion in 2001 to $13.4 billion in 2006 (Gabelhouse, 2002).

With e-learning as a cost-effective vehicle for extensive, multi-site training by corporate universities (Sauer, 2001), each company must develop its own experience using e-learning for its corporate university initiative to be productive. Will corporate universities continue to incorporate blended solutions or evolve into virtual Web-based entities? Also, with a growing tendency for the corporate university to be treated as a profit center, or at least to justify itself through positive ROI, e-learning becomes even more important. The good news is that the technology and software are maturing, and the seemingly endless number of vendors appears ready to start consolidating (Parks, 2002).

Corporate University's Today

As corporate universities continue to emerge, there are no universally accepted definitions, structures, or missions. From our discussions and on-site visits with a number of Chief Learning Officers and Directors of corporate universities, we explored the diversity and breadth of their corporate learning initiatives. For example, at Booz Allen & Hamilton's Center for Performance Excellence, the emphasis is on synchronizing corporate learning opportunities to business strategy. This is accomplished through focusing on individual personal development, and through linking career options and advancement to core competencies. They employ both face-to-face instruction and e-learning through a combination of fixed and Web-based virtual corporate university components. At Fidelity's Service Delivery University, a major goal is to surround employees with unlimited, seamless opportunities to enhance their capabilities through the use of professional courses, job-specific development, communities of knowledge/practice, and non-traditional learning. They use a blended learning approach that includes collaborative Web-based training, self-study Web-based learning, discussion groups/communities, Web-based testing, and traditional classrooms.

One corporate university stood out above the rest, the Defense Acquisition University (DAU) (www.dau.mil). In 2002, DAU received the Corporate University "Best-in Class" (CUBIC) award in recognition of its best practices, reflecting its clearly defined corporate university mission, its transformation of its learning environment to meet today's learners information and knowledge needs, the integration of technology into their learning products, and their ability to deliver the right training to the right employee at the right time.

DAU's Performance Learning Model (PLM) is at the core of its efforts. It is no accident that the name of the model blends the words performance and learning. DAU's initiatives meet the learning needs of its workforce while concurrently focusing on results or improvements in performance. PLM includes four components all aligned with the DAU mission: certification and assignment-specific training, continuous learning, performance support, and knowledge sharing/communities of practice. They have focused on providing an appropriate mix of Web-based, hybrid (or blended learning solutions), and case-based instruction. An important thrust of this mix has been their growth in their distributed learning program that includes computer-based and Internet instruction. Altogether, the DAU, based on the PLM model and tightly connected to the mission of the organization, creates a structured foundation for the new learner-centered environment. Today, the DAU serves over 130,000 individuals, and includes anytime, anywhere learning, making learning available seven days a week, 24 hours a day.

Each of the above-mentioned corporate universities has recognized and harnessed, to differing degrees, the three major trends that are driving the growth of corporate universities — the growing connection between organizational strategy and human resources, knowledge management, and technology/e-learning. DAU, in particular, has developed best practices in integrating these trends.

Emerging Research Models and Research Opportunities

Corporate universities are intended to function as the primary delivery mechanism that encompasses organizational strategy, HRM (and e-HRM), knowledge management, and e-learning, under one umbrella, with the goal of fostering a climate of continually improving organizational performance. As many more organizations gain experience with corporate universities and their underlying components — the changing role of human resources, the growing importance of knowledge management, and the rapidly evolving technologies that help develop, deliver, and assess learning initiatives — the more corporate university structures and activities will continue to evolve.

Fortunately, research models are being developed to support the investigation of corporate universities. Prince and Stewart (2002) have developed a descriptive and analytical framework that is based upon knowledge management, learning organizations, and organizational learning. Their "corporate university wheel" focuses on two concepts. First, there are four key functions a corporate university should perform:

- **Knowledge Systems and Processes.** This category recognizes the rapidly growing number of computer-based tools that can help an organization capture, organize, and disseminate knowledge—databases, expert systems, and decision-making software. It also recognizes the importance of finding ways to use these tools effectively.

- **Networks and Partnerships.** Partnerships that support learning include connecting people or groups together within an organization, connecting with experts in the broader community outside the organization, and developing outsource relationships for training and development activities where appropriate.

- **Learning Processes.** Most visibly, learning processes involve training and education programs. However, the corporate university should also be facilitating the creation of a culture of learning throughout the organization.

- **People Processes.** People processes include ways that people in the organization have to learn and "build and reinforce shared meaning" (Prince & Stewart, 2002, p. 807).

Secondly, the model emphasizes that the effectiveness of corporate universities today is limited, not as much by the functioning of the four key functions, but on the lack of sufficient integration, management, and nurturing of the four functions as an interrelated system—a system that supports the organization's learning.

Barley's (2002) corporate university design model clearly illustrates the importance of strategic alignment between the corporate university and the organization. She also highlights the need for evaluation at all levels — organizational assessment, strategic alignment, curriculum development, and program implementation — and the need to connect corporate university activities to performance improvement.

Finally, for those wishing to focus research specifically on the technology behind e-learning and how it relates to corporate universities, one can delve into specific technologies that support extensive e-learning initiatives — learning management systems, portals for information and collaboration, synchronous learning such as video and audio communication, and learning content management systems for developing and delivering both distance learning and blended learning.

These models provide researchers a means for exploring a number of interesting topics related to corporate universities, including:

- how corporate universities can increasingly develop learning opportunities that connect explicitly to improved job and organizational performance, including skills development, cultural changes, and development of better and more meaningful metrics;

- how corporate universities, through the use of e-learning, can continue to speed up the development and delivery of new training initiatives, making a just-in-time philosophy possible;

- how e-HRM and e-learning administration tools (e.g., learning management systems) can help manage and assess short- and long-term learning initiatives by an organization's corporate university;

- how knowledge management systems can be used by corporate universities to develop and share expertise on an organizational level, as well as identify and manage gaps in their knowledge competencies;

- how HR and corporate university job roles and job titles change as e-learning and e-HRM move from the experimental stage into becoming fully integrated into the HR workplace and workplace learning activities (e.g., the evolution of the Chief Learning Officer); and

- how corporate universities develop and experience the expanding use of outsource arrangements with suppliers of learning products and services.

In addition to research challenges, faculty who teach HRM and HRM practitioners alike need a way to "keep up" with the speed with which corporate universities are evolving. The next section provides a means to do just that, largely through the extraordinary resources available on the Internet to disseminate information and connect people.

Keeping Up

One thing is certain: Most of what we have recounted above is changing. As we pointed out, corporate universities differ; yet, in whatever form they take, their role in shaping organizational strategies, impacting knowledge management, and utilizing e-learning is increasingly necessary to organizations that wish to retain their best employees and remain competitive. For faculty, the challenge is in keeping up with a phenomenon that's evolving as rapidly as corporate universities are and, in addition to incorporating relevant information into courses, alerting our students that ongoing learning will, in the foreseeable future, be a critical part of their organizational job requirements. For human resources practitioners — especially for those designing, implementing, or managing a corporate university — the challenge is to keep abreast of the best and most current experience by colleagues and researchers in order to bring that experience and wisdom to their own particular organization.

At the end of this chapter, we have provided several resources for management and human resource faculty, with which they can stay connected to the important and pervasive changes being brought about by corporate universities, without the necessity of investing weeks in research. Faculty and HR practitioners may have the best of intentions, yet become discouraged because of the time needed to filter through the massive amount of resources on the Internet to identify a few useful, quality sites. We have attempted to provide that filter in order to make possible a less painful journey. In addition to key books, articles, and reports, an annotated list of relevant Web sites is included so that faculty and practitioners can easily update their knowledge of the latest changes in this field. The online resources, in particular, offer the most up-to-date knowledge and information for management and human resource faculty. Many of the sites listed contain extensive treatments of current news in the field, as well as convenient links to related periodicals, white papers, case studies, books, consulting companies, vendors, upcoming conference and event information, research centers, and online communities.

Conclusions

As corporate universities continue to emerge and redefine themselves, the three major trends — involving strategy, knowledge management, and e-learning —

will influence those institutions, shaping and expanding their impact on human resource development and workplace learning. Meister (1998) discusses a new model for workplace learning: "one that is offered 'just-in-time' and focused on the skills, knowledge, and competencies needed for success in a fast changing global marketplace" (p. 216). Corporate universities are playing a key role in creating and sustaining this new model for workplace learning. Corporate University Enterprise, a consulting firm in McLean, Virginia, states:

"The most progressive organizations will make a corporate university the centerpiece of their organizational culture — a university that will facilitate the kind of lifelong learning employees will need to make themselves and the organization more successful." (Prochaska, 2001)

Further, human resource academic faculty and organizational practitioners will play a critical role in introducing today's — and tomorrow's — corporate university concepts to our business students and in applying these concepts in organizations. Understanding the changing world of corporate universities will keep our faculty, students, and practitioners correctly focused on the essential ingredients for succeeding on the job, improving short- and long-term learning initiatives in their organizations, tightening connections between human resource practices and organizational goals, and increasing the ability of an organization to assess its learning initiatives.

Resources for Faculty

Corporate Universities

Books

Allen, M. (Ed.). (2002). *The corporate university handbook: Designing, managing and growing a successful program.* New York: Amacom.

Jarvis, P. (2001). *Universities and corporate universities: The higher learning industry in global society.* London: Kogan Page Limited.

Meister, J. (1998). *Corporate universities: Lessons in building a world-class work force* (2nd ed.). New York: McGraw-Hill.

Reports

Corporate University Xchange Fifth Annual Benchmarking Report. (2002). Available from Corporate University Exchange (http://www.corpu.com) for $595. Looking at year-to-year trends, the report examines how organizations shape their corporate universities based on building blocks such as funding, organization, products/services, learning partners, and technology.

The Corporate University: Measuring the Impact of Learning. (2000). Available from American Productivity and Quality Center (APQC) (http://www.apqc.org) $495. This report details how corporate universities in leading-edge organizations are measured, monitored, and reported. This APQC Best-Practice Report provides training measurement and evaluation (M&E) examples, with a focus on the alignment of employee training with corporate strategy, and the identification and reporting of learning measurements.

Web Sites

Chief Learning Officer (http://CLOmedia.com): Access to *Chief Learning Officer Magazine* (premier issue September 2002). The magazine features top experts in the corporate training industry writing to executives and officers about the importance, benefits, and advancements of a properly trained workforce.

Corporate University Xchange, Inc. (CUX) (http://www.corpu.com): CUX is a comprehensive Web site that offers research on learning best practices, consulting services, events listings, publications, and an e-newsletter on current trends and CU activities.

The New Corporate University Review (http://www.traininguniversity.com/tu_map.php): Includes a listing of corporate university human resource events, national and international conferences, and offers a free subscription to the Corporate University and Training E-Newsletter.

Strategy and Human Resources

Books

Aldelsberg, D., & Trolley, E. (1999). *Running training like a business: Delivering unmistakable value.* San Francisco: Berrett-Koehler.

Becker, B., Huselid, M., & Ulrich, D. (2001). *The HR scorecard: Linking people, strategy and performance.* Boston: Harvard Business School Press.

Boud, D., & Garrick, J. (Eds.) (1999). *Understanding learning at work.* London: Routledge.

Fitz-enz, J. (2000). *The ROI of human capital: Measuring the economic value of employee performance.* New York: Amacom.

Kirkpatrick, D. (1998). *Evaluating training programs: The four levels.* San Francisco: Berrett-Koehler.

Lengnick-Hall, M., & Lengnick-Hall, C. (2003). *Human resource management in the knowledge economy: New challenges, new roles, new capabilities.* San Francisco: Berrett-Koehler.

Raelin, J. (2000). *Work-based learning: The new frontier of management development.* Upper Saddle River, NJ: Prentice-Hall.

Rossett, A. (1999). *First things fast: A handbook for performance analysis.* San Francisco: Jossey-Bass.

Wexley, K., & Latham, G. (2002). *Developing and training human resources in organizations* (3rd ed.). Upper Saddle River, NJ: Prentice-Hall.

Reports

Spitzer, D., & Conway, M. (2002). Link training to your bottom line. ASTD Info-Line Report. Alexandria, VA: American Society for Training and Development.

Van Buren, M., & Erskine, W. (2002). Trends in employer-provided training in the United States. ASTD State of the Industry Report 2002. Alexandria, VA: American Society for Training and Development.

Web Sites

American Productivity and Quality Center (http://www.apqc.org): APQC is a nonprofit organization that provides information, expertise, and support for process and performance improvement for organizations. This includes benchmarking and best practices, knowledge management, customer-focused systems, organizational effectiveness, and performance measurement and improvement.

American Society for Training and Development (http://www.astd.org): ASTD provides individuals and organizations with up-to-date and comprehensive information on training and development through publication and research reports, online resources, white papers, customized research services, conferences, and so forth. Membership fee required for use of some resources.

Society for Human Resources Management (SHRM) (http://www.shrm.org): The world's largest association devoted to human resource management, SHRM serves 170,000 members and provides publications, research reports, online resources, networking opportunities, conferences and workshops, and so forth. Membership fee required for use of most resources.

Knowledge Management

Books

Allee, V. (1997). *The knowledge evolution: Expanding organizational intelligence.* Newton, MA: Butterworth-Heinemann.

Brown, J., & Duguid, P. (2000). *The social life of information.* Boston: Harvard Business School Press.

Davenport, T., & Prusak, L. (1998). *Working knowledge: How organizations manage what they know.* Boston: Harvard Business School Press.

Jurgen, K., Stein, W., & Licht, T. (2002). *Knowledge unplugged: The McKinsey & company global survey on knowledge management.* Palgrave Publishing.

Malhotra, Y. (Ed.). (2001). *Knowledge management and business model innovation.* Hershey, PA: Idea Group Publishing.

Pfeffer, J., & Sutton, R. (2000). *The knowing-doing gap: How smart companies turn knowledge into action.* Boston: Harvard Business School Press.

Stewart, T. (1997). *Intellectual capital: The new wealth of organizations.* New York: Currency Doubleday.

Article

Raybould, R. (2002). Building performance-centered Web-based systems, information systems, and knowledge management systems in the 21st century. In A. Rossett (Ed.), *The ASTD e-learning handbook* (pp. 338-353). New York: McGraw-Hill.

Web Sites

Knowledge Management Magazine (http://www.kmmagazine.com): "A case study-based journal featuring articles from global companies...reinforced with contribution from leading academics."

Knowledge Management World (http://www.kmworld.com): Contains online resources, solutions, news, conference information, and publications related to knowledge management.

The Knowledge Management Resource Center (http://www.kmresource. com): Offers online news, online communities focused on knowledge management, conference and event information, periodicals, books, and numerous other knowledge management-related links.

@brint.com, the BizTech Network (http://www.brint.com/OrgLrng.htm): "The premier portal and global knowledge network for business, information, technology, and knowledge managers, professionals, and entrepreneurs." Its knowledge management, organizational learning, and learning organizations portal has extensive resources including a virtual library, community discussion forums, quotes, a Knowledge Executives Network, conferences, and KM tools.

CIO's Knowledge Management Research Center (http://www.cio.com/ research/knowledge/): "Knowledge management is an evolving broad umbrella of topics and viewpoints, which takes a comprehensive look at the subject difficult. The KM Research Center has taken the approach of focusing on a few links to high quality content from CIO and Web sites that encompass most of the major trends." The site includes links to articles, Web sites, publications, forums, a glossary, and white papers.

Technology and E-Learning

Books

Lissak, R., & Bailey, G. (2002). *A thousand tribes: How technology unites people in great companies.* New York: John Wiley & Sons.

Rosenberg, M. (2000). *E-learning strategies for delivering knowledge in the digital age.* New York: McGraw-Hill.

Rossett, A. (2002). *The ASTD e-learning handbook.* New York: McGraw-Hill.

Schank, R. (2002). *Designing world-class e-learning.* New York: McGraw-Hill.

Reports

Corporate University Xchange's Pillars of E-learning Success. (2002). Available from Corporate University Exchange (http://www.corpu.com) for $495. Survey of 65 best-practice e-learning organizations with latest statistics on vendors, delivery, and trends in e-learning. Includes intensive interviews with leading practitioners to present best-practice case examples focusing on areas such as: managing vendors, assessing e-learners' readiness, providing support to learners, and understanding the critical elements needed to create an effective e-learning infrastructure.

Web Sites

Learning Circuits: ASTD's Online Magazine (http://www.learningcircuits. org): Offers up-to-date industry news, feature stories, reviews of technology products, a question-and-answer link, discussion board, calendar of events, and an archive.

2004 Chief Learning Officer SourceBook (http://CLOmedia.com/ sourcebook): The *Chief Learning Officer* magazine *SourceBook* is a free search engine listing hundreds of leading companies providing products, services, tools, and expertise to chief learning officers and other executives involved in workforce learning and development.

e-Learning Centre (http://www.e-learningcentre.co.uk/eclipse/index.html): "Contains links to thousands of selected and reviewed e-learning articles, white papers, research reports; examples of e-learning solutions; vendors of e-learning content, technology and services; as well as e-learning conferences, seminars, workshops, and other e-learning events. The main focus is on adult e-learning, i.e., e-learning in the workplace, in higher education, and in continuing professional development."

Syllabus Magazine (http://www.syllabus.com/): "*Syllabus'* mission is to inform educators on how technology can be used to support their teaching, learning, and administrative activities. Each issue includes feature articles, case studies, product reviews, and profiles of technology use at the individual, departmental, and institutional level. Regular features cover multimedia, distance learning, the Internet, quantitative tools, publishing, and administrative technology. The *Syllabus* Web site supports and expands upon the publication's content covering the latest technology for higher education."

click2learn (http://home.click2learn.com/): "Click2learn is the leading provider of enterprise software to help organizations improve workforce productivity and business performance through the strategic application of innovative learning software solutions and services." Click2learn is an example of a company that is "putting it all together" into a "one-stop-shopping" business, providing tools for e-training development, delivery (virtual classroom, collaboration, etc.), and evaluation (performance management, learning management).

References

Alavi, M., & Leidner, D. (2001). Review. Knowledge management and knowledge management systems: Conceptual foundations and research issues. *MIS Quarterly, 25*(1), 107-136.

Aldelsberg, D., & Trolley, E. (1999). *Running training like a business: Delivering unmistakable value.* San Francisco: Berrett-Koehler.

Allee, V. (2002). 12 principles of knowledge management: ASTD linking people, learning and performance. Retrieved August 26, 2003, from *www.astd.org/CMS/templates/index.html?template_id=1& articleid= 10595*

Allen, M. (Ed.). (2002). *The corporate university handbook.* New York: Amacom.

American Productivity & Quality Center (APQC). (2000). *The corporate university: Measuring the impact of learning. Consortium Learning Forum best-practice report.* Houston, TX: American Productivity & Quality Center.

American Society for Training and Development (ASTD). (2002). Retrieved September 3, 2003, from *www.astd.org/*

Anderson, L. (2001). Tailor-made for life-long learning [Electronic version]. *Financial Times (London)*, *1*(March 26). Retrieved September 3, 2003, from *web.lexis-nexis.com/universe*

Argote, L., McEvily, B., & Reagans, R. (2003). Managing knowledge in organizations: An integrative framework and review of emerging themes. *Management Science*, *49*(4), 571-582.

Baldwin, T., & Danielson, C. (2000). Building a learning strategy at the top: Interviews with ten of America's CLOs. *Business Horizons*, *43*(6), 5-14.

Barley, K. (2002). Corporate university structures that reflect organizational cultures. In M. Allen (Ed.), *The corporate university handbook* (pp. 43-65). New York: Amacom.

Barley, K. (2001). Finding golden nuggets: Making the most of corporate university benchmarking. Workshop presentation at Corporate University Enterprise, Inc., Corporate University Site Tour, McLean, Virginia, December 13-14.

Barth, S. (2002). Defining knowledge management. Retrieved August 16, 2003, from *www.destinationcrm.com/print/default.asp?ArticleID=1400*

Bean, M. (2002). Methods that work in global enterprises. *Chief Learning Officer*, *22*(September).

Becker, B., Huselid, M., & Ulrich, D. (2001). *The HR scorecard: Linking people, strategy, and performance.* Boston: Harvard Business School Press.

Bellinger, G. (2002). Knowledge management—emerging perspectives. *Outsights.* Retrieved August 16, 2003, from *www.systems-thinking.org/kmgmt/kmgmt.htm*

Berry, J. (2000). Corporate training—the e-learning center—companies using metrics to justify e-learning's impact on strategic business goals. *Internetweek*, *836*(November 6), 61-64.

Carter, L., Giber, D., & Goldsmith, M. (Eds.) (2001). *Best practices in organizational development and change.* San Francisco: Jossey-Bass/Pfeiffer.

Dillich, S. (2000). Corporate universities. *Computing Canada, 26*(16), 25.

Fitz-enz, J. (2000). *The ROI of human capital: Measuring the economic value of employee performance.* New York: Amacom.

Fulmer, R. (2002). Best practices in corporate universities. In M. Allen (Ed.), *Corporate university handbook* (pp. 107-120). New York: Amacom.

Gabelhouse, G. (2002). Enterprise learning: A spending summary. *Chief Learning Officer*, (September), 60-62.

Galvin, T. (2002). 2002 industry report. *Training, 39*(October), 24-52.

Global Learning Resources. (2001). The uses and misuses of the term "corporate university". Retrieved August 16, 2003, from *glresources.com*

Graunke, T. (2002). E-learning—the second wave. *Chief Learning Officer, 13*(September).

Hall, B. (2002). Six steps to developing a successful e-learning initiative: Excerpts from the e-learning guidebook. In A. Rossett, *The ASTD e-learning handbook* (pp. 234-250). New York: McGraw-Hill.

Jackson, S., & Schuler, R. (2003). *Managing human resources through strategic partnerships* (8th ed.). Mason, OH: Thomson/Southwestern.

Jarvis, P. (2001). *Universities and corporate universities: The higher learning industry in global society.* London: Kogan Page Limited.

Kaplan, S. (2002). KM the right way. *CIO Magazine,* (July 15). Retrieved August 12, 2003, from *cio.com/archive/071502/right_content.html*

Kirkpatrick, D. (1998). *Evaluating training programs: The four levels.* San Francisco: Berrett-Koehler.

Koprowski, G. (2000). Online learning: The competitive edge. *Informationweek, 801*(August 28), 124-128.

Malhotra, Y. (2001). Knowledge management for the new world of business. Retrieved August 26, 2003, from *www.brint.com/km/whatis.htm*

Mathis, R., & Jackson, J. (2003). *Human resource management* (10th ed.). Mason OH: Thompson/Southwestern.

Meister, J. (1998). *Corporate universities: Lessons in building a world-class work force* (2nd ed.). New York: McGraw-Hill Trade.

National Alliance of Business. (2002). Corporate universities. Retrieved September 3, 2003, from *www.nab.com/corpuni.htm*

Noe, R., Hollenbeck, J., Gerhart, B., & Wright, P. (2003). *Human resource management* (4th ed.). New York: McGraw-Hill Irwin.

Parks, E. (2002). Dr. Parks' top 10 2003 predictions for e-learning. Retrieved September 3, 2003, from *askintl.com/index.cfm/1,0,794,4389,693,441, html*

Prince, C., & Stewart, J. (2002). Corporate universities—an analytical framework. *The Journal of Management Development, 21*, 794-811.

Prochaska, S. (2001). Is a corporate university in your organization's future? Society for Human Resource Management White Paper. Retrieved August 16, 2003, from *www.shrm.org*

Rossett, A. (1999). *First things fast: A handbook for performance analysis.* San Francisco: Jossey-Bass.

Rossett, A. (2002). *The ASTD e-learning handbook.* New York: McGraw-Hill.

Santosus, M., & Surmacz, J. (2002). The ABCs of knowledge management. CIO Magazine's Knowledge Management Research Center. Retrieved September 3, 2003, from *www.cio.com/research/knowledge/edit/ kmabcs.html*

Sauer, P. (2001). E-learning energizes as the next horizon in corporate training with promises of cost savings. *Chemical Market Reporter,* (September 3), F8-F12.

Schank, R. (2002). *Designing world-class e-learning.* New York: McGraw-Hill.

Schettler, J. (2003). Defense acquisition university: Weapons of mass instruction. *Training, 40*(2), 20-30.

Spitzer, D., & Conway, M. (2002). Link training to your bottom line. ASTD Info-Line Report. Alexandria, VA: American Society for Training and Development.

Sveiby, K. (2001). What is knowledge management? Retrieved September 3, 2003, from *www.sveiby.com/library.html*

Van Buren, M., & Erskine, W. (2002). Trends in employer-provided training in the United States: ASTD State of the Industry Report 2002. Alexandria, VA: American Society for Training and Development.

Vine, P., &, Palsule, S. (1999). Corporate universities: Back to school. *The British Journal of Administrative Management,* (March/April), 18-21.

Wexley, K., & Latham, G. (2002). *Developing and training human resources in organizations* (3rd ed.). Upper Saddle River, NJ: Prentice-Hall.

Chapter VIII

E-Learning Strategies of Italian Companies

Anna Comacchio, University of Ca' Foscari, Italy

Annachiara Scapolan, University of Ca' Foscari, Italy

Abstract

The chapter gives a contribution to the understanding country-specific e-learning models, focusing on the e-learning experience of Italian companies in the pharmaceutical and banking industries. The chapter analyzes the antecedents of a corporate e-learning adoption process, asking whether it is forced by the rational search for economic benefit, or by bandwagon pressures, whereby companies are more interested in their reputations. The chapter also aims at understanding how companies are implementing e-learning, analyzing the most important features of the e-learning strategies: users, contents, infrastructures, and services and supports. After having discussed the result of the research conducted on a document analysis, a survey, some interviews, and two in-depth case studies, the emerging B2E strategy for e-learning is explained. In the conclusions the main issues related to the e-learning processes in the Italian companies are summarized, and the research methodology and the possible future research lines are discussed.

Introduction

In recent years, corporate e-learning has been the subject of several studies. On the one hand, it has been identified as one of the latest best practices in HRM (Nacamulli, 2003) because it enables companies to meet new intellectual capital investment requirements (ASTD, 2001). These include the need to enhance quality and effectiveness in program development while reducing costs, to update the skills base throughout the organization (at all levels, across a wide geographical area, etc.), and to increase the organization's learning capability by integrating online training and strategic knowledge management (Ley & Ulbrich, 2002).

On the other hand, due to the exponential rate at which this innovation was adopted in the USA, in the last years the experience of pioneers, in both the public and private sectors, and their best practices have become one of the main issues dealt with in corporate e-learning research and literature (Shank, 2002; Horton, 2001; Rosenberg, 2001).

However, corporate e-learning is not spreading worldwide as fast as expected, and it is far from being applied extensively in Europe and Italy, despite a number of enthusiastic forecasts (Anee, 2003; IDC, 2002). Furthermore, if we look at companies' e-learning experiences, it appears that organizations are approaching it in an incremental and experimental manner. Among other explanations, three factors (partially related) can help to understand this controversial rate of diffusion. First of all, many benefits promised on paper are not what e-learning is really providing (Prandstraller, 2001). Secondly, even if the standardization process does seem to simplify the identification of some main features of a corporate e-learning strategy, it is still rather difficult to relate them to ROI. Thirdly, technological and organizational best practices are not simply introduced as they are by companies, but adoption of best models is a learning process and depends on specific organizational capabilities such as absorptive capacity (Martin, Robson, & Jennings, 2002; Cohen & Levinthal, 1990).

These considerations suggest that the study of e-learning should take a more in-depth view of the ways it is adopted and of the context-related factors that, nationally and within organizations, may promote or prevent it and influence the way companies implement corporate e-learning.

From this perspective, the chapter aims to give a contribution to understanding the e-learning adoption process in Italy. First of all, the chapter will focus on what makes a company adopt e-learning, asking whether it is forced to by the rational search for economic benefit, or by institutional pressures whereby companies are more interested in their reputation and image. The adoption process will be analyzed, considering who the decision makers are in companies, the main sources of information, and the perceived and achieved organizational aims.

Secondly, the chapter will contribute to understand how companies are implementing e-learning and the main issues related to this process. From an organizational point of view, it will analyze the main features of the e-learning strategies that are emerging in Italian companies.

Since the spread of e-learning in Italy is in its infancy, research has been undertaken in two industries — pharmaceuticals and banking — where e-learning has been adopted more extensively than in others, and where both companies with very early and more advanced experiences can be analyzed. An empirical study has been developed in each industry based on a survey, interviews, and document analysis.

Corporate E-Learning: How Companies Adopt It

Corporate E-Learning and Its Main Drivers

Corporate e-learning can be defined as an extensive computer and Internet-based method (Piskurich, 2003) for a company's training and development policies.

Today's new browser-based HR portal technology is changing the way organizations manage human resources (Walker, 2001), specifically the way firms train their employees. The debate around this latest killer application of

Figure 1. Benefits of e-learning

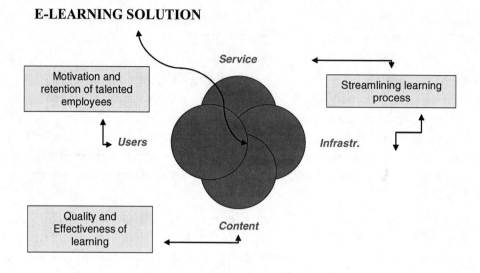

ICT, as John Chamber, Cisco CEO, has defined it, has contributed to the knowledge about e-learning being codified, by updating common languages and frames of reference. Networks of research projects, consultants, and companies continuously rationalize experiences at a national and company level, comparing different alternatives and building common theoretical assumptions on e-learning strategy (Nacamulli, 2003; Cunningham, 2001; Rosenberg, 2001). Researchers and practitioners mainly agree that by investing in e-learning, companies try to gain three types of benefits (Hartley, 2003; Shank, 2002):

1. **Streamlining learning processes** through cost savings (instructional costs, opportunity costs, administrative costs, travel costs, scalability resulting from the repeatability of courses or modules). Cost reduction and flexibility can be achieved in many ways, mainly by choosing the level of interactivity and cooperation of a learning experience and its synchronicity or asynchronicity.

2. **Quality and effectiveness of learning** through flexibility (just-in-time access to knowledge/information) and by tailoring time, methods, and content of courses to work requirements and learning by doing.

3.   **Motivation and retention of talented employees** through customization and learning on demand. The delivery of online courses fitting personal learning style seems to enhance the learning experience. Learning on demand and free choice of courses may also develop employees' employability.

Recent debate is questioning why these benefits are not accomplished yet, why there are more failures than successes in achieving economic and quality benefits (Prandstraller, 2001). One main question to address is that the adoption of e-learning is not a rational choice but an ambiguous decision process, characterized by "opaqueness or lack of clarity surrounding an organizational assessment of an innovation" (Abrahamson & Rosenkopf, 1993, p. 494). As a company cannot evaluate the technical efficiency or the returns of an innovation, because of ambiguity of goals, of means-end relationships, and environment (March & Olsen, 1976), it will rely more on social as opposed to economic factors, in order to decide whether to adopt an innovation or not.

Considering the innovation of e-learning, we may find that ambiguity does matter. Doubtless there is a codification of best practices process going on within the international e-learning marketplace. It is driven by academic studies, research centers (Astd, Idc, Masie, etc.), and providers, and it is also facilitated by the actions of standardizing groups (AICC, IEEE Ltsc, EU Ariadne project, ADL) (Rosenberg, 2001) and by the emergence of shareable courseware object reference models (reusable learning objects). This codification process of e-learning best practices seems to make it easier to identify both strategies' dimensions and advantages. Considering this process, managerial literature and research centers (Astd, Masie, IDC) maintain that a company can rationally identify the best e-learning model and decide which to adopt after evaluating the ROI of this type of investment. But even if the standardization process does seem to help companies identify some main features of an e-learning solution and its main benefits, it is still rather difficult to relate them to economic performance.

First of all, it appears that companies are suffering from *ambiguity of goals*, especially in the early-stage adoption. Considering the Italian context as an example of early-stage adoptions, results of research into e-learning in Italy in 2002 by A.D. Little 2002 highlighted that, while companies seem mainly efficiency driven, when they choose an e-learning solution, their decision process is far from being rational. Companies do not plan the adoption of e-learning taking into consideration each phase of the introduction process and do not specify the related objectives and measurements of performance.

Secondly, considering the type of innovation e-learning triggers, *ambiguity of means-ends relations* has an effect. E-HRM policies like e-learning should be considered more than just a simple technological change of people management tools and more than online delivery of HR services (Hansen & Deimler, 2001). From this point of view, firstly, e-learning adoption implies not only technological but also organizational changes and, secondly, for this reason, their impact on efficiency could be less clear. Quality results can be achieved by CBT asynchronous courses, but also by blended solutions. Moreover, even though some indicators of efficiency and also of effectiveness of training are widely adopted (Kirkpatrick, 1998), individual learning processes are "soft" issues. Their results are mainly of an intangible nature, and even though skill or competency development can be achieved and partially measured, it is rather difficult to isolate its impact on job performance and individual motivation from several other causes. It is also more difficult to measure increased employability that people can gain thanks to online training. For this reason measurements are not univocally quantifiable, related indicators have an ambiguous meaning, and the evaluation process is still time consuming and costly. Thus, the adoption process of e-learning could be difficult to evaluate on a traditional basis (Schank, 2002).

Under these conditions, companies rely more on information about who has adopted an innovation (Abrahamason & Rosenkopf, 1997). Moreover, adopters choose an innovation because of the threat of lost legitimacy under *institutional bandwagon pressure*. Recent studies of the managerial best practices (e.g., quality management or teamwork) (Staw & Epstein, 2000) demonstrated that what forces the adoption of a new organizational solution is the pursuit of reputation within a social and cultural environment (DiMaggio & Powell, 1983; Granovetter, 1985).

E-learning is a particularly relevant innovation from a corporate point of view. For example, it impacts on the issue of lifelong learning, which is one of the priorities of the EU (2003), national governments, trade unions, and training institutions. Furthermore, the flexibility and the connectivity of such solutions facilitate remote learning from home, and this is an important issue for workforce retraining from a trade union point of view. From this perspective, as e-learning impacts on the investment in human capital and lifelong learning, it may attract the attention of institutions operating in the labor market such as unions, training associations, and public institutions. Secondly, companies seek standardized responses to cope with uncertainty related to innovation. They do this by imitating those organizations that, thanks to their competitive capabilities or their international dimensions, are considered a reference model (for example, Cisco is often referred to as a benchmark in E-HRM and e-learning in many conferences, studies, and consultants' reports) (Haberberg & Binsardi, 2002). Finally, the managers' choice of e-learning is influenced by the professional community with which they share common learning paths and the same social networks (Haberberg & Binsardi, 2002).

When the adoption process is uncertain and results are ambiguous, there might also be *competitive bandwagon pressures* towards the introduction of an e-learning strategy by companies (Abrahamson & Rosenkopf, 1993, 1990). Companies will adopt innovations because of the threat of lost competitive advantage. Bandwagons occur if potential adopters perceive the risk that an innovation is a success and that if they do not adopt it, their performance will fall below the average performance of adopters.

From a bandwagon perspective, benefits like cost cutting, scalability, and flexible delivery of skill training to a spread number of trainees can be easily communicated because they are measurable in the short term and quantifiable, and so are perceived as a threat of a competitive disadvantage. If this threat, in the utility scheme of companies, outweighs the perceived value of an equally large competitive advantage (Abrahamson & Rosenkopf, 1993), bandwagon pressures exceed the company's adoption threshold — that is, a company's reluctance in the face of innovation and change.

E-Learning in Italy and the Adoption Process

As discussed previously, institutional and competitive bandwagon pressures may be main determinants of e-learning adoption. In the following paragraphs we will also concentrate on the knowledge creation process related to an adoption process. We will discuss how external pressures are translated within an organization in company-specific solutions, by analyzing four main dimensions of a corporate e-learning strategy: *content* delivered (asyncronicity, learning object, information, knowledge, and competency issues), *infrastructure* (learning portal, authoring system, LMS, interoperability issues), *users* (issues related to the role of HRM, push or pull learning, learners' problems, and motivation), and *services and supports* (tutoring, tracking functions, feedback, culture building, etc.).

Empirical Research: Research Design and the Sample

The research presented in this section focuses on two industries—pharmaceutical and banking—that both have undergone significant changes in recent years. Considering the competitive environment of the two industries, which were highly protected until a few years ago, they have both been caught up by new challenges like technological innovations, deregulation, globalization, and M&A. On the one hand, both types of companies have been forced to reorganize their structures (making them flatter and decentralized) and to manage more efficiently and effectively their supply chain processes as well as staff services like human resource management policies. On the other hand, in order to increase their response to the market and competitors, they have been induced to reskill their workforce, thereby increasing their investment in human capital (for instance, those staff who deal with end customers). For these reasons the two industries are among those in Italy where e-learning seems to be widespread (Anee, 2001), and where both early and more advanced experiences can be studied. Another reason to study them is their different institutional contexts, especially from an industrial relations point of view. This aspect matters if we consider institutional pressures as determinants of e-learning adoption.

The empirical study has been developed on a survey, interviews, and document analysis. The survey was conducted through structured questionnaire e-mailed to the main companies in both sectors between September and December 2002.[1] Some interviews of HRM managers of leading companies in the two industries were conducted before and after the survey, in order to prepare the cross-sectional analysis, to assess triangulating sources of data, and to develop some case studies. Two cases (Unicredit and BPM) are discussed in the following sections. Finally, document analysis was carried out on collective agreements and on a secondary source of data provided by ABI (the Italian association of banks).

The pharmaceutical sample[2] includes 20 organizations, both multinational and Italian, and represents both large and medium-sized companies. Five of the companies interviewed (25%) belong to the top 10 pharmaceutical companies in Italy.

The banks[3] surveyed include 22 companies: both large banking groups and very small banks like cooperative banks. Six of the companies interviewed (27%) belong to the top 10 banks in Italy.

Adoption Decisions

We started our analysis by looking at the rate of adoption of e-learning in relation to the different institutional and competitive bandwagon pressures that characterize the two industries.

With regards to labor market institutions in the pharmaceutical industry, even though the national collective contract (CCNL) mentions *"the arrangement of remote training modules on subjects specific to workers of the pharmaceutical industry,"* and since the end of 2002 the Bilateral National Organization (created by the same CCNL) has had the task of investing in lifelong training of employees, e-learning is not explicitly taken into account by the agreement between employers' associations and unions. Besides, the national employers' association (Federchimica) has not yet adopted policies or realized activities aimed at promoting or studying e-learning. These considerations lead to the conclusion that regulatory institutional pressures are rather low in the pharmaceutical industry.

In the banking sector, by contrast, the use of e-learning for continuous training is recognized by the labor market's institutions. First of all, the CCNL says that continuous training of personnel is an essential tool for developing human capital, and it has a strategic role in the transformation of the banking system. For this reason the collective contract states that the Bilateral National Organization has the task of promoting training by applying for European, national, and regional funds. It also states that from the year 2000, banks have to provide all employees with not only a fixed amount of training hours during working time, but also 26 hours per year spare time "through self-training using appropriate computing tools". Furthermore, the employers' association is promoting e-learning adoption through its training company (ABIFormazione), which is also one of the main e-learning providers in the banking industry. ABIFormazione also promotes e-learning awareness in the industry through conferences and researches. For example, during 2002, ABIFormazione carried out two surveys on state-of-the-art e-learning in the banking industry. Finally, Bank of Italy (the Italian central bank) also did a survey, contributing to the development of e-learning awareness.

Adoption Rate

The rate of adoption in the two industries has been measured by three indicators: level of adoption (number of companies in the sample that have adopted e-learning), length of experience (number of years), and type of experience (an initial experience vs. a consolidated one).

The survey results show that in the pharmaceutical industry, the rate of adoption is in its infancy. Only 45% of pharmaceutical companies have adopted e-learning. However, in the banking industry, 91% have adopted it. Pharmaceutical companies are still at an initial phase, the majority have no more than two years experience, and the solutions are still sporadic. Only one company has well-established experience in e-learning and two organizations are at an intermediate stage.

Figure 2. Adoption of e-learning and quality of experience

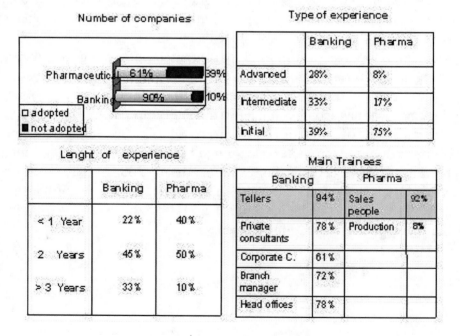

Number of companies

	adopted	not adopted
Pharmaceutic.	61%	39%
Banking	90%	10%

Type of experience

	Banking	Pharma
Advanced	28%	8%
Intermediate	33%	17%
Initial	39%	75%

Lenght of experience

	Banking	Pharma
< 1 Year	22%	40%
2 Years	45%	50%
> 3 Years	33%	10%

Main Trainees

Banking		Pharma	
Tellers	94%	Sales people	92%
Private consultants	78%	Production	8%
Corporate C.	61%		
Branch manager	72%		
Head offices	78%		

In the banking industry, nine banks have already experienced e-learning solutions for about one to two years and, in six cases, this training experience started more than three years ago. In 65% of the banks that have adopted e-learning, the application rate is intermediate/high. A confirmation of the spread of e-learning in the banking industry comes from an ABI survey, which shows that the majority of the banks interviewed (mostly the larger ones) have experienced distance training, with a high number of courses already supplied technologies by advanced. Moreover e-learning in banks is delivered to more segments of personnel than in pharmaceutical companies.

Decision Makers

As regard the decision makers, the unit in charge of the e-learning strategy is usually the HRM one in both industries. It manages the budget for e-learning (on average less than 25% of the total investment in training) and decides on the adoption of e-learning solutions. In half of the pharmaceutical companies interviewed, the adoption of e-learning solutions is decided by a single person who, in 70% of cases, is a human resources professional (HR director or training manager). In another nine companies, the responsibility is shared among the personnel management staff or with the IT manager. In banks, this decision is made mainly by the training director (18 banks); only in seven cases (35% of the total sample) is it made by both the training director and the HR manager.

Figure 3. E-learning decision makers

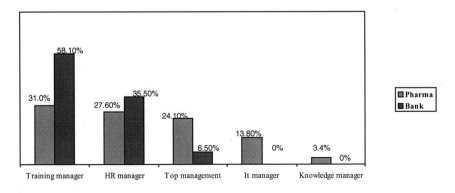

Main information sources are not only consultants but also colleagues. They are used to make decisions about e-learning adoption and to select the provider, which is chosen considering its capability to help companies during the implementation and maintenance phases. The advice of other users is a source for 23.4% of companies in the pharmaceutical industry. In 45% of the cases, these two sources are used together. In half the cases, companies indicate that conferences are important sources for gathering information, together with the advice of other users. This result seems to indicate that a social network is activated, helping the exchange and gathering of information necessary for the choice.

Table 1. Main sources of information for choosing e-learning providers in the pharmaceutical industry*

	% of answers
Newspapers and magazines	6.4%
Internet	6.4%
Consultants	31.9%
Professional associations	4.3%
Management studies	10.6%
Conferences/fairs	17.0%
Advice of other users	23.4%

* multiple choices were possible

Table 2. Main sources of information to decide on e-learning adoption in the banking industry*

	w.a.**
Colleagues	2.8
ABI	2.2
Rules	2.5
Training companies	2.2
Unions	2.0
ICT provider	1.9

*multiple choices were possible

**weighted average on a scale1-4: 4=very important, 3=important, 2=less important, 1=not important

These outcomes are confirmed in the banking industry. The interviewed banks state that the advice given by colleagues in the human resources area are decisive for the adoption of e-learning. Secondly, the companies interviewed stated that training regulations have a significant influence on their adoption of e-learning. Another notable influence comes from the indications given by ABI or other public institutions, which deal with training. It is interesting to note that ICT providers are the least used source of information from the companies' point of view.

Concluding Remarks about the Adoption Decisions

Data suggests that institutional pressures could explain the different rate of adoption in the two industries. In both industries, social professional networks are an important source of information and advice. This is particularly true in banks where the decision is made mainly by human resources professionals. Moreover, the analysis of sources of information also seems to demonstrate that banks' decision makers rely on labor market institutions, namely ABI.

The presence of institutional factors that impact on the adoption decision is also demonstrated by the level of e-learning effectiveness stated by the interviewed companies. In fact, it seems that, despite its diffusion, e-learning is not perceived to be very effective. In the pharmaceutical industry, three companies out of the nine experimenting with e-learning find this experience non-effective (two of them have a well-established experience of over two years). Furthermore, it has to be underlined that on an evaluation scale from 1 (not effective) to 4 (very effective), none of the companies attributes the maximum score to e-learning. In the banking industry, only one organization states that e-learning is a highly effective training tool and another eight (5% of the banks that use e-learning) say it is effective, while six (30% of the banks that use e-learning) admit that its effectiveness is limited. Among these last six, one bank is at an initial stage in the application of e-learning, while the other five have a longer established experience. The choice of investing in e-learning, although the effectiveness is not high, can be considered a signal of the presence of search of reputation rather than of ROI.

One can argue that competitive bandwagon pressures are also present: if competitors apply e-learning because they perceive that it can allow flexibility and efficiency in the training processes even if in the short term there are a few problems, then the fear of competitive disadvantages related to non-adoption of e-learning (in terms of higher training costs) is a pressure that exceeds a company's resistance to adoption costs.

E-Learning Strategy

As seen in previous paragraphs, Italian companies belonging to the two industries analyzed have invested in e-learning in the last few years. Thus most of them do not yet have a well-designed and implemented e-learning strategy. However, their reply to the question on objectives shows that a common trend among banks and pharmaceutical companies can be identified. Data from the survey show that the main benefit expected from e-learning is flexibility of designing and delivering courses (anywhere and anytime). A second advantage is connectivity that fosters communication and diffusion of knowledge in the company. In addition to these factors, there is cost reduction. Objectives, as expected, are mainly associated with efficiency and flexibility, those more easily related to competitive bandwagon pressures.

Table 3. Aims of e-learning*

	PHARMA OBJECTIVES w.a.**	BANK OBJECTIVES w.a.**
Anywhere, training closest to the trainee	3.0	3.2
Anytime, when I want, at the right time	3.0	3.4
Updating training content rapidly and efficiently	3.1	3.0
Fostering the spread of knowledge within the organisation	3.0	3.4
Flexibility, coherence with learning style of trainees	2.9	2.9
Cost savings	2.9	2.7
Fostering communication processes within the company	3.0	2.8
Monitoring how much the trainee has learnt	3.3	2.7
Faster learning than traditional training	2.3	2.1
Coherence among training and individual and company objectives	2.7	2.9
Self responsibility of trainee towards training	3.1	3.1
Attracting talent people	2.5	2.2

* multiple choices were possible

** weighted average on a scale 1-4: 4=very important, 3=important, 2=less important, 1=not important

E-Learning Users

The issue of e-learning users (Figure 1) should be considered from three perspectives. The first is the HRM perspective. E-learning implementation could be an opportunity to reorganize the training processes and also HRM processes from a functional approach (policy-based) towards a more customer-based approach, to match two different and sometimes opposite drivers. One is the need to reorganize the training and development function in order to focus it on key roles and their competencies profile. The second is to cut administrative costs. This type of change has been made by some companies in both the industries studied, where the adoption of e-learning is associated with a reorganization of training activities (75% of the pharmaceutical companies and 80% of the banks). The most common impact is the redefinition of training processes by targets (professional families).

A second perspective is that of the end user. First of all, the full exploitation of efficiency advantages, namely cost reduction and flexibility of delivery, are related to the fact that specific roles, such as a sales force, are geographically spread. They need to be in continuous contact with the clients/customers and the market on the one hand, and on the other with the companies to stay up to date regarding new products or procedures. Thus, courses that can be delivered anywhere and anytime are particularly suitable for them. Secondly, to the extent that e-learning leaves more freedom to users, trainees' commitment is critical. Thirdly, e-learning needs basic ICT knowledge to access material and tests. Finally, the problem of isolation could undermine the learning process and results.

Data from both industries confirm that the sales force is the main user of e-learning courses. In the pharmaceutical industry, the main trainees are sales

Table 4. Impact of e-learning on the reorganization of training activities*

	PHARMA No. of companies	BANK No. of companies
Reorganization by targets	7	15
Reorganization by processes	5	4
Reorganization by geographical area	1	1
No impact	5	4

* *multiple choices were possible*

Figure 4. Self-responsibility of trainees

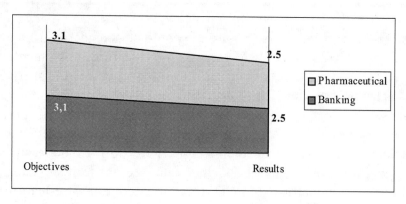

people and, in a few cases, the personnel in charge of production (training in standard procedures). In the banking industry, 95% of the banks that adopt e-learning use this tool to train counter staff. E-learning is also used to train private consultants (80% of the banks that adopt e-learning) and corporate consultants (61% of the banks that adopt e-learning). Only a few larger companies with consolidated e-learning experience also train branch managers and head office personnel. Five banks (25% of the banks that use e-learning) stated that they use e-learning with all their personnel.

Basic ITC knowledge among learners is a problem in the early stages, but companies do not think that this will still be a problem in the future. This is related to the fact that the first courses provided online are ICT and language courses, as data show.

Different results regard trainee commitment. Comparisons of objectives and problems highlight the fact that Italian companies consider the self-responsibility of trainees one of their main objectives but, at the same time, this is one of the critical problems of the future. To force people to take ownership of their learning will be a big challenge for companies that want to move from just-in-case to a just-in-time and "just-for-me learning".

The third perspective regarding users concerns the line managers. Line managers are particularly relevant in the early stages, when e-learning needs a culture-building process, managerial support, and communication. Managers themselves could be learners. Data on Italian pharmaceutical and banking companies confirm that among the most frequent problems cited, there is a lack of e-

Table 5. Main problems of e-learning strategies*

	Pharmaceutical EXPERIENCED (w.a.)**	Pharmaceutical FUTURE (w.a.)**	Banking EXPERIENCED (w.a.)**	Banking FUTURE (w.a.)**
Changing the training processes and structure	3.0	3.2	3.3	3.0
Blended learning	4.0	2.8	3.4	3.5
Basic IT knowledge among learners	4.0	2.6	2.1	2.0
Limited cooperation between HR and IT	4.0	2.5	2.2	1.8
Showing the benefits of e-learning to the management	3.7	3.3	3.1	2.6
Increasing bandwidth	3.7	2.6	3.2	2.3
E-learning culture	3.6	3.3	3.5	3.3
Showing the benefits of e-learning to the trainees	3.4	2.9	3.1	3.3
Measuring effectiveness	3.0	2.6	2.9	3.3
RU knowledge	3.0	2.3	2.9	2.7
Platform choice	2.7	2.8	3.1	2.5
Infrastructure	2.5	2.9	2.8	3.0

* multiple choices were possible

** weighted average on a scale 1-4: 4=very important, 3=important, 2=less important, 1=not important

learning culture and a difficulty to show the benefits of e-learning to the management. These problems can be seen not only among past problems but also among future issues (Table 5).

Content

The choice of content is driven by three factors. First of all content may be defined as being related to the type of learning it will support. In the IBM content model, there are four e-learning levels. At the first level, content is information (*learning by information*: Web lecture, Web books, etc.). At a second level, content is knowledge, multimedia, and interactive learning objects (*learning by interaction*: CBT, interactive games, self-directed learning objects, coaching, and simulations). At a third level, the main content is collaboration (*learning by collaboration*: e-labs, real-time awareness, live conferences). At the fourth level, the content is delivered off-line (*learning by face-to-face*: mentoring, coaching, case studies).

Secondly, content may be identified by taking into consideration the type of result it would obtain: provide *information* about products and processes, enhance job-specific or company-specific *knowledge* and develop best performers' *behaviors*.

Finally, a third approach to content concerns the architecture of the course-product. A course like a product could be considered as an integral product or a modular product. In the first case, a company is much more constrained by its choices, and the course can be changed at a higher cost than a product in modules. The search for modularity through the granularity of a learning object is driven by the advantages of costs (scalability) and flexibility. Designing learning objects, however, requires a metadata index and a reference for the content of the learning objects, like skills required for a job.

As regards e-learning contents, pharmaceutical companies develop technical-operative skills by e-learning courses; they also train in product and service knowledge, and computing and foreign language skills. The majority of companies do not believe that managerial skills can be taught effectively through e-learning. Training contents delivered mainly by e-learning in the banking industry are information concerning new products and banking ser-

Table 6. Main contents*

	PHARMA REALISED w.a.**	PHARMA FUTURE w.a.**	BANK REALISED w.a.**	BANK FUTURE w.a.**
Technical-operative skills needed to perform one's job	3.0	3.5	3.2	3.7
Organizational systems and processes	1.7	3.4	2.9	2.8
Basic and specialist knowledge	2.3	3.2	3.1	3.3
IT training	2.7	3.1	3.2	3.3
Linguistic training	2.8	3.1	2.7	3.2
Distance coaching	1.7	3.0	1.7	1.5
Company's product and services	2.7	2.8	3.5	2.8
Managerial competencies (communication, project management, etc.)	1.0	2.6	2.6	2.0

* multiple choices were possible

** weighted average on a scale1-4: 4=very important, 3=important, 2=less important, 1=not important

vices. E-learning is also considered very important for teaching basic and specialist knowledge (e.g., basic finance, counter operations, and credit management), technical-operative skills (anti-money laundering, privacy and security, Lira/Euro conversion procedures), as well as the company's internal systems and processes. E-learning is also considered effective in teaching ICT skills and foreign language skills. It is considered far less effective though as a tool to create managerial skills (selling or project management) or organizational skills such as the ability to communicate, and even less important as a distance coaching tool.

In both industries, e-learning allows companies to deliver courses anywhere and at any time thanks to modular and asynchronous solutions. It also allows quick redefinitions of the courses in order to face changes in regulations or the reduction of time to market of new products.

In brief, Italian companies seem mainly to deliver learning by information (about product and process) and only in part learning by interaction, and they aim mainly to develop job-specific knowledge.

Infrastructure

Technology is not the main driver of an e-learning strategy. From a company's point of view, the right learning management system does not ensure the quality of the e-learning. As some authors maintain, the choice of technology is related to a comparative analysis of costs and effectiveness: CBT may be an alternative tool to online training (Shank, 2001).

Data from top companies in the U.S. revealed that they are still struggling with technological problems (Kruse, 1999). From the trainees' point of view, technology matters in the daily or weekly access to e-learning courses. Some technological problems (slowdown or failure to access the Intranet) may undermine the delivery process and should be considered when a company decides what type of services and support it must provide learners with.

In the Italian pharmaceutical industry, the technological solution considered most effective is the virtual classroom, together with the personalized LMS platform, computer-based training, and training via mobile phones. In two cases, CBT is supported by other tools (laptop and virtual classroom).

In the banking industry, the technological solution used mainly and very effectively is indeed personalized LMS platforms. Computer-based training is

*Table 7. Technological solutions**

	PHARMA w.a.**	BANK w.a.**
Customized LMS platform	3.0	3.6
LMS platform in ASP solution	0	3.3
Standard LMS platform	1.0	3.0
LCMS	0	3.0
CBT	3.0	2.5
Virtual classroom	3.5	2.0
Tools used jointly	0	2.4
Mobile phones	3.0	2.0
Business television	0	0

* *multiple choices were possible*

** *weighted average on a scale1-4: 4=very important, 3=important, 2=less important, 1=not important*

the second choice in terms of the number of interview responses, even though it is considered less effective. Virtual classrooms and training via mobile phones are used less.

As for the main problems for the future, both the banks and the pharmaceutical companies declared that there are infrastructure problems, while increasing bandwidth (a present issue) will no longer be a priority in the future.

Services and Supports

Services and supports means that e-learning can be delivered and utilized by trainees, if they are assisted by organizational and technological solutions at the different stages in the e-learning process. In order to foster satisfaction with e-learning, to reduce drop-out rates, and to create an e-learning culture within the organization, Italian companies are implementing a number of organizational solutions.

Most companies in the pharmaceutical industry use internal tutoring and consider it pivotal in the process of e-learning training. Another solution is the support given by unit managers. A positive judgment is given to collaborative learning such as online discussion forums and chat sessions. However, these tools are still not diffused.

Table 8. Organizational supports to technological solutions*

	PHARMA w.a. **	BANK w.a. **
Internal tutoring	3.4	3.2
Support of unit manager	3.0	2.7
Online forum	3.0	2.5
External tutoring	2.5	2.3
Chat rooms	3.0	2.2
Virtual classroom	2.5	2.0

* multiple choices were possible

** weighted average on a scale1-4: 4=very important, 3=important, 2=less important, 1=not important

Figure 5. Control systems

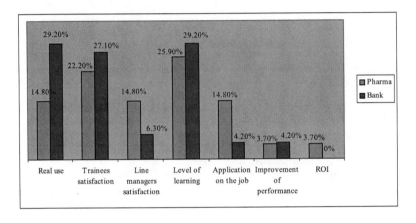

Tutorship is also the most widely adopted solution in the banking industry. In particular, an internal tutor is considered more effective than the external one. The support of unit managers is less common (six banks), but is considered effective. Eleven banks (55% of the companies that use e-learning) also mention online discussion forums, however, they are not considered to be as effective as internal tutoring.

As regards the *control* systems used in order to assess the results of courses and learning processes, pharmaceutical companies use more than one indicator. On average they use three different ones. Feedback information about e-learning performance is obtained mainly by testing how much employees have learned and how satisfied they are with the courses. Other criteria adopted in 15% of the cases are the assessments of how satisfied the whole organization is and the extent to which the knowledge acquired through training applies to one's job. Evaluation criteria such as ROI or improvement of performance are not used.

In the banking industry, companies assess the level of learning attained in order to measure the effectiveness of an e-learning program; moreover, they compare the aimed targets with how effectively the training programs are used and measure the satisfaction level of users. Three banks also measure the satisfaction level of the whole organization. The application of knowledge and skills learned on the job and the improvement of performance are both measured only in two cases (10% of the banks that use e-learning). ROI is definitely not contemplated. It should be noted that 15 banks (75 % of the banks that use e-learning) use at least two measurements, nine banks (45%) use three, and in two cases, five indicators are used.

To summarize, the results indicate that on average more than one indicator is used in both industries, pharmaceutical and banking, but the most that are adopted are traditional; monitoring systems that focus on means-ends relations (like improvement of trainees' performance) or on returns on this innovation (like ROI) are rarely used, confirming the hypothesis that the assessment of e-learning returns is difficult and ambiguous.

Future Trends

A B2E Strategy for E-Learning

Both institutional and competitive pressures seem to have a twofold effect on adoption processes. On the one hand, they prompt a search for information and best practices through social networks. On the other hand, they provide a frame of reference to companies that have to choose. They seem to highlight two issues from among others emerging from the debate on e-learning. Pressures are forcing companies towards a B2E strategy, through which it may increase both the value to employees and the value to the company. Institutional pressures highlight the added value to employees of e-learning solutions. Competitive pressures seem to highlight a firm added value more related to the aspects that can most easily be recognized by companies: cost savings and up-rating a flexibly deployed workforce.

Recent research into e-HRM (Hansen & Deimler, 2001) developed a model conceiving both sides of added value. If we apply the model developed by Hansen and Deimler to the whole system of e-HRM applications, specifically to e-learning, we may identify three facets of a *B2E strategy for e-learning*:

- **Online business processes:** The primary driver of this facet is to reduce interaction and coordination costs and effort within the organization to do the business with e-learning solutions (Maxey, 2003). A first objective is the codification process of knowledge and information about product and processes—for instance training in common processes in companies interested by M&A strategies, or training on new products — in innovating companies. A second objective is enhancing individual information exchanges by facilitating the creation of discussion groups and communities of practices as a by-product of an e-learning course. Third, e-learning could help customer/employee interaction by providing just-in-time information and integrating knowledge management tools with e-learning, such as an information desk.

- **Online people management:** The primary driver of this facet is to provide easy tools to help employees to develop personal skills and competencies. This facet on one hand comprises bundles of policies like online performance management and/or competency management complementary with e-learning. On the other hand a new direction of this policy is to facilitate "learning in the context of work rather than in the context of training" (Rosenberg, 2003) — increasing not only the freedom of employees to choose the courses they think they need and the way they learn through them, but also providing online access to something (knowledge, information, material, etc.) that people need for a better performance, when and where they want.

- **Online services and processes:** The primary driver of this facet is to provide services and information useful for benefiting from e-learning courses such as counseling, educational advice, or tutorship. E-learning B2E applications may reduce costs and effort associated with delivery and training courses, for instance by an online search for courses and information on course availability.

Emerging B2E Strategy for E-Learning in Italy

In the actual experience of Italian companies, some weak signals of an emerging *B2E strategy for e-learning* can be seen (two in-depth case studies are in Appendix Box 1 and Box 2):

- **Online business processes:** Respondents are interested in a company's benefits of streamlining learning processes. The importance of connectivity shows that online business processes of B2E e-learning strategy, thus the coordination of employees spread throughout the organization and in the field (sales force), is a primary driver. Another objective is the codification process of knowledge and information of product and processes, as the two cases of Unicredit and BPM illustrate. As previously mentioned, companies are in search of cheaper, faster solutions for providing learning by information and by doing so in the context of work.

Figure 6. "B2E" perspective of e-learning

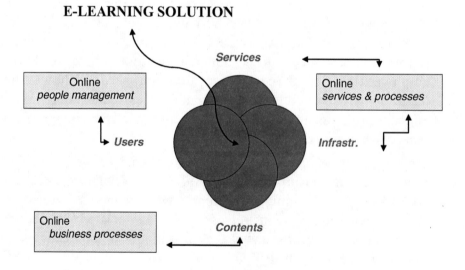

- **Online people management:** Italian companies analyzed seem to implement e-learning with a push approach instead of a demand pull one. Moreover, in the more advanced experiences, such as the cases of BPM and Unicredit, e-learning is planned and delivered mainly by following companies' training programs and scheduling. Also, companies are not investing in other policies related to e-learning, like knowledge management and performance management. However, they pay a great deal of attention to properly designed courses and tests, in order to overcome individual problems and increase motivation. Companies interviewed seem to be oriented to facilitate "learning in the context of work rather than in the context of training" by providing just-in-time information.

- **Online services and processes:** Tutoring is, among other things, the solution Italian companies favor most, even if companies approach it in different ways: internal vs. external, push or pull tutorship, or both. As the two cases (BPM and Unicredit) in the banking industry suggest, there is no one best solution. This facet, as well as online people management, aims to arouse the interest and the motivation of people, by providing services and roles that make e-learning less "cold" and isolated.

Conclusions

This research was aimed at studying the adoption of e-learning in the Italian pharmaceutical and banking industries and their e-learning strategy.

The ambiguity of decision gives importance to bandwagon pressures, and to external networks of colleagues who HR professionals use when they need information and suggestions about adopting e-learning. Results seem to confirm that e-learning is more widespread and sophisticated in the banking industry, where there are more bandwagon pressures. Some common traits can be identified in the e-learning strategies of companies of the two industries. However, the two cases studied, Unicredit and BPM, show that e-learning is adopted by an implementation process that leads to firm-specific solutions.

By analyzing the main objectives and problems cited by companies interviewed, the learners' motivation is the current and future main issue of both pharmaceutical and banking management. On one hand, e-learning, especially based on self-directed training courses, allows more autonomous learning. This means that e-learning helps a participant choose how and when to access the course. On the other hand, people face problems in terms of isolation, complexity of multimedia tools, slowness in running cooperative tools, and technological problems. Consequently, firms should care for their people commitment by investing on the four features of their e-learning strategy.

Finally, with respect to our research methodology, it is worthwhile highlighting that, given the explorative nature of the research, we have favored the analysis of a small but significant group of companies, together with case studies, in order to study in greater depth the dynamics of the adoption process at the organizational level. A line of research could be the extension of the analysis to other cases within the same industries, for stronger literal and theoretical replication (Yin, 2003; Eisenhardt, 1989). The study of other industries, characterized by different institutional and competitive pressures, could help to test the bandwagon model.

References

Abrahamson, E., & Rosenkopf, L. (1993). Institutional and competitive bandwagons: Using mathematical modeling as a tool to explore innovation diffusion. *Academy of Management Review, 18*(3), 487-517.

Abrahamson, E., & Rosenkopf, L. (1997). Social network effects on the extent of innovation diffusion: A computer simulation. *Organization Science, 8*(3), 289-309.

Anee. (2002). *E-learning 2001*. Report of the Associazione dei Servizi e dei contenuti multimediali, April.

Brewster, C., & Hegewisch, A. (Eds.). (1994). *Policy and practices in European human resource management*. London: Routledge.

Cohen, W.M., & Levinthal, D.A. (1990). Absorptive capacity: A new perspective on learning and innovation. *Administrative Science Quarterly, 35*, 128-152.

Comacchio, A., & Camuffo, A. (1999). Diffusion patterns of lean practices: Lessons from the European auto industry. In A. Comacchio, G. Volpato, & A. Camuffo (Eds.), *Automation in automotive industries*. Berlin: Springer

DiMaggio, P.J., & Powell, W.W. (1983). The iron cage revisited: Institutional isomorphism and collective rationality in organizational fields. *American Sociological Review, 48*, 147-160.

Eisenhardt, K. (1989). Building theories from case study research. *Academy of Management Review, 14*(4), 532-550.

European Commission. (2003). Lifelong learning: An overview of national measures in the EU Member States and Candidate Countries, *European trend chart on innovation*, Brussel.

Granovetter, M. (1985). Economic action and social structure: The problem of embeddedness. *American Journal of Sociology, 91*, 481-510.

Haberberg, A., & Binsardi, A. (2002). Institutional influences on organisational consensus. Paper presented at the *British Academy of Management Conference,* Hammersmith, London, UK. September.

Hansen, M.T., &Deimler, M.S. (2001). Cutting costs while improving morale with B2E management. *MIT Sloan Management Review, 43*(1), 96-100.

Horton, W. (2000). *Designing Web-based training.* New York: John Wiley & Sons.

IDC. (2002). *European corporate business skills training market forecast and analysis 2000-2005.*

Kirkpatrick, D.L. (1998). *Evaluating training programs: The four levels* (2nd ed.). San Francisco: Berrett-Koehler.

Kruse, K. (1999). Real world WBT: Lessons learned at the Fortune 500. Paper presented at the *ASTD International Conference & Exposition,* Atlanta, Georgia.

Ley, T., & Ulbrich, A. (2002). Achieving benefits through integrating e-learning and strategic knowledge management. Retrieved from *www.eurodl.org/materials/2002*

Martin, G., Robson, I., & Jennings, A. (2002, September). When absorptive capacity meets institutions and e-learning: Adopting, diffusing and exploiting e-learning in organizations. Paper presented at the *British Academy of Management Annual Conference,* Hammersmith, London, September.

Maxey, J. (2003) E-learning brain trust, ASTD, learning circuits. Retrieved from *www.learningcircuits.org/2003/sep2003/braintrust.htm*

Nacamulli, R.C.D. (Ed.). (2003). *La formazione, il cemento e la rete.* Milano: Etas.

Piskurich, G.M. (2003). Editor's introduction: What is e-learning? In G.M. Piskurich (Ed.), *The AMA handbook of e-learning.* New York, Amacom.

Prandstraller, F. (2001). Corporate e-learning: Myths and reality. Paper presented at the *Hawaii International Conference of Social Science.*

Rosenberg, M.J. (2001). *E-learning. Strategies for delivering knowledge in the digital age.* New York: McGraw-Hill.

Rosenberg, M.J. (2003). E-learning brain trust, ASTD, learning circuits. Retrieved from *www.learningcircuits.org/2003/sep2003/braintrust.htm*

Schank, R.C. (2002). *Designing world-class e-learning.* New York: McGraw-Hill.

Staw, B.M., & Epstein, L.D. (2000). What bandwagons bring: Effects of popular management techniques on corporate performance, reputation, and CEO pay. *Administrative Science Quarterly, 45,* 523-556.

Walker, A.J. (Eds.). (2001). *Web-based human resources.* New York: McGraw-Hill.

Yin, R.K. (2003). *Case study research: Design and methods.* Thousand Oaks: Sage Publications.

Endnotes

[1]   The collection of data for the survey in the pharmaceutical industry was carried out by Business International with Sfera's sponsorship.

[2]   Companies interviewed in the pharmaceutical industry were: 3M, Air Liquide Sanità, Astrazeneca, BristolMeyers Squibb, Chiesi, Farmaceutici Caber, Farmaceutici Damor, Gsk, Informa, Lilly Italia, Merck&Sharp, Organon, Pfizer, Procter&Gamble, Sanofi Sythelabo, Taked Italia Farmaceutici, Sigma Tau, UCB Pharma, Wyet Lederle, and Zambon.

[3]   Companies interviewed in the banking industry were: Credem, Deutsche Bank Spa, San Paolo IMI S.p.A, Banca Popolare di Milano, Bipielle, Cardine Finanziaria S.p.A., Banca S. Biagio del Veneto Orientale, Banca

121 S.p.A, Banca di credito cooperativo di Cartura, Banca Fideuram S.p.A., Banca delle Marche S.p.A, Banca Carige S.p.A, Banca Popolare dell'Emilia Romagna, Banca Popolare di Verona e Novara, Banca popolare di Vicenza, Banca Antonveneta, BNL, Cassa di risparmio di Trento e Rovereto, Banca Intesa, Banca di Roma, Unicredit, and Bancaintesa.

Appendix

Box 1. Unicredit

Unicredito Italiano, created in 1998 by the union of seven Italian banks, is the top banking group in Italy in terms of stock exchange capitalization and, furthermore, it is one of the major European groups. The group overall has a network of 4,115 branches and 66,000 employees. Following a reorganization process, which was concluded in 2003, the group operates through three national banks specializing in customer-based operations: Unicredit Banca (families and small businesses), Unicredit Banca d'Impresa (medium-sized and large companies and corporations), and Unicredit Private Banking (for major customers). In 2002, UnicreditBanca launched an e-learning project that was implemented through a company belonging to the group, TradingLab, which coordinates the project and handles most of the matters together with two of the group's other companies, jointly with marketing management and personnel management, and in collaboration with Sda Bocconi-Milano, which acts as consultant and content auditor.

Infrastructures

For some two years now, the Unicredit Group has already had a platform that carries out online training activities and is supported by an overall strategy of computer literacy. In the context of this strategy, the group has decided to provide each employee with a free home computer, which gives comprehensive access to the Internet. The group is equipped with a network of 400 multimedia stations, which will be expanded in time to 600 stations.

From a technological point of view, TradingLab's e-learning project is part of a general, wider initiative that seeks to use the digital approach in order to accomplish an expertise and information development strategy, which not only benefits the abilities of the individual but the entire know-how of the Unicredit Group. In addition to Banca Unicredit's e-learning project, other examples of this strategy are a commercial desk, which is at the disposal of all the members of the group, and the presence of an online group investment desk.

Content and Learners

The goal of the TradingLab project is to develop and certify the distinctive expertise profile of the private customer consultants. The goal is also to develop the competencies present in the group, at the same time standardizing the know-how of the seven member banks.

Planning of the content takes place internally and, as a whole, concerns 10 areas relating to investment services and to the skills required to sell them (financial mathematics, risk analysis, shares and bonds, the working of the capital markets, managed savings or funds, warrant certificates, and financial derivatives). Training is at three levels of expertise and therefore involves three courses: Level A, the most basic, through to C for a senior consultant. The content for each level is subject to constant checking and re-editing. A preliminary online self-assessment test, in which nearly all the consultants have participated freely, has allowed the training level and the course or modules for each learner to follow to be established. Certain consultants had direct access to the B-level/course.

Box 1. (continued)

The 10 modules planned for each level/course are structured in an integrated manner, especially at the higher levels: the preparatory material for the Level B modules is obligatory, while in the case of Level A, being the basic, they are only recommended. Blended-learning is envisaged at each level, which integrates eight online modules with two in the classroom. The classroom activities are spread over four days and are thus aimed at the modules that are more difficult to manage online (for example, in the case of Level A, warrants, financial derivatives, and bonds), and the administering of an evaluation test on all 10 of the course's modules.

Also as part of a path established by *company push*, the access to each online module (which lasts two to four hours) is *learner pull*. The internal structure of each of the eight online courses is divided into three sections. Unrestricted navigation within each section is possible, just as it is from one section to another. Each module can be used at different times and flexibly, according to individual requirements. Therefore, for a module with an average duration of two to four hours, individual utilization time is extremely variable.

The bookmark function is included to make the program even easier to use. This will allow the user to pick up again from exactly where he/she stopped in the previous session. Furthermore, there will be an interactive exercise every three or four slides that has the purpose of keeping the user's attention and monitoring the learning. Each module has a glossary and perhaps a link to further the study of a particular point (for example, the cross-reference to a law).

There will be a test at the end of each module that can only be accessed if the entire module has been completed, and it is recommended that at least a week be dedicated to study after the e-learning is finished. In the event the test is not passed, the examination can be taken again after doing the complete course once more.

Services and Supports

Services and support materials are aimed at facilitating access to the online course and minimizing the perception of isolation. To support e-learning courses, printed material is distributed to make it easier for people who find it hard to follow the online course alone to study. This solution has meant an improvement in the results in the testing of certain modules, which recorded a 90% pass rate.

As regards the offices equipped with a multimedia station for e-learning, there is a person in charge of the local organization who fixes the dates for use of the courses during working hours. Each person in charge coordinates about 40 employees. Even though he is closely involved in the quality and the development of the online training process, this person does not perform the function of tutor—a role that has not as yet been activated.

From the project's outset, the group's portal has had a section dealing with the instructions and to the recommendations for use of the online courses. There is also a mailbox for users that provides (within 48 hours) answers to problems both of a technical and organizational nature (method of use). This activity is managed by an internal structure currently consisting of two people who telephone the users who have taken the examination the previous week to congratulate them on the positive examination results, and to give advice on the rest of the course on the basis of an examination of the weekly attendance and exam result statistics. The principal aim of the service, which is most appreciated by the learners, is that of maintaining the motivation to learn and, above all, to establish a relationship that the trainees will then have to recreate with the final customer.

Box 1. (continued)

Tracking and Assessment

The tracking activity is currently aimed at monitoring the access to a module (that is freely chosen by the employee) and the test results. In the future, the plan is to activate more of the platform's functions for more in-depth tracking of the use of the courses. Moreover, to check the satisfaction of the e-learners, a "your opinion of the course" approval test has been prepared, which can only be completed after the whole course has been attended and which concerns course satisfaction and how clear and usable the course content was.

Box 2. Banca Popolare di Milano

The Banca Popolare di Milano (BPM), founded in 1865, is an interregional commercial bank and one of the largest in Italy. The group is developing an expansion strategy nationally, and at the European level, through internal growth and mergers and acquisitions.

Infrastructures

The Banca Popolare di Milano started using internal distance learning back in 1988, making it one of the pioneers of distance learning in Italy. It has had training activities available on CD-ROM and videoconference forums since 1997 and, starting from 1999, it has introduced blended solutions (FAD and classroom) supported by tutorship.

The BPM group is equipped with a widespread technology. The platform has become an extranet and the courses are used from learning points wherever the bank operates through an LMS. Depending upon the number of people, there are one to three learning points per branch dedicated to distance learning,. Consequently, the network of 600 branches has one learning point available for every 15 employees, with a total of about 6,700 workers involved. The workstations are also present in the head office and in the training unit, where there are 10 computers available. The distance training activity currently covers 65-70% of the total training delivered to the employees. The main advantage of the high investment in e-learning is considered, from a business point of view, to be efficiency in terms of the times and codifying of the company know-how, as, for the first time, new profiles of expertise are identified and widely developed within the organization.

Content and Learners

Training in BPM is structured on the basis of professional families. For each professional family (private managers, private plus managers, retail company managers, portfolio managers), a competency model has been identified on the basis of which a specific blended learning training path is designed, which provides for the combination of online modules and classroom modules. The competency analysis process, which was begun in 2000, has been implemented with the cooperation of external companies and through interviews with branch and office managers.

Box 2. Banca Popolare di Milano (continued)

The most consolidated competency profile within BPM is that of the *private* manager and includes knowledge pertaining to the products and services offered to the customer which in recent years have broadened to include insurance and the complementary security, as well as knowledge of regulations (national and internal memos). The skills to manage relations with the customer such as negotiation, customer care, and customer satisfaction skills also fall under the expertise of the *private* manager.

Starting with the expertise model thus identified, a training path was designed in seven steps, each of which could consist of online or classroom modules. As part of planning a modular approach, the learning path is sequential and each of the didactic units is therefore a preparation for another. On average a course lasts two hours and is broken down into didactic units of about 20-40 minutes. The individual user time envisaged for an hour of e-learning is about one week (during working hours), branch activities permitting. The contents of the modules have been designed with attention to the interactive elements: self-evaluation tests for the quantitative part, cases, tasks, and interactive games. Each module also comprises supplementary activities such as commercial proposals or bibliographies that can be called up by clicking on the screen at the user's discretion. Among the new professionals involved in training is that of the *information broker,* who is particularly significant, as s/he is responsible for finding, researching, and cataloging data and materials useful for the definition of the content. S/he acts, for example, as the story boarder at the moment when a certain amount of information concerning a particular subject is necessary, and s/he also has the task of organizing the alternative subjects.

Each module is designed to include a final meeting in the classroom which has an evaluation as well as a training purpose. The post FAD is considered to be a motivational element that is very important to stimulate the learners at the end of the course. The path lasts nine months overall.

Services and Supports

The distance training modules are published on the learning management system, which has an initial "Welcome on Board" session in the classroom or in a videoconference that lasts about three hours. This session has the aim of introducing the tutors, the training environment, and the planning of the start of the individual modules. During the Welcome on Board session, the tutors provide all the instructions necessary for how to use the course. Two types of tutorship are used in BPM: pull tutorship and push tutorship. *Pull tutorship* is done through a call center managed by outsourcing. *Push tutorship* is internal and based upon the monitoring data (what and amounts) obtained. It provides the trainees with motivation, coaching, and counseling services. The tutors telephone the learners during the course to give ongoing encouragement and advice to do with the course.

Box 2. Banca Popolare di Milano (continued)

The permanent pool of tutors forms part of the training management and is composed of a minimum of two up to a maximum of six people. The tutor is neither associated with an individual course nor a determined number of people; he can, therefore, follow different courses and can manage an average of 150-200 learners. The push tutor does not carry out any expert subject matter activities, which are entrusted externally to a network of content experts. Second-level tutorship is, therefore, active upon demand, even if generally the number of questions is filtered by the tutors. The tutors' pushing activities and the classroom activity at the end of the e-learning course are considered fundamental factors of success of the training path. With the activation of the orientation and pushing services, the people who completed the training in an effective and satisfactory manner went from an initial percentage of 13-17% (completion percentage in line with European data) to the current percentage of 85-95%.

Tracking and Assessment

The data on the training path are gathered through an evaluation and tracking system. *Dependent-learner* monitoring is done at the end of each module and during the classroom meeting at the end of the overall training path, when both the approval evaluation by the trainees and the evaluation of their level of learning is ascertained. *Independent-learner* monitoring refers to the information concerning the work done and the way people learn (amount, times, methods of use, etc.), collected through the platform's tracking facility. This type of information is given to the tutors on a daily basis and is used by them in planning the push calls. The tracking data and those of the evaluation questionnaires (both individual and as a whole) are used either during the path or thereafter to evaluate the overall progress of the path or the time actually taken by the learners to use it, and to review (for example the duration) and design activities for subsequent courses.

Section IV

Managing IT and Organizational Changes

Chapter IX

Is Organizational e-Democracy Inevitable?
The Impact of Information Technologies on Communication Effectiveness*

Bernadette M. Watson, University of Queensland, Australia

Gavin M. Schwarz, University of New South Wales, Australia

Elizabeth Jones, Griffith University, Australia

Abstract

In this chapter, we consider the relationships between social identity and e-democracy in organizations that exist in the constantly changing global business and technological environment. We also consider the inevitability of organizational e-democracy in organizations undertaking information technology (IT) changes, the technology at the base of e-democracy. Through an examination of employees' experiences of change, we

*investigate their perceptions of changes in effective communication
during major organizational change implementation in a hospital context.
While the changes were far reaching, we mainly focus on the introduction
of information and communication technology (ICT). We use an empirical
examination of an Australian public hospital's IT change experience as
the backdrop to assess the accuracy of the statement that there is an
improvement in the autonomy within organizations as a result of IT
changes. We discuss our findings in light of the implications that arise for
HR practitioners.*

Introduction

In this chapter, we consider the relationships between effective communication, social identity, and e-democracy in organizations that exist in the constantly changing global business and technological environment. We also consider the inevitability of organizational e-democracy in organizations undertaking information technology (IT) changes, the technology at the base of e-democracy. Through an examination of employees' experiences of change, we investigate their perceptions of changes in effective communication during major organizational change implementation in a hospital context. While the changes were far reaching, we mainly focus on the introduction of information and communication technology (ICT).

We define e-democracy as the technological advances in communication media that provide employees with more information and more direct access to other employees (supervisory and subordinate levels) than previously existed. These changes to communication channels provide organizational connections and lead to e-democracy practices that seek to improve the autonomy of organizational members. Thus there is a freeing of information to help erase or ease organizational boundaries, which changes the relationship between executive and middle management parties.

The chapter uses an empirical examination of an Australian public hospital's IT change experience as the backdrop to assess the accuracy of the statement that there is an improvement in the autonomy within organizations as a result of IT changes. We assert that while hospitals are a very specific type of organization, they represent a typical hierarchical organization that uses the same human

resource (HR) practices and principles that underlie all successful ICT implementations. We adopt the theoretical framework of *social identity theory*
(SIT) (Tajfel, 1978) to understand how communication effectiveness and e-
democracy evolve during IT change. SIT proposes that individuals understand
their self-concept through their identification with salient social groups (1978,
p. 63). Such groups include gender, profession, nationality, and religion — to
name just a few. Individuals derive their sense of self-worth and positive self-
esteem by viewing their group memberships (in-groups) as better than other
groups to which they do not belong (out-groups). Employees will often tend to
make favorable in-group comparisons to ensure that their workgroup is
perceived as more successful and prestigious than comparable out-groups.
Such comparisons lead to positive evaluations of one's own self-worth. This
theory, which is discussed in more detail below, has important implications for
the ways in which individuals will react to and manage ICT change.

ICT often changes the environment in which individuals work. As the work
environment changes, so to do work-related tasks and roles. Changes to role
and work functions alter the composition of workgroups and so impact on an
employee's identification with his or her workgroup and intergroup relations
between groups. From an SIT perspective, we view organizations as cultures.
Thus the hospital environment has its own culture; within this, subcultures or
groups (e.g., work units, departments) co-exist. We argue that SIT is a
theoretical framework that provides insights into how employees absorb and
manage ICT-enabled changes.

Thus our chapter highlights the social side of organizational change that is often
ignored by the planners and implementers of change. We emphasize the need
for HR managers to recognize these social issues. In this way HR practitioners
will maintain the good employee environment that they have developed, as well
as improve the outcomes of organizational change for members of that
organization. Using a longitudinal study, we examine how employees' work
identities impact on their understanding and adoption of ICTs. Bearing in mind
the chapter's focus on e-democracy, we examine employees' perceptions of
communication effectiveness and discuss these findings in the context of the HR
focus that frames this book.

The chapter highlights two important issues within the area of organizational
change and new technology introduction:

1. the changes in employees' perceptions of their role and the groups within the organization that they identify with that are brought about by ICT-enabled change, and

2. the implications of these changes for HR practitioners.

Focusing on the ways that individuals in traditionally hierarchical organizations understand and adapt to the changes in their work, we examine the process of change from the viewpoint of both the implementers of change and the employees who must adapt to change. In so doing, we investigate how communication processes and their level of effectiveness change with IT implementation. Our intention is to provide e-human resources management with key recommendations that need to be in place to successfully implement an organization's planned ICT change.

This research is framed by the arrival of the knowledge economy that allows e-democracy practices to exist. As the knowledge economy has evolved, as part of more widespread changes to organizations including ICT, some researchers have examined how employees' identification with organizations explains change outcomes (Terry, 2001).

We recognize that there is a gap in our understanding between the emergence of organizational e-democracy and the potential changes to the organizational structure and communication that can result from ICT implementations. We bridge this gap by highlighting the fact that, because individuals identify with their workgroups, when the current status or existence of these groups is threatened, resistance to the change may result. HR practitioners need to understand the composition and function of employee workgroups — both formal and informal. They will then develop an understanding of how and why members of these groups resist the changes within the organization and can seek to remedy the issues.

Organizations that typify the knowledge economy are viewed as dynamic and organic (Alvesson, 1995). As a consequence, the nature of organizational change in such organizations can be unpredictable. Understanding that change will bring about unexpected alterations to the way that employees respond to change is, therefore, key to being able to manage these people. In line with this view, Carlopio (1998) notes that the implementation stage of organizational change, while crucial to successful change, has been wrongly considered to be a rational and linear process.

In the subsequent pages we discuss the implementation of ICT change to stimulate discussion on the nature and place of organizational e-democracy. We seek to promote debate on the ways that social identification adapts and modifies itself within an organization undergoing ICT change. We focus on the implications for HR practice as we examine the uptake of ICT changes, the emergence of e-democracy, issues of identification, and the role of effective communication.

In this chapter, we first briefly describe the theoretical background to our research, focusing on the overlap between organizational democracy, change, and social identity. Using the experiences of a large public hospital undergoing change, we then provide evidence to demonstrate the value of connecting ICT innovation with social identity processes and e-democracy outcomes. We discuss the role that social identification with an organization or workgroup plays in an organization during ICT change. Finally, we examine the outcomes of such change as it affects the core business of an organization and make recommendations for HR practitioners. These recommendations will equip HR practitioners with a more appropriate and relevant knowledge base from which to plan and operationalize technology change.

Research Background

The Paradox of Democracy in Organizational Research

Over 100 years after de Tocqueville's (1835) discussion on the triumphs, hazards, and powers of democracy, Slater and Bennis (1964) argued that "democracy is inevitable." They offered democracy as the most efficient and practical form of social organization, mimicking Weber's (1924/1968) philosophy on bureaucracy. At the time of their argument, the Cold War was the center of world attention, making the issue of democracy both topical and compelling. In the context of the global and technological changes occurring over the past five years, our research borrows from Slater and Bennis' thesis, but considers the same issue from an organizational perspective.

Today we live in a knowledge economy whose core assets are the intelligence, understanding, skills, and experience of employees, not the machinery, buildings, or real estate of yesteryear (Drucker, 2001; Manville & Ober, 2002). This environment has focused attention on the role of ICTs and their ability to disseminate information. The emergence of a knowledge economy, where effective information transfer and the decentralization of organizational power structures is paramount, however, raises questions about the nature of organizational democracy.

Despite its prominence in change research (e.g., Beer & Nohria, 2000), organizational democracy within the knowledge economy is confusing. In the contemporary workplace, knowledge is regularly portrayed as the primary resource for individuals (Drucker, 1992). The simultaneous sharing of information through sophisticated technology is viewed as a primary tool of organization (Orlikowski & Iacono, 2001). This process assumes that the militaristic conditions of the industrial organization are antiquated and perhaps even unnecessary. Consequently, changes to traditional bases of power and influence are believed to occur through decentralization and information access (e.g., Applegate, 1994; Halal, 1996). Change initiated in the knowledge economy is regularly presented as a constant feature of the modern organization, despite the dissatisfaction that exists with the nature of change research (see Tsoukas & Chia, 2002). This perspective that change is constant in the knowledge economy adds a paradoxical tangent to organizational e-democracy.

These changes do not necessarily foster democracy (Mantovani, 1994), even though there are implied benefits of the evolving, boundary-less, and pluralistic nature of organizations in the current global economy. Many organizations are still organized autocratically (Kraemer & Dedrick, 1997; Schwarz, 2002). Corporate ownership structures, governance systems, and incentive programs are still firmly entrenched in the industrial age. Organizations are still primarily organized through small management groups typical of hierarchies (Markus, 1983; Robey & Boudreau, 1999). Any features of employee empowerment are limited.

It would, of course, be negligent not to recognize the advances made in the use of more democratic governance methods, such as participatory management practices (e.g., Drehmer, Belohlav, & Coye, 2000), organizational citizenship (e.g., Lambert, 2000), and communities of practice (e.g., Wenger, 1999). Nonetheless, change research is often too concerned with two aspects of change. First, the research concerns itself with re-evaluating the authority, power, and control features that normally exist in institutions (Scott, 2001). Second, it concerns itself with the promotion of alternative organizational designs and practices (Schilling & Steensma, 2001).

Organizational change in a knowledge economy context is regularly hypothesized to bring about a more democratic organizational shape than previously existed. For example, we expect more information connectivity and freer communication than before. We expect more autonomy, but less centralization and less hierarchy than before. Yet there is enough research, and a growing line of argument, to undermine this assumption. Is organizational democracy in the knowledge economy (i.e., e-democracy) inevitable? If organizations change, then logically, so too must employee perceptions of their role in the organization. In a consideration of the objectives of this chapter, we therefore invoke social identity theory (SIT) as a guiding framework that may help understand the outcomes from change and whether or not e-democracy emerges as a result of ICTs.

Social Identity Theory and its Organizational Context

In the section that follows, we provide a preliminary overview of the theory, referring readers to Hogg and Terry (2001, 2000) for a comprehensive review of the theory and its links to organizational contexts. Social identification "is the perception of oneness with or belongingness to some human aggregate" (Ashforth & Mael, 1989, p. 21), encompassing salient group classifications. Social identity theory, therefore, is based on the premise that most often it is our group-based identities that are important in our interactions with others.

The central tenet of this approach is that belonging to a group is largely a psychological state. This grouping confers social identity, or a shared representation of who one is and how one should behave (Hogg & Abrams, 1988). In this way, group belongingness reduces our uncertainty about where we fit in society (Hogg & Mullin, 1999). More recently, SIT has been applied to the organizational context. Implicit in this understanding of organizational identity function is the recognition that organizations are composed of the people in that organization. In essence then, "Organizations are internally structured groups, which are located in complex networks of intergroup relations that are characterized by power, status, and prestige differentials" (Hogg & Terry, 2001, p.1). As a result, organizations are implicitly dynamic, continually changing entities. Changes that affect the organization can therefore have serious effects on employees in terms of their identification with workgroups and the relationships between workgroups.

While there has been a longstanding research tradition examining organizational identification, more recently SIT researchers have viewed organizations as being composed of individuals possessing multiple group identities. These identities range from the employees' overall identification as members of an organization, to their identification with specific work units and professions. At any one time different group membership may be salient for an employee. Accordingly, when a manager interacts with a subordinate, he or she is likely to identify with their respective roles of manager and subordinate as most salient in the work situation (Gardner & Jones, 1999). Yet in another context the person's professional identity may be most salient.

SIT has been used by organizational scholars to better understand how the individual relates to these collectives, and the intergroup relations that accompany the process of identification (see Pratt, 2001, for a comprehensive review of this trend). Such a perspective does not deny the importance of an individual's personal identification, but sees it as often less relevant than group identification in the workplace.

Social identity theory proposes that individuals will tend to make favorable evaluations about their in-group ('us'), but make unfavorable evaluations concerning the out-group ('them'). If we identify at the organizational level, we perceive all employees of our organization as in-group members and employees of competing organizations as members of an out-group. More often though, it is at the sub-organizational level that we make the most relevant comparisons. The result is that employees will then tend to favor their workgroup or department and evaluate it more positively than other workgroups or departments. Organizational change, including the development of the knowledge economy, may not only lead to the formation of new identities, but may challenge/threaten existing identities and intergroup relations. Thus mergers, acquisitions, and downsizing have increasingly become the subject of research examining organizational change and SIT (Terry, 2001; van Knippenberg & van Leeuwen, 2001).

Such research has been crucial in understanding change from an SIT perspective, but as Hogg and Terry (2000) note, they do not address important developments of SIT in the last decade that are particularly relevant as to whether e-democracy may emerge in response to ICTs. Recent developments include research on identification problems dealing with (1) loyalty, and (2) nested and cross-cutting identities. Looking first at the issue of loyalty, as information intensity becomes more relevant to organizational functioning, many of the traditional roles of identity are undercut (Neef, 1998). Group identification is a process whereby individuals become connected with others and where joint interests may overtake those of the individual. When there are changes in perceived membership or competing identities emerge which make the lines of group belongingness unclear, questions concerning group loyalty may arise. Specifically, employees ask whether their loyalty should be conferred to the group, the organization, the professional association, the occupation, or to workmates?

Thus, before individuals can act in a given organizational context, they need to situate themselves, allowing certain identities to be nested or embedded within others (Ashforth & Johnson, 2001). Nested identities exist at the higher order level, such as an employee's identification with his or her division, which is nested under the organizational identification. Lower order identities are those of identification with an individual's job. Job identification would be nested under an individual's workgroup. Conversely, cross-cutting identities refer to an employee's committee or task force identification that runs across the hierarchical structure. Cross-cutting identities and lower order level nested identities are more likely, more salient, and more proximal than are higher order level identities (see Ashforth & Johnson, 2001, for a full discussion on this topic). Internal conflicts may arise when an individual perceives competing demands across two of his or her work identities. The cognitions and identity changes that occur during change therefore need to be thoroughly investigated in order to better understand the change outcomes.

The longitudinal study that we present in this chapter acknowledges these aforementioned complexities and seeks to raise awareness levels of HR managers to these issues. Specifically, we contend that an examination of any change implementation without due consideration to the psychological processes that underlie an employee's perception of the change will not provide an accurate picture of the evolution process during change. Nor will such an examination provide an understanding of the potential subsequent changes in e-democracy.

The empirical review that follows describes how employee workgroup identification interacts with technology change and communication effectiveness, and the outcomes in terms of e-democracy. Employee responses include perceptions about changes to their levels of job satisfaction and commitment, as well as changes to the status and prestige of their workgroup and other groups within the organization. For HR practitioners, these are important considerations that, if managed well, allow for smooth transitions during change. Researchers have typically neglected the intergroup nature of change, despite the fact that corporate change involves major reallocations of status, power, and resources across divisions of an organization (Gardner, Paulsen, Gallois, Callan, & Monaghan, 2000).

We present change as a process that impacts on an organization in at least two ways. First, there is the individual impact upon employees in terms of their levels of job satisfaction and organizational commitment. Second, researchers — and by implication, HR practitioners — need to consider the significant impacts upon employees' levels of identification with their workgroups or the social categories with which they identify. This second impact is demonstrated by employees' perceptions of changes in the groups they identify with, perceived status, and the levels of in- and out-group bias.

Our approach adds to previous research by considering whether e-democracy is an inevitable consequence of ICT changes, and how a social identity perspective helps us understand the effects of ICT changes. We argue that social identity theory provides an alternative (socially) evaluative insight into the nature of change and the process of how organizations evolve and adapt to the knowledge environment economy. In this chapter, we concentrate on how group memberships within organizations are influenced by change. Our approach differs from other researchers who have applied democracy at the organizational level in debating what the organization and organizational change will look like (e.g., Lammers & Szell, 1989; Mason, 1982).

Social identity argues that organizations are internally structured groups that are located in complex networks of intergroup relations characterized by power and status (Hogg & Terry, 2000). In referring to the processes that underlie the development and maintenance of individual and group identities, social identity allows us to better deconstruct the process of organizational democracy using this prestige differential.

As part of this examination, we discuss change and organizational democracy by focusing on how the social identity of health professionals in a large metropolitan hospital affects their understanding of and adaptation to new ICTs. Our analysis was guided by two research questions:

RQ1: What is the relationship between employees' perceptions of their workplace identification and e-democracy change?

RQ2: How do the features of ICT change and organizational e-democracy relate to employees' perceptions of communication effectiveness during change?

Method

Context

Information and communication technologies are regularly promoted as drivers that take costs out of the supply chain, improve the management of customers, and enhance the capability of the organization to quickly respond to a changing marketplace (Glover, Prawitt, & Romney, 1999). ICT developments are perceived as key organizational tools that can alter reporting structures, cultures, job roles, and the identities of employees and their groups. These technologies have been an excellent means of expanding access to information across an organization, empowering employees through added flexibility and enhanced functional integration. These new capabilities have occurred despite the increasing recognition that in reality many very expensive IT systems are abandoned or never realize their full potential (Fahy, 2001). To date, we know that while organizations often have high expectations for change when new systems are commissioned, technology implementations regularly result in the reduced or failed adoption of complex, integrated technology architectures (Koch & Buhl, 2001).

Nonetheless, as with most industries, ICTs are an increasingly essential part of contemporary healthcare. The healthcare industry has recently experienced substantive changes brought about by this new technology, with consequences for health providers, professionals, and patients. These include changes to the way healthcare is delivered through the emergence of new medical professions (e.g., genetic specialists), the devolution of minor medical treatments as nursing staff become more highly trained in new technology, and less invasive treatments. Future medical ICT-related developments include the use of robotics and telemedicine, enhanced drug design through the use of computerization, and the trend towards electronic services (e.g., e-procurement) as a way to deliver healthcare services. Ongoing developments related to ICTs that will change the nature of healthcare in the next 20 years include emerging medical communication technologies and increasing application of evidence-based healthcare globalization. It is within a hospital context that we sought to examine examples of such industry changes.

The Studies

As previously noted, we focus on change in a large Australian metropolitan public hospital that was undergoing significant organizational re-engineering change both in its infrastructure as well as in the introduction of new technology. We used a sample from a series of 85 in-depth, unstructured interviews with a cross-section of healthcare employees. We examine how these employees described and identified with the change process. This change included staff restructuring; the introduction of innovative wards to trial changes that were planned to occur in the new hospital building; the devolution of finance from management to department level, with the introduction of new financial technologies (i.e., enterprise resource planning system: ERP); and the phasing in of new medical technologies (e.g., the picture archive communication system: PACS). These changes had implications for increasing the knowledge and authority levels of staff. Management of department finances by charge nurses rather than by higher management levels meant that senior nurses were now responsible for the budget of specific wards and units. Thus they would have access to information databases that were previously not available. In theory such changes should empower these nurses. Similarly, the PACS would provide easy access to patient x-rays across the hospital, and lead to more efficient and effective communication between hospital departments. In fact improved and more fluid communication was a vision for the new hospital with more communication between units and wards than had previously existed. The participants in our study represented a cross-section of different levels and roles in the hospital, including executives (often with medical backgrounds), doctors, nurses, and allied health professionals (e.g., physiotherapists, psychologists, occupational therapists).

In our interviews, we were particularly interested in the ways in which employees' work units or professional identities influenced their understanding of the changes being implemented. To this end we focused on the health professional employees within the hospital as identified above. We investigated the relationship between changed organizational structure and employee perceptions about their role and identification in the organization. In particular, we examined the ways that new IT implementation altered the dynamics of the organization in terms of lines of communication (including communication effectiveness) and democratic structure.

Our research for this chapter was conducted at two stages between 1998 and 2000. At Time 1 (1998), we conducted 67 in-depth, unstructured interviews. From this data collection period, we selected 19 interviews for in-depth analysis. The sample included five executives, four doctors, six nurses, and four allied health professionals. During this time period, the hospital was at the beginning of undertaking many changes (e.g., downsizing and changes to work practices—including ICT implementations such as ERP and PACS). For Time 2 (2000), we conducted 28 in-depth unstructured interviews from which we have drawn a sample of 18 interviewees. During this time period, the implementation of changes initiated at Time 1 were quite advanced (e.g., hospital rebuilding, changes to work practices, and the ICT changes).

For this chapter, we analyzed the interviews of nine executives, one doctor, five nurses, and three allied health professionals. It is unfortunate that at Time 2 we were only able to interview one doctor. For each period of data collection, interview transcripts were analyzed with the use of the QSR qualitative software package called NVIVO. Trained coders identified common themes throughout the data. The interviews conducted at Times 1 and 2 were open and unstructured. The aim at Time 1 was for the interviewees to describe what they felt was good and bad about the changes that were to occur. At Time 2, the interviewees again described what they felt was good and bad about the changes that were occurring. They also described their perceptions concerning the implementation process.

Empirical Examination of the Relationship between e-Democracy, Communication Effectiveness, and Social Identity in a Hospital

In the following results we examine the findings in relation to our two research questions. To this end, using hospital employees' descriptions of change, we summarize our results as they relate to the nature and place of e-democracy, HR practice, and more generally to employees' workplace identification during a period of change. We will include specific examples of hospital staff descriptions as they relate to both our research questions in order to illustrate their perceptions of the change process. We examine our findings across the two times to investigate whether there are distinct differences between the two phases as they relate to identification, e-democracy, and communication effectiveness.

Overview of Findings

With respect to RQ1, we examined the emergence of e-democracy by looking for perceived changes in health professionals' levels of reporting, their increased access to knowledge, and increased levels of authority. Results suggested that over the period of change, while there were modifications to nomenclature and associated rhetoric to describe the change process, control over employee behavior and management authority remained as it was prior to the changes in infrastructure and ICT implementations (e.g., PACS and ERP technology). Thus, despite the potential of the new systems to provide a greater availability of information, serving as a means of empowerment, no changes to the democratic structure occurred. Such systems, while offering employees the opportunity to manage their departmental accounting themselves or to rapidly access patient information in digital format, did not increase employee input or strengthen the knowledge economy. Rather, as shown at Times 1 and 2 respectively, failure to sufficiently train and support the staff led to frustration and reduced efficiency. Nurses and doctors tended to highlight their professional memberships in terms of patient care and did not embrace the ICT changes that would change their management of patients. Regardless of the implied benefits of change, substantive role, function, or empowerment adjustments did not occur.

Hospital executives never perceived their roles or positions to be threatened, and therefore perceived or represented most of the changes (technology and others) as a positive step for the hospital. Doctors were negative about the proposed changes and focused their attention on challenges or problems associated with the hospital's functioning and staff feelings towards the change process. Nurses also spoke negatively of the change in the belief that they were not involved in decisions made by executives, and that the changes implemented would not enable promised efficiencies. Interestingly, many allied health workers were the most positive about overall change. However, it is interesting to note that one group of allied health workers who worked permanently in one unit rather than moving throughout the hospital (as do physiotherapists, dieticians, and speech therapists) was more affected by ICT changes and was not positive about the outcomes.

With respect to RQ2 — communication effectiveness — health professionals noted that maintaining their perceived levels of communication effectiveness prior to the change was problematic. Their concern stemmed from the fear that because of some ICT innovations (e.g., PACS), there was a reduction in face-to-face communication with other health professionals — a key aspect of communication for health careers. Thus in this organization maintaining effective communication did not align well with aspects of the proposed ICT change.

Clearly, employees who control aspects of their work and working conditions are going to be happier than employees who do not. With relation to our findings, hospital executives who possessed the macro picture of the change and monitored the changes were more positive than those staff members who were confronted with change implementation and new ICTs. Just as clearly, however, despite the potential of an organizational community through ICTs, participatory management and empowerment is not an inevitable component of technology change. Results relating to RQ1 and RQ2 suggested that despite goals of enhanced performance, there was no redistribution of authority. Thus, while the hospital executive perceived that there would be staff empowerment through better ICT systems, this expectation was not realized.

Specific Findings

Workgroup Identity

Social identity theory posits that when change occurs, some employees will react with perceptions of threat to their in-groups. As a consequence, they will act to protect their social group status. Thus in-group bias may increase, but the group may also seek to create a new group identity. If the group does strive to create a new group identity, then social identity theory would predict a new energized in-group identity, as was seen in the creation of the "black is beautiful" new identity in the 1960s for black Americans. When doctors and allied health professionals spoke about the technology change, they identified with two in-groups, the hospital (distal in-group) and their profession (proximal in-group). When discussing the change implementation in more general terms (e.g., patient care), however, both their proximal in-group and out-group salience were more evident, that is, they spoke more about work units and professional identity. Interestingly, nurses did not make their professional identity salient when talking about ICT changes — rather they identified with the more distal in-group of hospital. The reasons underlying this finding are unclear. In contrast, when nurses talked about other general change issues, their identity as a nurse and in particular their unit was salient. This point is taken up below,

Overall, executives identified as being part of the hospital first and foremost. Doctors talked about how medical professionals (the in-group) felt threatened by the change process that was being managed by the executive board (the out-group). For example, at Time 1, a senior doctor commented on a computerized patient file system that he thought would be phased in at a later stage of the change:

"I'm not so sure it [the new patient file system] will be a success. I suspect they're trying to save on clerical staff and turn us, all the clinicians, into mini-clerks." (Participant A, Senior Doctor, Time 1)

This doctor was reporting his perceptions that executives were imposing new work roles on clinicians. The hospital's non-executive medical employees understood that their roles had changed because of the new system's information-sharing or task-related initiatives. They were compelled to adapt to these role changes as prescribed by the executive level. In the quote, the doctor stated that his in-group felt threatened as a group by the out-group of executives. The episode demonstrated the broader principle that rather than create a new identity, built on ICT-based participatory practice, the strength of traditionally instituted group affiliation and group status remained in place. A Level 3 nurse at Time 1 also spoke about the executive as the out-group and his perception of threat.

"They [the executives] all say we're cutting back on jobs, but nobody knows what numbers and to who[m] they're looking at or who[m] they're keeping on. It's that big question mark that everybody's a little bit scared." (Participant B, Registered Nurse, Time 1)

At Time 2 a different senior doctor commented on the role of the executive and their power in relation to the government control of the executive.

"Well they [the executives] neither have the given authority nor management skills. They might acquire the management skills if they were delegated the authority, but [health state government] is very much rule and structure, and authority comes from the top down. And any attempts to give individuals management authority are very rapidly squashed by reversal of their decisions when they are not liked." (Participant C, Senior Doctor, Time 2)

These comments still focused on the executive as the out-group, but this participant was also viewing the bigger picture of where the executive sat in terms of their power. The comments again validated the lack of change in respect to overall structure and democratic process during ICT change.

Effective Communication

Health professionals expressed concern about the effects of new technology on communication. For example, an allied health professional was of the opinion that the new PACS technology led to reduced communication between health professionals, leading to a loss of relationship with other clinicians and trainee staff. She commented that the medical staff [people] would lose the network connections that currently existed.

"...new residents may not be super-familiar with the techniques ...but by seeing them face to face, you can say well, look, you know, how you can determine priorities...the personal [contact] will be lost. People won't know who to contact when they really need something in a hurry. It's just punching into a screen [ordering using a computer screen]...rather than coming down and seeing someone and say, 'Look, what can you do about it?'" (Participant D, Allied Health Professional, Time 1)

A member of the executive level focused on this reduced level of communication at Time 2. However, she looked to the level of efficiency that would be achieved.

"We have images available throughout the organization at the same time, but [do] not have to run around with only one person having access at the one time." (Participant E, Member of Executive (and doctor), Time 2)

The sentiments regarding the PACS technology expressed by the allied health professional at Time 1 demonstrated the view of non-executive health professionals that communication still needed to take place at the physical rather than the electronic level. Face-to-face communication was viewed as an important feature of the intra-hospital networking system. A perceived lack of such communication brought about by the ICT change was therefore viewed as a threat to communication efficiencies. For example, PACS technology meant that x-ray requests could now be requested electronically. The old system had meant that forms were filled out and taken down to the x-ray division. As a result of the archaic manual system, however, interns got a better understanding of x-ray procedures and could ask for advice from the radiographers and radiologists because they interacted with them. As exemplified by the allied health professional quote at Time 1, ICT change thereby paradoxically allowed both a reduction in information connectivity alongside an increase in autonomy. But rather than enable the ease of information sharing, as e-democracy practices forecast, our results revealed an atrophying of inter-disciplinary contact and subsequently lower effective communication than previously existed.

In presenting much the same belief in the need for face-to-face communication, doctors suggested that PACS changes did not allow important information relayed by people to be received effectively. A doctor related the medical professional perspective of the PACS change:

"I think that probably medical staff prefer to communicate in person and by voice. That's the way we spend our day talking to people...and we [doctors] don't like communicating so much by paper, and yet administrative staff communicate with us via paper which is seen as impersonal." (Participant F, Doctor, Time 1)

This doctor implied that owing to the culture of medical staff (i.e., his in-group), important information was continuously lost, ignored, or overlooked as the systems changes started to take effect.

At Time 2 a nurse commented that the structure of the hospital would improve the communication. His comments supported the notion that health professionals recognize the need to communicate on a face-to-face basis. Interestingly, he also addressed the issue of work identities. While this comment does not directly address ICT, it highlighted the face-to-face culture that exists in the hospital context.

"Because of the way the building is laid out, it flows on, there is no defined point of one ward ending and the next ward starting. A lot of units overlap each other as well, so it's going to force communication between them. That has, I mean, it's positive in one aspect, but negative in that they don't have their own identities as such." (Participant G, Nurse, Time 2)

Change and Adjustment as an Outcome of Social Identity and Communication

Workgroup identity and communication work against each other or together to influence both intergroup and individual adjustment to change. In the hospital setting described in this chapter, the outcomes were such that the hospital remained a highly stratified institution. Both executive and non-executive groupings were able to develop justifications and explanations for the lack of participatory change and for existent structural arrangements. Specifically, although some executives expressed concern for lower level staff as they were experiencing a high workload and stress associated with the changes, they were simultaneously convinced that there were more positive issues brought about by the change than there were negative. The system and the processes it set in place did not bring about an amalgamation of different groups, nor did it equalize the way authority was transferred. Non-executive groups adopted a far more reactive outlook to the change, as one doctor states:

"There are some clinicians [who are] very computer literate and very keen on computers — both in work and recreation. Others like me are not the slightest bit interested, and that technology's going to be forced on us, and I think it's foolish. I mean we're not trained and we shouldn't be paid to put information into computers and operate computers. We are trained and should be paid to be skilled clinicians, not computers jockeys." (Participant A, Senior Doctor, Time 1)

Such a reaction to changes suggested a difficulty in adapting to some kinds of changes. The view held by this doctor was that medical practitioners should not have to be involved in technology unless they wish it. This reaction also reflected a belief that a lot of time was being spent on change-related activities, without adequate compensation or proper attention being paid to those being forced to use the new system. In particular, doctors believed that executives were making decisions based on budgetary constraints rather than patient care. This opinion clearly emphasized the different group identity outlook (i.e., healthcare professionals versus healthcare managers). Doctors were resistant to technological changes, and perceived that their job was to treat patients and everything else was secondary. Nurses presented a resistance with ICT-enabled changes, based on similar reasoning, and focused on role changes and possible staff reduction.

The difference in individual and therefore intergroup adjustment was further typified by the executive group's perception of how adjustment to change should be managed. A senior executive commenting on the voluntary retrenchment of 40 workers as their jobs became obsolete observed that working with the staff who would be laid off made for a smooth transition.

"Most people were quite happy with the outcome. Instead of building it up into something that had to go to an Industrial Relations Commission type thing, we actually managed it at the shop floor level, with the local managers and us giving them some guidance instead of bringing all the heavies all the time." (Participant H, Senior Member of Executive, Time 1)

The inference made by this very senior executive who was brought in to manage the change was that adaptation to changes is easily made if the correct internal procedures are followed. In his mind, this procedure included talking to staff at the shop floor level and discussing the need for redundancies for the hospital's own good. This reaction emphasized the view that the hospital's cumulative needs over-rode those of the group. For this executive, in his mind, he was reaffirming that communication about change is effective if it is well managed through staff involvement. There was, of course, some level of involvement at the non-executive level, with some employees happy to be part of an internal arrangement rather than take industrial action, generally. Nonetheless, the individual risk associated with ICT change overwhelmed the change rationalization offered by executives. In particular, as the change implementation progressed, nurses became increasingly agitated by the potential job losses expected to occur. This concern was linked to frustration about the level of care that would occur as an outcome of the resultant devolution of responsibility. Other nurse concerns related to training and patient care outcomes as a result of role changes.

"...like computers in the wards. They're everybody's headache at the present moment, because the system is not set up to deal with everybody's needs and there are loop holes [problems] getting computers up and running, [and] getting staff [to] use it." (Participant I, Nurse, Time 1)

This observation reflected a common perception that while new technology resources were welcome, they were introduced for spurious budgetary reasons, rather than to improve patient care. Consequently, they initiated a series of problems at the ward level. A belief among some nurses was that the hospital was not prepared for ICT change outcomes. In short, they argued that the hospital's infrastructure was not equipped for the planned IT changes.

The executives were viewed by some medical staff as interested in the benefits to the hospital that arose from the introduction of new technology rather than health benefits. The most visible outcome of this divide was that the good change outcomes brought about by the new system were obscured, as a nurse observes:

"For me personally, it feels like [executives] are only interested in money, more so than patients. Now I don't know whether that's a nursing perspective or the way I've been taught or anything like that, but I feel that they seem to make decisions, but it's not in the interests of the patients. It's always in the interest of the dollar." (Participant J, Nurse, Time 1)

The disparity between identities across employee groups brought about by the different technology change focus led to the new technology being undermined. Whereas the new system offered healthcare professionals a plethora of sophisticated new functions, the widespread belief that the executive grouping was more interested in financial gains than patient care created a serious breach in faith. As a doctor and nurse noted, far from embracing new roles and participatory regimes, caregivers concentrated on the legitimacy of the new system:

"The computerized x-ray facility [is] foolish because I think we're putting in unproved systems. We're going to be the first [using PACS] almost and it's always a very silly thing to do." (Participant A, Senior Doctor, Time 1)

"It's annoying in a way because lots of …the things that seem to get the most money or the most attention are things that aren't for patient care. So even while using the technology for paperwork and things like that, the things that could make nurses' jobs easier, we're not really spending any money on that technology." (Participant K, Nurse, Time 1)

These comments highlighted the inference that patient safety was not improving with the innovations because the hospital is first and foremost interested in institutional outcomes. Thus, while technology advances can aid the patient, they were perceived to also put the patient at risk if the new technology is not supported at all levels of the hospital. Hospital executives may have cultivated a belief that some technology was installed for the sake of the hospital being seen as a state-of-the-art organization, without prioritizing the needs of the patients. Clearly patient outcomes in this context were not as focal as they might be. In this context, ICT change implied patient risk when executives imposed changes on the roles of health professional roles. Health professionals may resist the changes and so resist the ICT.

Democracy is Inevitable … But Maybe Not Just Yet

In this chapter, using the hospital case study, we advance the view that how employees perceive group memberships and their relations with other groups during the introduction of ICT change reinforces the regulatory, evaluative, and obligatory dimensions of organizational life over e-democracy practices. These findings should generalize to other hierarchically structured organizations, particularly those employing a range of professional groups.

Using a social identity framework, we reiterate that organizations suffer from problems of intergroup relations. Unlike other research and commentary, however, we assert that group identity and status differences simultaneously impede and enable e-democracy. For instance, whereas Semler (1989) suggests that the participatory features of organizational e-democracy are "just hot air" (1989, p. 3) that needs to be minimized, our results reveal that the features of democracy are embedded in the organization under review, but may not be able to penetrate traditional bases of power and influence. In other words, the organization chooses to appropriate parts of the democracy features of a new technology that seem to best fit its preexisting structure or institutional arrangement. IT-enabled changes therefore paradoxically reinforce normative institutional practices (after Scott, 2001). In response to our focal research question that examines the inevitability of e-democracy, Slater and Bennis (1964) were correct in asserting the place of and importance of democracy. Our results suggest, however, that while aspects of e-democracy are inevitable (i.e., symbolically more information is available to staff), social identity provides a barrier that reduces the extent to which e-democracy will occur.

Our findings have important implications for HR practitioners. Our results show that ICT brings changes to the ways in which employees focus on their roles and identities. In particular, we argue that group identification is a key part of the successful adoption of e-democracy change. At the two phases of changes described here, when ICT changes were highlighted, findings suggest that compared to doctors and allied health professionals, higher order identities (e.g., hospital) are more salient for nurses. This result may reflect that fact that the nurses were less involved with the technology changes than the doctors and allied professionals at these two phases of change. For example, PACS was highly relevant for some allied health professionals and doctors. Thus, groups who find themselves immersed in the new system, and affected by it, do present their proximal roles as salient. By contrast, when change implementation and patient care was the focal topic, all health professionals identified with their professional in-group.

Individual empowerment through PACS was not translated upward into group changes in the organizational hierarchy. As noted above, our findings focus on a healthcare industry, but their relevance to other organizations with hierarchical structures is self-evident. This finding, concerning employee identities, also raises a second implication that HR practitioners need to bear in mind during ICT change. That is, they need to be aware of the salient identities within organizations and not simply focus on the formal roles and functions that are outlined in the organizational charter. Our findings reveal that, at least for some groups, higher order identities during IT implementation seem to be more salient. We would have predicted that lower order level identities would be more salient in the ICT context, but this is not so. Thus the management of ICT changes is a complex phenomenon that may differ from the implementation of other types of changes. Specifically, rhetoric of empowerment and authority voiced by senior management do not equate to high levels of e-democracy with staff who historically did not have such responsibilities — nor is it sought by these staff. This observation highlights that, at least in our context, the overall good of the organization (the hospital) and professional roles are paramount. This finding goes some way to explaining why role relations remain intact during ICT implementation, regardless of the collaborative practices organizations adopt during new information technology implementations.

A third implication that HR practitioners need to focus on is that employee identity can act as a barrier to the uptake of change. Resistance to change is not a new phenomenon, but in this chapter we have begun unpicking the elements of that resistance. If ICT brings with it significant changes to a professional's job description and duties, HR must acknowledge this change and address the changes directly with the professionals involved. This last point relates closely to the following two HR implications that arise from our findings.

HR practitioners must recognize the importance of ensuring the participation of key groups in the planning and implementation of changes. They must also recognize the importance of effective and relevant training procedures in the newly acquired technology. The former implication suggests that HR practitioners should put in place an appropriate program of focus groups and workshops for employees which will serve to encourage key personnel to engage in and champion the changes. From such programs, these employees will gain an in-depth understanding of the rationale for each aspect of ICT change. With their increased knowledge and understanding of the change, they will then be able to impart their knowledge to other employees affected by the change. Specifically, the rationale that underlies each ICT introduction needs to be openly explained to the staff. In turn, staff should be allowed to provide input as to their perceptions of the value of the implementation. HR practitioners need to be aware of the critical importance of this level of dialogue throughout all phases of change.

The latter implication, regarding training, relates to our results that reveal that despite the potential sophistication of the new systems, such technology requires effective training procedures to be put in place. Staff training programs need to timed so that they integrate smoothly with the introduction of new technology. Training must be viewed by the change agents as another important aspect of the change and implemented at the appropriate time in the change program, with back-up and training assistance available as needed. Clearly then, HR managers need to address resource and training issues and, in the case of some professions, create an environment where the professional will want to engage in the technology. While there are some professionals who will seek to resist new technology, it is important that education and training be aligned with technology preparation and a clear outline of the benefits to the organization. Again, active dialogue at all stages of change is critical.

A final implication for HR is the need to recognize the communication culture of the organization. If the organization is one that relies on face-to-face and one-on-one communication, HR practitioners must not only address the impact of the new technology, but must monitor how employees manage the change in their traditional channels of communication. Not to recognize the huge culture change that new communication media bring to traditional organizations is to jeopardize the efficient functioning of the organization and risk increases in miscommunication and disharmony.

We have highlighted the unintended consequences of new technology implementation. By illustrating the problems with assuming the inevitability of e-democracy, we indicate that integrating HR practices with the task of designing information systems is much more than simply specifying particular equipment parameters. Rather the process is about designing, inscribing, and configuring the system both for users and recipients alike — in this case, health professionals and their patients. This process needs to include ongoing negotiation as the system evolves. We would suggest that patients or other clients may not benefit from new ICTs, at least in the short term and in the current climate of HR-managed change. This disadvantage to patients/clients needs to be addressed by HR practitioners through the suggestions above. Our SIT framework highlights the need for attention on human resource issues during the implementation of new information technology. The impact of information technology improvements on the workforce needs careful evaluation beyond a simple assessment of technology outcomes or organizational benefits.

Conclusions

In this chapter, we illustrate how social identity processes drive organizational e-democracy change outcomes. We emphasize how an organization's communication processes and its levels of effectiveness may change with ICT implementation. Our findings suggest that IT implementations are sometimes installed at the expense of other systems, which may be more directly beneficial to the patient. To generalize to other organizations, we ask: Are organizations installing IT for IT's sake without due consideration of the needs? Paradoxically this approach to IT and, in particular, ICT change may disadvantage the original aims of the organization.

ICT changes do not necessarily equate to improved communication between employees or workgroups. Our findings highlight that as new ICT systems are put in place, communication channels and dynamics alter. This alteration may not align with staff empowerment or increased communication effectiveness. HR practitioners need to examine current communication procedures and involve employees in the potential changes to communication that the new ICT brings. With the introduction of new technology, communication networks within organizations such as hospitals are often likely to break down. If the organizational culture has a tradition of face-to-face communication (as do hospitals), HR practitioners need to be aware that ICT implementation will have a huge impact on practice and on culture. Open discussion of disadvantages in a new system can only be acknowledged and constructively dealt with if there is genuine staff input and dialogue. Our findings suggest that HR managers need to be cognizant of the fact that effective communication may be compromised. Further they need to ensure that the change program is communicated and managed effectively. In this way, further miscommunication issues may be reduced or even avoided.

Our current findings suggest that e-democracy is not enhanced through IT change. Rather, we have found that the contrary is true. HR must respond to the frustration expressed by professionals concerning the actual changes and the implementation process. To address these concerns effectively, HR must understand both the formal and informal organizational charter. Without due consideration to the opinions of professionals throughout the change process, our findings suggest resistance.

References

Alvesson, M. (2000). Social identity and the problem of loyalty in knowledge-intensive companies. *Journal of Management Studies, 37*, 1101-1123.

Applegate, L.M. (1994). Managing in an information age: Transforming the organization for the 1990s. In R. Baskerville, S. Smithson, O. Ngwenyama, & J.I. DeGross (Eds.), *Transforming organizations with information technology* (pp. 15-94). Amsterdam: North-Holland.

Ashforth, B.E., & Johnson, S.A. (2001). Which hat to wear? The relative salience of multiple identities in organizational contexts. In M.A. Hogg & D.J. Terry (Eds.), *Social identity processes in organizational contexts* (pp. 31-48). Philadelphia, PA: Psychology Press.

Ashforth, B.E., & Mael, F. (1989). Social identity theory and the organization. *Academy of Management Review, 14*, 20-39.

Beer, M., & Nohria, N. (2000). Resolving the tension between theories E and O of change. In M. Beer & N. Nohria (Eds.), *Breaking the code of change* (pp. 1-34). Boston: Harvard Business School Press.

Carlopio, J. (1998). *Implementation: Making workplace innovation and technical change happen.* Roseville, NSW: McGraw-Hill.

de Tocqueville, A. (1835/1966). *Democracy in America.* New York: Harper & Row.

Drehmer, D.E., Belohlav, J.A., & Coye, R.W. (2000). An exploration of employee participation using a scaling approach. *Group and Organization Management, 25*, 397-419.

Drucker, P.F. (1992). The new society of organizations. *Harvard Business Review, 70*(5), 95-104.

Drucker, P.F. (2001). *The essential Drucker.* Oxford: Butterworth Heinemann.

Fahy, M. (2001). *Enterprise resource planning systems.* London: Chartered Institute of Management Accountants.

Gardner. J., & Jones, E. (1999). Problematic communication in the workplace: Beliefs of superiors and subordinates. *International Journal of Applied Linguistics, 9,* 198-205.

Gardner, J., Paulsen, N., Gallois, C., Callan, V., & Monaghan, P. (2000). An intergroup perspective on communication in organizations. In H. Giles &

W.P. Robinson (Eds.), *Handbook of language and social psychology* (2nd ed.). London: John Wiley & Sons.

Glover, S.M., Prawitt, D.F., & Romney, M.B. (1999). Implementing ERP. *Internal Auditor*, (February), 40.

Halal, W.E. (1994). From hierarchy to enterprise: Internal markets are the new foundation of management. *Academy of Management Executive*, *8*(4), 69-83.

Hogg, M.A. (2001). A social identity theory of leadership. *Personality and Social Psychology Review*, *5*, 184-200.

Hogg, M.A., & Abrams, D. (1988). *Social identification*. London: Routledge

Hogg, M.A., & Mullin, B.A. (1999). Joining groups to reduce uncertainty: Subjective uncertainty reduction and group identification. In D. Abrams & M.A. Hogg (Eds.), *Social identity and social cognition* (pp. 249-279). Oxford, UK: Blackwell.

Hogg, M.A., & Terry, D. (2000). Social identity and self-categorization processes in organizational contexts. *Academy of Management Review*, *25*, 121-140.

Hogg, M.A., & Terry, D. (2001). Social identity theory and organizational processes. In M.A. Hogg & D.J. Terry (Eds.), *Social identity processes in organizational contexts* (pp 1-12). Philadelphia, PA: Psychology Press

Koch, C., & Buhl, H. (2001). ERP supported team working in Danish manufacturing. *New Technology, Work and Employment, 16*, 164-177.

Kraemer, K.L. & Dedrick, J. (1997) Computing and public organizations. *Journal of Public Administration Research and Theory*, *7*, 89-113.

Lambert, S.J. (2000). Added benefits: The link between work-life benefits and organizational citizenship behavior. *Academy of Management Journal*, *43*, 801-816.

Lammers, C.J., & Szell, G. (Eds.). (1989). *International handbook of participation in organizations*. Oxford: Oxford University Press.

Mantovani, G. (1994). Is computer-mediated communication intrinsically apt to enhance democracy in organizations? *Human Relations, 47,* 45-63.

Manville, B., & Ober, J. (2003). Beyond empowerment: Building a company of citizens. *Harvard Business Review*, *81*(1), 48-53

Markus, M.L. (1983). Power, politics and MIS implementation. *Communications of the ACM, 26,* 430-444.

Mason, R.M. (1982). *Participatory and workplace democracy.* Carbondale, IL: Southern Illinois University Press.

Neef, D. (Ed.). (1998). *The knowledge economy.* Boston: Butterworth-Heinemann.

Orlikowski, W.J., & Iacono, C.S. (2001). Research commentary: Desperately seeking the "IT" in IT research – a call to theorizing the IT artifact. *Information Systems Research, 12,* 121-134.

Pratt, M.G. (2001). Social identity dynamics in modern organizations: An organizational psychology/organizational behavior perspective. In M.A. Hogg & D.J. Terry (Eds.), *Social identity processes in organizational contexts* (pp. 13-30). Philadelphia, PA: Psychology Press.

Robey, D., & Boudreau, M.C. (1999). Accounting for the contradictory organizational consequences of information technology: Theoretical directions and methodological implications. *Information Systems Research, 10*(2), 167-185.

Rothschild, J., & Whitt, J.A. (1986). *The cooperative workplace: Potentials and dilemmas of organizational democracy and participation.* Cambridge: Cambridge University Press.

Schilling, M.A., & Steensma, H.K. (2001). The use of modular organizational forms: An industry-level analysis. *Academy of Management Journal, 44,* 1149-1168.

Schwarz, G.M. (2002). Organizational hierarchy adaptation and information technology. *Information and Organization, 12*(3), 153-182.

Scott, W.R. (2001). *Institutions and organizations* (2nd ed.). Thousand Oaks, CA: Sage Publications.

Semler, R. (1989). Managing without managers. *Harvard Business Review, 89*(5), 76-84.

Slater, P., & Bennis, W.G. (1964). Democracy is inevitable. *Harvard Business Review, 2,* 51-59.

Tajfel, H. (1978). Differentiation between social groups: Studies in the social psychology of intergroup relations. *European Monographs in Social Psychology, 14.* London: Academic Press.

Terry, D. J. (2001). Intergroup relations and organizational mergers. In M.A. Hogg & D.J. Terry (Eds.), *Social identity processes in organizational contexts* (pp. 229-248). Philadelphia, PA: Psychology Press.

Tsoukas, H., & Chia, R. (2002). On organizational becoming: Rethinking organizational change. *Organization Science, 13*, 567-582.

van Knippenberg, D., & van Leeuwen, E. (2001). Organizational identity after a merger: Sense of continuity as the key to post-merger identification. In M.A. Hogg & D.J. Terry (Eds.), *Social identity processes in organizational contexts* (pp. 249-264). Philadelphia, PA: Psychology Press.

Weber, M. (1968). *Economy and society: An outline of interpretive sociology.* Edited and with an introduction by G. Roth & C. Wittich. New York: Bedminster Press.

Wenger, E. (1999). *Communities of practice: Learning, meaning and identity.* Cambridge: Cambridge University Press.

Endnote

* The authors wish to acknowledge that the data from this publication formed part of a large 3 year project funded by the Australian Strategic Partnership with Industry – Research and Training (SPIRT), Ref C0010720 entitled *Employee Adjustment to Continued Organisational Change.*

Chapter X

Managing and Practicing OD in an IT Environment:
A Structured Approach to Developing IT Project Teams

Joseph Logan, AstraZeneca Pharmaceuticals, USA

Abstract

This chapter introduces a framework for improving success in information technology (IT) projects by leveraging the organization development (OD) practitioner's expertise in fostering cooperation and learning in teams. It argues that IT project failure can be addressed and prevented by building teams that anticipate and recover from issues of communication, goal clarity, and internal support. The author intends this framework to provide a foundation for OD practitioners and IT project teams to engage the domain knowledge of each in order to successfully execute projects that are cooperative, focused on improvement through learning, and ultimately dedicated to more productive outcomes for the organizations they serve.

Introduction

Failure was not an option for the eRecords project. The health, safety, and lives of its constituents were at stake. The initiative sought to create a client-server application and database to replace the hundreds of thousands of paper files a government agency used to track those in its care. These files contained the most sensitive bits of information on each benefit recipient, and the decisions made from these files were literally a matter of life and death. The government had allocated millions of dollars in funding to eRecords (a pseudonym), and the project was publicly supported and promoted at the highest levels of government. Multiple agencies contributed financial and human resources. The best-known, most expensive contractors formed an integrated team to develop and implement the new system. The project personnel were virtually an all-star team of the best and brightest in their field. Every possible resource was devoted to the initiative's success, and the lives and careers of thousands were riding on it.

And yet, eRecords failed.

In fact, it didn't just fail — it failed spectacularly. eRecords failed in the most public possible ways, leading to internal investigations, government audits, and an ongoing presence on the front page of the newspaper. Its staff fled for safer positions, its management scrambled to shift blame, and its sponsors were publicly humiliated and demoted. The project exceeded its schedule more than threefold, consumed many times its projected budget, and delivered fewer than half of its promised benefits. The application continues in use to this day, and every day it is used it exacts an escalating cost in lost time, unnecessary work duplication, and user frustration. Far from being an isolated example of IT project failure, it illustrates the norm.

Kurt Lewin on the last day of his life told Ronald Lippitt, "Interdependence is the greatest challenge" (Weisbord, 1987, p. 104). He was remarking on the hazards individualism presents to groups working together toward common goals, and, 60 years after his death, the father of organization development (OD) could just as easily have been addressing a group of information technology (IT) project managers. Despite linking people around the world with new and innovative uses of technology, IT project teams continue to contribute tremendous waste and dysfunction to their organizations and clients through their failure to work together effectively.

IT professionals, the premiere knowledge workers, are among the most individually gifted professionals in the world. They are able to interpret the processes of the physical world to a digital form, enabling quantum leaps in productivity and creating new opportunities in industry, government, and service organizations. Their work contributed US$255 billion in IT project spending in the United States in 2002 (The Standish Group [Standish], 2003), and over US$1 trillion globally (Microsoft Corporation [Microsoft], 2002). Yet, project waste reached $55 billion in the U.S. that year, over 20% of total IT project spending (Standish, 2003). Assuming a proportional global success rate, IT project waste could easily top a quarter of a trillion U.S. dollars each year.

If global IT project waste is over a quarter of a trillion U.S. dollars each year, is it the case that modern technology is too complex to be developed and deployed predictably? No. Graduates of elite project management programs like the one at Boston University — many of whom manage knowledge work in large IT projects — consistently cite the following reasons for the failure of IT projects:

- poor communication,
- unclear goals, and
- lack of senior management support.

Ten years of research into project success and failure by the Standish Group supports these findings (Standish, 2003). In other words, these hundreds of billions of dollars in waste are attributable not to failures in the technology itself, but rather to the human systems that create the technology.

OD is a field devoted to improving organizational effectiveness. The recurrent issues in IT projects — communication, clarity about objectives, and leadership alignment and support — are precisely the opportunities OD addresses. While the OD practitioner has not traditionally been a key member of IT project teams, the persistent issues these teams face indicate a strong need, integral role, and clear challenge for teachers, managers, and practitioners of OD.

Perspectives on OD and IT

Failure in IT projects can be defined as exceeding a projected budget, taking longer than the estimated schedule, failing to meet agreed-upon quality requirements, or (most common) some combination of the three. Some of the more common types of IT projects include:

- software application development (creating new software packages),
- hardware and software implementation (implementing new computers or software),
- database management and revision (ensuring proper data storage and access),
- hardware and software upgrades (replacing or enhancing existing assets), and
- network infrastructure improvements (continuing to involve the paths data travel).

While there are differences among these and other types of IT projects, one commonality is that most IT projects take longer, cost more, or contribute less than originally planned.

OD practitioners specialize in addressing the issues of organizational learning and alignment that plague IT projects, and yet OD practitioners are usually absent or marginal in such projects. IT professionals instead use project management techniques to exert greater control over uncertainty in projects, but IT projects continue to experience cost and schedule overruns, as well as unmet requirements. These gaps indicate a need for complementary roles between IT project managers and OD practitioners. IT offers a substantial market for increasingly underused OD practitioners, and OD offers relief for the cycle of dysfunction that drains IT budgets. The key to realizing these benefits is to eliminate the traditional barriers between these fields and frame a new working relationship.

IT and OD suffer from stereotypes that create barriers between them. IT professionals are often cast as aloof, antisocial, arrogant, analytical geeks. OD is usually dismissed as being too "touchy-feely" and largely useless for producing real results. These stereotypes mask the potential for each field to complement and extend the other. Working together, these two fields are far more effective than either is alone. To be accepted in IT projects, OD practitioners must respect the purpose and pace of IT, working with accountability toward its success. In return, IT professionals must be receptive to the presence and outcome-oriented approaches of the OD practitioner. The short-term result will be immediate savings in technology budgets. Long-term benefits include more strategic use of technology, more and better jobs for both IT professionals and OD consultants, and the promotion of innovation and growth.

Note that the lack of OD practitioners is not the source of project failure. The source of project failure is an inability or unwillingness to work cooperatively (as evidenced by the previously cited issues of poor communication, lack of clarity about objectives, and absence of leadership support) and to collectively learn from self-reflection (as evidenced by problem repetition within and across IT projects). Nor are OD practitioners the only way to address such issues; in fact, an OD practitioner without a framework for engaging the IT project team can hasten its demise. Success in IT projects can be improved when IT project teams work cooperatively and learn from experience, two behaviors that qualified OD practitioners understand and cultivate. The key to unlocking that success is to build a framework for enabling the IT project team's cooperation and learning.

Objectives of This Chapter

The objectives of this chapter are to:

- explain the most common issues resulting in IT failure and waste;
- explain how OD can address these issues;
- present a model for managing and practicing OD in an IT environment;
- describe how to use the model to create effective teams, organizational alignment, and organizational learning in IT projects; and
- prescribe practical strategies for ensuring success in IT projects.

This chapter establishes a framework for using OD to minimize common IT issues. Its focus is neither technology nor OD technique. The chapter does not discuss such technical distinctions as whether the IT project comprises software development, implementation, network configuration, or other objectives. It also is not concerned with specific OD approaches or orientations. This chapter presents a general approach that can be used in most technical projects and with many OD approaches. This chapter brings IT and OD together to minimize the recurrent issues that consume a quarter of a trillion U.S. dollars in IT project waste each year, and to realize significant, lasting technological and organizational change.

The primary intended audience for this chapter is the manager or practitioner of OD interested in engaging with IT projects as a means of improving and influencing the organizations they serve. This chapter may also be of interest to the IT project manager or executive interested in new approaches to the persistent, expensive issues plaguing IT projects.

Background

A thorough overview of the issues and opportunities facing OD practitioners in IT projects requires a common set of definitions and some background information on the issue. The next sections discuss common terminology and present a foundation of theory for this discussion.

Definitions

When discussing two fields as disparate as OD and IT, it is essential to clarify the terminology of each at the outset. In the case of these particular fields, where a word such as "system" or "process" may have different meanings in each, such definition is absolutely necessary. IT and OD are fundamentally distanced from each other by their terminology, and each views its work through its own metaphors. Agreement on terms or at least the differences between similar terms is a logical first step toward bridging that distance. Defining terms is also a good investment of time in the early stages of IT-specific OD efforts, minimizing misunderstandings later in the project. The following terms are key to this discussion.

- **Organization development:** Though there are nearly as many definitions as people purporting to practice it, organization development in the context of this discussion can be defined as "a process that applies behavioral science knowledge and practices to help organizations achieve greater effectiveness, including increased financial performance and improved quality of worklife" (Cummings & Worley, 1997, p. 1). Marvin Weisbord (1987) notes that high-quality work requires a creative interaction of the three perspectives of people, economics, and technology. This definition of OD accommodates that essential interaction, and the pace and investment in IT projects demand the successful management of that interaction.

- **Information technology:** Information technology also has a variety of definitions, most of which are largely derived from the perspective of the person doing the defining. John Thorp defines information technology as "a general term used to refer to all aspects of computing and communications technology, including hardware and software (both system and application software) that encompasses the creation, storage, processing, distribution, and display of information for a variety of uses, including business, educational, artistic, scientific, recreational, or personal" (Thorp, 1998, p. 257). For the purpose of succinctness, let's consider IT to be software systems that process information and the technologies supporting these systems. This definition accommodates office applications, communications systems such as e-mail and groupware, specialized systems such as accounting packages, and Internet and World Wide Web sites and applications. While the field of IT is as broad and diverse as the organizations and individuals that use it, this discussion will place IT in a much more focused context.

- **Projects and project management:** IT is executed in discrete efforts called "projects." The Project Management Body of Knowledge (PMBOK) defines a project as "a temporary endeavor undertaken to create a unique product, service, or result" (Project Management Institute [PMI], 2000, p. 204). Projects may be as short as a few weeks or as long as a few years, but they are distinct from an ongoing business concern in that they have a planned beginning and end. The field of project management, defined as "the application of knowledge, skills, tools, and techniques to project activities to meet the project requirements," is the *lingua franca* of IT projects, and the PMBOK is its bible (PMI, 2000, p. 205).

While it is not necessary for the OD practitioner to be certified as a project manager in order to understand these terms of art, it is useful to have a copy of the PMBOK as a reference.

- **Systems, processes, and process consultation:** As mentioned earlier, IT and OD have different meanings for the same terms, and being clear on these dual meanings will help in establishing rapport. It will also save time and confusion during the more critical points in the project. A "system" in IT terms usually refers to some combination of software, hardware, or both that work together to perform a specific function or set of functions. The OD practitioner is likely more familiar with human "systems" such as organizations or groups. Similarly, IT professionals understand "process" as an activity that receives inputs and acts upon them to produce outputs. For example, a personal finance software system might take one's bank balances as an input and act upon them to produce a pie chart, comparing these balances as an output. OD practitioners compare "process" with "task," where the "task" is what is to be done and the "process" is how (Weisbord, 1987, p. 221). Weisbord (1987) notes that process reflects perceptions, attitudes, feelings, and reasoning, a definition that will likely sound quite foreign to those accustomed to mapping processes in flow-charts.

  Edgar Schein defines "process consultation" as "a set of activities on the part of the consultant that help the client to perceive, understand, and act upon the process events that occur in the client's environment in order to improve the situation *as defined by the client*" [italics added] (Schein, 1988, p. 11). This definition comes closest to the OD practitioner's role described here, and the emphasis on the customer's definition helps to frame that role. However, in this discussion the OD practitioner will be presented with a model that specifies inputs, outputs, and quality in relation to the activities of process consultation, in essence merging the OD definition of process with the technical one. The technical definition of process considers an input to be any product, service, or piece of information that comes into a process from a supplier (Pande, Neuman, & Cavanagh, 2000, p. 397). In this model, inputs will be information about the functioning of the IT project team, and the suppliers will be the team, its members, and its customers. Similarly, an output is any product, service, or piece of information coming out of, or resulting from, the activities in a process (Pande et al., 2000, p. 399). The outputs from this model are new information about the IT project team's functioning and new behaviors that improve that functioning.

- **Customers, requirements, and quality:** Three important and related terms in this discussion are "quality," "requirements," and "customer." "Quality" is defined as "measurable standards of comparison so that applications can be consistently directed toward business goals" (Pande et al., 2000, p. 401). Note that "business goals" in this sense refers to the business of the organization, whether that business is making cars or abating global warming. "Requirements" are specific statements of those measurable standards of comparison for a given process. A "customer" is any person or organization who receives the output of a process (Pande et al., 2000, p. 395). In this context, **quality** is the degree to which a process **acts upon inputs** to **produce outputs that meet the (process) customer's requirements**. These terms are important in this model because the IT project team (the customer) has very specific requirements (including schedule and cost), and the OD practitioner will select the inputs into and seek outputs from the OD process that meet these requirements (quality). The OD practitioner in the IT project is using Schein's process consultation, with the more technical definition of "process" framing the data going into and the outcomes resulting from the process consultation. In essence, this is one type of process embedded within the other.

- **Teambuilding:** One final term needs to be defined for this discussion: "teambuilding." William Dyer lists four criteria for success in teambuilding:

  - Top management must provide clear support.
  - Organizational rewards should support teamwork.
  - Time for team development should be encouraged and made available.
  - People must clearly understand what teambuilding is and what it is not. (Dyer, 1995, pp. 13-15)

Dyer goes on to satisfy the last item by defining teambuilding as an activity whose purpose is "to help those who must work together to accomplish results, to identify any condition that impedes effective collaboration, and engage in actions that improve the quality of teamwork" (Dyer, 1995, p. 15). In contrast to the common perception of teambuilding as an activity that helps people feel good about working with each other but drains time and money from the organization, this definition emphasizes results, effective collaboration, and quality. These are the priorities of the IT project team, and they are what the OD practitioner will help to achieve as a part of that team.

The terminology used by IT and OD in their respective domains may seem obscure and contradictory, but in working together, simplicity and directness are key. The better the two fields are able to understand each other, the more effectively they can work together to produce the results they jointly seek.

Literature

The 2001 IDC IT Economic Impact study estimated annual global spending on information technology — computer hardware, software, and services — at US$1 trillion (Microsoft, 2002). The most recent Standish Group CHAOS Report on project success and failure noted that of the US$255 billion in IT project spending in the United States, only a third of these projects are successful (completed on time, within budget, and according to requirements). The report asserts that US$55 billion of IT project spending is wasted (Standish, 2003). The report goes on to note that IT projects overrun their schedules an average of 82%, and that only 52% of required features and functions appear in the released product (Standish, 2003). These are astounding statistics. If global IT project success and failure rates are even close to the U.S. averages — and trends suggest they are even worse — those projects are contributing hundreds of billions of dollars in waste even as they drive global economic development. Conservative estimates extrapolating the rate of U.S. IT project waste to global IT spending pegs annual global IT project waste at over US$250 billion.

IT expenditures have been growing 20-30% annually for 20 years and account for about 40% of annual business equipment expenditure in the U.S. (Thorp, 1998, p. xxi). In 1997 IT accounted for about 7% of total corporate costs, and about 60% of corporations depended to some extent on IT systems (Thorp, 1998, p. 4). These figures have risen substantially since then. Yet, project success rates indicate severe inefficiencies in realizing a return on IT investment. In 1996, 73% of corporate IT projects were late, over budget, or canceled (Thorp, 1998, p.12). As these rates of failure increase, their costs will also increase with global IT spending. The U.S. Government alone spends over

US$59 billion annually on IT, and non-profit organizations are becoming increasingly reliant on IT's power (Executive Office of the President, Office of Management and Budget, 2003). Global IT spending is projected to top US$1.4 trillion by 2005 (Microsoft, 2002).

IT success and failure is interesting (and shocking) at a global level, but it is experienced at the organizational and IT project level. IT is created and disseminated through discrete projects, and these projects cumulatively and exponentially influence the organizations that are their customers. Change in the organizational, societal, and global effects of IT must begin at the IT project level. Margaret Mead believed in the importance of the small, face-to-face group as the link between the person and 'macro' system. The IT project team is such a group. While only a small subset of the body of organizational theory targets project teams and their limited life cycles, the link between project team and organization is a link between tactics and strategy (PMI, 2000, p. 110). The IT project team offers an opportunity to translate the individual IT professional's talents into productive group, organizational, and global results (Weisbord, 1987, pp. 85-86).

Most IT professionals are familiar with the maxim "garbage in, garbage out." Buried within this *bon mot* is the assertion that so long as technical inputs are of good quality, outputs will be as well. The underlying assumption in the maxim is that the system or process acting on the inputs works perfectly. The reality is that few systems or processes are perfect. Processes are at least important as inputs and outputs when seeking performance improvements. When an IT project team comprising numerous talented individuals begins working toward a common purpose, the result is often a shared set of processes that can be improved to lead to better results.

The project manager is the person responsible for managing the technical aspects of a project (PMI, 2000, p. 205), but Dyer notes that the manager is also responsible for the development of the work team (Dyer, 1995, p. 87). The IT project manager is usually so focused on the content and scope of the project that team development is an afterthought, if a thought at all. Also, given that the IT project team is often a mix of people from different divisions or companies, and that an IT project team is usually designed to be a temporary unit (PMI, 2000, p. 204), the IT project manager may not have formal responsibility for team development. Still, there is a connection between teamwork and the content and scope of the IT project. Weisbord (1987) explains Mike Blansfield's identification of universal processes (purposes, in/ out, elbow room, discussion, use of skills, conflict, support) that work teams rarely connect to results, noting that most managers define positive results as higher productivity, better quality, more profits, and lower costs. Blansfield directly links the key processes to the managerial definition of results in his Team Effectiveness Theory, indicating a strong, though often unacknowledged, causal relationship (Weisbord, 1987, p. 303). The implication is clear: Focusing on improving IT project teams' processes can have a positive effect on their results, and thus on the organizations they serve. In fact, the very act of bringing the team to reflection about its behaviors can result in a sort of Hawthorne effect, improving performance through the act of change despite the intent of the change (Roethlisberger & Dickson, 1939).

Participation in decision-making processes would seem a natural operating mode for one as highly skilled as the IT professional. Yet, project management works at cross-purposes with participation in practice if not in theory. The tendency in a fast-paced, high-pressure environment like IT is to control, and one person in control can always make decisions faster than many. Project management as a controlling mechanism may produce temporary results, but will ultimately create more issues than would participation. Similarly, Lewin knew that participation alone would also fail absent careful diagnosis and application, reflecting the uniqueness of each situation (Weisbord, 1987, pp. 93-94). Involving people is more than just a technique. A truly effective IT project team operates from an integration of the structured theory of project management and the proven foundation of participation in the decision-making process. The key is in finding a way to integrate the two.

Main Thrust of the Chapter

OD has a tremendous opportunity in the IT field. OD practitioners who want jobs, influence, and an opportunity to make a meaningful difference can find all three in IT by first building the effectiveness of the IT project team. Eric Trist wrote, "Information technologies, especially those concerned with the microprocessor and telecommunication, give immense scope for solving many current problems — if the right value choices can be made" (Trist, 1981, p. 59). More than two decades after Trist's observation, IT is the single largest capital investment in most organizations today (Thorp, 1998). IT drives tremendous changes in organizations and is one of the most powerful organizational interventions. The way IT products and services are created and deployed significantly influences an organization's culture, structure, development, and survival (Beckhard & Harris, 1987). OD practitioners seek but seldom find this level of influence in organizations, and the IT project team provides access to that influence. The process of creating IT products and services also produces the issues associated with IT projects: poor communication, unclear or competing objectives, and lack of leadership buy-in. While these issues are common, approaches to overcoming them are not. The IT project management process does not by itself offer mechanisms for learning and improving during projects. The OD process does.

OD "applies behavioral science knowledge and practices to help organizations achieve greater effectiveness" (Cummings & Worley, 1997, p. 1). The major issues in IT projects — poor communication, lack of clear objectives, and lack of leadership support — are targeted and minimized by OD interventions that create participation and learning. OD addresses the issues with which IT struggles. In this sense, the relationship between OD and IT is — or should be — symbiotic.

Yet, IT continues to repeat its mistakes, and OD continues to be considered more a luxury than an IT project necessity. The next section discusses the issues, controversies, and problems that maintain distance between these seemingly complementary fields.

Issues, Controversies, Problems

IT and OD remain distanced by differences in priorities, undefined relationships, and incomplete approaches. Each pursues different — and often conflicting — goals and values. Similarly, the relationship between IT and OD — and the benefits of creating such a relationship — has not been defined and does not have many models to emulate. Perhaps most important, IT and OD continue to employ incomplete, insular approaches when more robust, complementary, and collaborative approaches are required. This section discusses each of these issues.

Differences in Priorities

The persistent issue in the way IT projects are currently conducted is the astounding waste in cost and schedule overruns and in unmet requirements. The human and opportunity costs of such waste are tremendous, both globally and locally. Yet, this big problem masks an equally disturbing issue: Few people seem to really care about solving the big problem.

IT professionals rarely occupy a level in their organizations that requires or even offers a clear view of the organization's strategy and finances. Their concerns often focus on producing IT products and services that meet immediate or near-term needs, and the boundaries of their current projects often define their spheres of concern. The larger organizational picture is often missing. IT professionals who do have a view of the larger organizational picture — usually mid- to upper-level managers — are often caught up in the political struggles common in the upper levels of organizations. While both groups believe in the holy IT trinity of cost, schedule, and requirements, that trinity serves different ends for each. Neither directly feels the mounting losses of IT project waste, and almost no one comprehends the magnified costs downstream. These are measured in lost opportunities, lost revenue, and lost jobs.

OD practitioners are seldom more strategic than IT professionals in their orientation, but they do care about lost opportunities and lost jobs. When markets expand, people have secure jobs and growing room (Weisbord, 1987, p. 2). When there is waste that results in lost jobs and shrinking opportunity, the opposite is true. OD practitioners usually work toward personal and organizational growth, and are often stymied by the economic conditions that make jobs less secure. Their work resides in the diagnosis and correction of organizational issues such as poor communication, clarity about objectives, and issues of organizational alignment and support. The espoused theory is that eliminating these problems will produce organizations that are more productive and rewarding places to work. The unfortunate reality is that when times get tough, OD is considered an expendable luxury rather than a strategic tool.

Undefined Relationships

While the most common, persistent issues in IT projects are the very sorts of issues OD addresses, few IT projects have an OD practitioner as a team member or consider OD critical to success. The historic role of the OD practitioner in IT projects has been limited to narrowly focused efforts such as training, project communication, and documentation. While these functions are important in any IT environment, the OD practitioner has far more to offer to the IT organization. The real OD work lies within the IT project team itself.

Why haven't IT projects traditionally had OD practitioners as part of the team? Three reasons immediately present themselves. First, both IT and OD value competence, and asking for help is analogous to admitting fault. IT and OD practitioners are experts brought into an organization to solve the toughest problems, not to introduce new ones. Whether from arrogance or insecurity, people in both fields often opt for working problems out alone rather than seeking help. Second, IT and OD tend to approach issues differently. While OD practitioners tend to take the broad, big-picture view of organizations with the human element as a primary concern, IT professionals are narrowly focused on the technical requirements, schedule, and cost of their particular project, often to the exclusion of individual and organizational concerns. Yet, the most important reason IT and OD people do not often work together is also the most obvious: Most have never done it before.

There are very few examples of successful IT-OD partnerships. Despite failing in exactly the areas OD seeks to improve, IT professionals tend not to notice or value OD practitioners. Ask most IT professionals their impression of OD and they will gladly recount the pointless teambuilding session that cost them half a day of work or the boring "people skills" training their manager made them attend. Ask OD practitioners about IT projects and they will likely offer blank stares or nervous laughter. Despite having complementary needs and talents, the two fields remain separated by ego, approach, and ignorance.

Incomplete Approaches

The field of OD has not invested the effort in defining its relationship to IT in the same way project management has. As a result, IT professionals know little about OD, and OD takes little notice of IT. In the past several years, OD has become increasingly technique-focused while minimizing the importance of the outcomes of using those techniques, a shift that runs counter to the most pressing needs of IT. IT demands results, and OD is seldom held accountable for them. While OD practitioners seem to believe that newer and better techniques will produce more consistent, meaningful — though vague — outcomes, IT continues to invest its faith in the controlling (and often creativity-starving) mechanisms of project management, and both are the worse for it.

It seems clear that OD and IT can play a role in each other's success, and the challenge at this point is in defining that role. IT can no longer afford to spend a quarter trillion dollars each year on ego and ignorance, and OD is equally challenged in establishing its relevance and credibility. Through careful, systematic, sensitive application of OD theory and approach within the specific project management context of the IT project, both IT and OD can achieve the cost savings and organizational impact as yet unrealized by each.

Solutions and Recommendations

In order to stop the cycle of IT project failure and waste, IT project teams must learn to learn, correcting recurrent behaviors that impede their success. OD efforts to facilitate these improvements must respect the boundaries of the project, delivering results while working within the schedule and budget of the IT project. Time and cost are at a premium in the IT project; this is perhaps the strongest element of the IT culture. The OD practitioner interested in working with IT project teams must understand that their work will be evaluated in these terms.

The OD practitioner can contribute to the success of the IT project by using a model for integrating IT and OD, adapting the model to each IT project with a customized project charter, and employing a structured team-building approach that focuses the model on the process level. Once the proper context has been established, teambuilding is a logical first approach to addressing the most cumbersome problems of IT. While there are many interventions that can produce positive results in the IT project, the structured team-building approach is the one that most directly addresses the most troublesome issues in IT projects. The goal in this approach is to promote a structured, results-driven methodology for engaging and promoting productive learning in these projects. Working with the IT project manager — the formal leader of the IT project — the OD practitioner builds the team's capacity to plan and manage its own work within the parameters of the project's scope, purpose, and organizational goal.

A Model for Integrating IT and OD

Differences in priorities, undefined relationships, and incomplete approaches have impeded IT-OD collaboration. A model for integrating and defining shared priorities, relationships, and approaches creates a way to overcome these barriers and begin the work of developing the IT project team. The IT Project Success Funnel is that model.

Figure 1. IT Project Success Funnel (The elements of IT project success are considered by working downward through the levels of the funnel.)

The IT Project Success Funnel (Figure 1) brings together the priorities of the OD practitioner and the IT project manager in one unified, consistent approach to the work of the project. The model takes the primary concerns of the OD practitioner — organizational strategy and project purpose — and merges them with the on-the-ground imperatives of the IT project manager: project requirements, schedule, and cost. The combination dictates the alignment essential to creating and demonstrating value through IT projects. This alignment creates the foundation for consistent communication, clarity about project objectives, and support throughout the organization.

- **Organizational strategy:** At the top of the funnel is organizational strategy. Organizational strategy is the broadest context within which an IT project is conducted. Every IT project should be able to be directly traced to the organizational strategy. If not, the project is likely not something on which the organization should be spending time and energy. While this may seem a somewhat extreme view, IT investment is too large a part of organizational investment to be anything other than perfectly clear about how the IT project supports organizational strategy. When the project's benefit is unclear, so is its entitlement to be a part of the organization.

- **Project purpose:** Under organizational strategy is project purpose. Project purpose is the specific objective or objectives met by the IT project, and these are where the most direct links to organizational strategy are emphasized. The project purpose is the means by which the IT project supports the organizational strategy. The project purpose is ideally a very brief (one- to two-sentence) statement of how the project supports an organizational strategic objective.

- **Requirements:** The next level is requirements, which refer to the specific things the product or service of the IT project must do. These are the means for achieving the ends of the project purpose. The requirements specify what the IT project's end product or service is supposed to *do*. While IT project teams sometimes confuse requirements with features (such as "Oracle database" or "Microsoft Word-like spell check feature"), IT project requirements specify the outcomes of the project that make the project purpose a reality.

- **Schedule:** Next is the project schedule; this element in the funnel defines the time by which the requirements of the project can be delivered upon. The project schedule plays an important role in supporting the requirements, purpose, and strategy in that the IT project's role is often time sensitive. IT projects' ability to deliver value upward into the organizational strategy usually depends on being able to deliver that value within a particular window of time, especially when that strategy focuses on competitive advantage. Lapses in the project schedule can push an IT project's outcomes from indispensable to irrelevant.

- **Cost:** At the bottom of the funnel is cost. Cost is the smallest part of the funnel but is the part (along with schedule) most likely to receive attention throughout the project, especially from the IT project team and manager. Cost and schedule are the most clear indicators in any IT project, though meeting these requirements says nothing about the value delivered by the IT project. Cost is at the bottom of the funnel for the purposes of OD intervention because problems throughout the funnel's levels always trickle down to cost, whether through serving the wrong goals and purposes, unmet or unnecessary requirements, or — most commonly —

lapses in schedule. All these issues exact costs, and these costs can ultimately stop an IT project cold.

The IT Project Success Funnel very clearly defines the boundaries of the IT project in such a way that the OD practitioner can begin addressing issues of alignment and leadership support while planning an approach to the IT project team's process needs.

Using the Project Charter

The model is a useful theory for thinking about the parameters of an IT project, but the OD practitioner has to bridge the gap between theory and practice to create real results in the IT project. One of the most useful tools for an OD practitioner in contracting and working with an IT project manager is a project charter specifying the IT project's organizational strategy linkage and the purpose of the project, and laying out the highest level of requirements, schedule, and cost. These should ideally be laid out at a level appropriate for an executive, omitting unnecessary details in order to present a high-level view of the IT project's intent and the scope of the OD practitioner's efforts.

The charter is not a binding contract, but rather a tool for confirming shared understanding at the outset of the partners' work together. The project charter announces that a new project has begun, and it demonstrates management support for the project and the project manager (Verzuh, 1999, p. 53). Ideally the OD practitioner would be present at the inception of the IT project, and thus would recommend the use of a project charter at the outset, but the OD practitioner may also arrive after a project is already underway. In this case, the OD practitioner may encourage the IT project manager to collaborate in creating a charter that describes the high-level specifics of the project. If the IT project manager already has a working charter — and many will — the OD practitioner should obtain it, verify that all necessary information is included, and negotiate a relationship with the IT project manager and team based on the existing charter and the team's development opportunities.

The IT Project Charter captures the common understanding of the elements of the project funnel at a level that is specific enough to guide the project, but general enough to be shared among all members of the IT project team and its customers. The charter establishes the definition of quality for all involved, and

Figure 2. Example of an IT Project Charter

Project Charter for ABC Project Management Framework Career Development (Version 4)

Objective	Scope	Benefits
To define and recommend the capability framework for career development of project professionals across ABC.	Career Development of ABC Project Professionals* — Accreditation of ABC Project Leaders. *(Portfolio Managers, Sponsors, Leaders, Team Members)	This project will: • Support ABC project maturity. • Improve project professionalism as a core capability with ABC. • Provide professional development support for project professionals.

Sponsor/s
- ABC Project Management Framework Core Team (leader: ▒▒▒▒▒).
- GL&D Leadership Team (leader: ▒▒▒▒▒).

Deliverables

This team will deliver recommendations and high level implementation plans for the following:
- Generic career pathways for project professionals.
- Generic capabilities for project professionals.
- Generic role descriptors for project professionals.
- Definition of current organisational obstacles and change implementation plans.
- Characteristics and benefits of a suitable accreditation process.

Benefits (continued)
- Contribute to maximising the impact of project work on Business performance.
- Improve the retention of skilled project professionals within ABC.
- Improve the ability to attract external project professionals.

Key Stakeholders
- Project Professionals in ABC.
- Projects support groups in ABC.
- Functional L&D specialist
- HR Business Partners.
- ABC Line Managers who manage project professionals.
- Cite/Function CMTs.

Team

Project Leader:
Mark Marx (Operations).

Team Members:
(* Specialist Advisors)
- Marianne Smith (R&D).
- John Jones (IS).
- Peter Piper (HRBP).
- Annisa Gates (HR)
- Joanna Roseanna (PSA)
- Chris Kringle (Corporate)*
- Larry Logan (US Business)*

Critical Success Factors
- Support from senior line management in all functions.
- Support from senior HR management.
- Good alignment with ABC PMF and ABC People Strategy (including the timetable for roll out of the PMF).
- Credibility of the deliverables with the ABC project professionals.

Timetable/KPIs
- Project starts end March 2004.
- Recommendations for career path definitions by end Q3 2004.
- Recommendations for associated capabilities by end Q3 2004.
- Definition of organisational obstacles and change implementation plans by end Q3 2004.
- Recommendations for potential accreditation processes by end Q4 2004.

thus should be validated and shared across the IT project team. The IT project manager may also wish to use the charter as a tool for framing interactions with the project sponsor and stakeholders.

The IT Project Charter is usually created by the IT project manager and OD practitioner together at the outset of the project, or when the OD practitioner joins the team. The charter should include:

- the name of the IT project,
- the name of the IT project's sponsor,
- the unit of the organization that is requesting and/or sponsoring the project,
- the beginning and ending dates of the project,
- the name of the OD practitioner (or manager): the person responsible for increasing communication, clarity, and alignment in the project,
- the date the OD practitioner (or team) joined the project,

- the organizational strategic objective the project supports: the specific element of the organization's strategy that is directly served by this project,

- the purpose of the project (phrased to indicate how the strategic objective is supported): what the project will be doing to directly support that objective,

- a list of three to five high-level requirements for the project, and a reference to where the complete requirements are recorded: the main activities performed by the product of this project,

- a high-level project schedule with major milestone dates and deliverables: the key dates in the project, and

- a high-level statement of the project's budget and funding source: the broad financial parameters that form part of the definition of project success.

The project charter should ideally be no more than a page or two, and it should serve as a touchstone throughout the project. Rather than occupying a binder on a shelf, the IT project manager and OD practitioner should seek ways to use the charter as an orienting device throughout the project. Figure 2 provides an example of a template for the IT Project Charter.

The IT Project Charter establishes clarity about the IT project in a way that provides the OD practitioner and the IT project team the initial data to begin the work of improving communication and other processes. The very act of creating and validating the charter is itself an intervention addressing both clarity about objectives and an understanding of leadership and stakeholder support. Once created, the charter is a vital foundation document for the work of addressing the IT project team's functioning. If the charter already exists, it is an invaluable link between the IT Project Success Funnel and the structured teambuilding approach to improving team effectiveness.

A Teambuilding Approach to IT Project Success

Once the elements of the IT Project Success funnel are established and agreed upon, the OD practitioner must design ways to use the model as a lever for positive change with the IT project team. The IT project team is able to improve performance and minimize the historic issues of poor communication, lack of leadership support, and unclear objectives through focused teambuilding, organizational alignment, and organizational learning. Warner Burke notes that when a workgroup has at least one goal common to all members and when accomplishment of that goal requires cooperative, interdependent behaviors on the part of all group members — as for the IT project team — teambuilding may be an appropriate intervention (Burke, 1982). Teambuilding is an especially effective intervention for addressing the common issues in IT projects because its structure provides a framework for addressing organizational alignment and organizational learning. An IT executive in the U.S. government once remarked that creating organizational change while continuing to deliver mission-critical services is like attempting to paint a Boeing 747 in full flight. The structured framework of teambuilding, organizational alignment, and organizational learning attempts to do a better job of painting the airplane while keeping the flight on schedule.

Burke, citing Beckhard, notes that there are four purposes of teambuilding:

1.   to set goals or priorities;
2.   to analyze or allocate the way work is performed according to team members' roles and responsibilities;
3.   to examine the way the team is working (its processes such as norms, decision making, communications, etc.); and
4.   to examine relationships among the team members. (Burke, 1982)

Burke elaborates on Beckhard's purposes by emphasizing that while all these purposes are operating in a teambuilding effort, one purpose should be defined as the primary purpose in order to avoid conflicting notions among team members of the purpose of the effort. In the IT project, the primary purpose of teambuilding is to address the processes of the team, especially those specific to the team's communication behaviors. The reason for this emphasis is that poor communication among team members is by far the most commonly cited issue in IT projects, and that better communication may provide clarity about objectives and leadership support needs.

Burke also notes that Beckhard's purposes are most effectively used in the order listed (Burke, 1982). The reason for working from the top of Beckhard's model downward is that each level sets context for the levels beneath it. Burke notes that it may be a misuse of energy to begin work at the interpersonal relationship level because these issues may result from misunderstanding in the other domains. This approach is particularly useful for the IT project team and its typical issues because it addresses objectives and roles (leadership and otherwise), two of the most common issues in IT projects, in the process of working toward the process level, where communication issues can be identified and resolved.

The work of the IT-focused OD practitioner begins with the first level of Beckhard's model, goals and priorities, and continues through roles and responsibilities toward the focus of the OD effort, the processes of the team itself, and the interpersonal concerns in its work.

- **Goals of the IT-focused OD practitioner:** The mission of the OD practitioner in an IT project — and that of the IT project team — is to increase the IT project's contribution to the organization's strategy. The OD practitioner's goal as a part of the IT project team is to increase the likelihood of project success by facilitating better communication, clearer objectives, and support for the project throughout the organization. To achieve these ends, the OD practitioner in an IT project takes into account alignment of the organization's strategy, the purpose of the IT project, and the requirements, schedule, and cost of the project. This orientation aligns the organizational concerns of the OD practitioner with the project-specific concerns of the IT professional to define the value boundaries of work within the project.

  The process of completing and validating the project charter is the most meaningful approach to satisfying the goals and priorities level of the IT project. With shared understanding of the IT project's organizational alignment and project boundaries, the IT project team comes to a clear, common vision of their work together.

  A common issue found at the goals and priorities level is a misalignment through the project funnel, such as contradictions between project purpose and organizational strategy, requirements and project purpose, or any combination of requirements, schedule, and cost. These issues should become fairly obvious during the OD practitioner's contracting phase with the IT project manager, and they should be noted and addressed or flagged as likely trouble spots.

Since the focus of the teambuilding effort is at the process level, the goals and priorities level defines the context and objectives for the project team's processes. The goals and priorities level, through the model of the project funnel, also establishes the boundaries for the inputs to both the IT project team and the OD practitioner's processes. If the data the OD practitioner obtains from the organizational or project system (the inputs to the process level) do not fall within or demonstrably affect the boundaries of the IT project funnel, they are irrelevant. In short, the OD practitioner must deliver value in the eyes of her customer, the IT project team.

• **Roles and responsibilities of the IT-focused OD practitioner:** Because of the prominence of the project management approach as a means to deliver value and increase the probability of success in IT projects, roles and responsibilities in IT projects tend to be exceptionally well defined. Project managers usually employ a Responsibility Assignment Matrix (RAM) such as the sample in Table 1 (PMI, 2000), and OD scholars have advocated similar approaches in teambuilding and organizational structure interventions (Dyer, 1995; Weisbord, 1987; Burke, 1982).

A key concern of the IT-focused OD practitioner is the specific outcomes to be delivered as a result of having worked with the IT project team. Specifying desired outcomes and behaviors establishes the parameters of that relationship. The OD practitioner has a responsibility to select inputs, interventions, and outputs that fall within the funnel, and thus serve the

Table 1. Responsibility Assignment Matrix (Adapted from Guide to the Project Management Body of Knowledge, 2000 Edition)

Phase	Person A	Person B	Person C	Person D	Person E	Person F
Requirements	S	R	A	P	P	
Functional	S		A	P		
Design	S		R	A	I	P
Development		R	S	A		P
Testing			S	P	I	P

P=Participant; A=Accountable; R=Review Required; I=Input Required; S=Sign-off Required

goals of the project and the strategy of the organization. This responsibility is demonstrated at the process level in Burke's model.

- **The process of OD in the IT environment:** The process level of Beckhard/Burke's model is the focus of the teambuilding approach, and it is where the most critical work with an IT project team is performed. The most common issue contributing to IT project failure—poor communication—is a result of dysfunction in the IT project team's processes. With the foundation of clear goals and priorities and mutually understood roles and responsibilities, the OD practitioner can employ the action research process to diagnose and positively intervene in the IT project team's processes, especially those that produce the symptoms of poor communication.

It is helpful to think of the action research process in the same way an IT professional thinks of technical processes: a set of steps that receives inputs and acts upon them to produce outputs. In the case of the IT-focused OD effort, the inputs to the process are selected from within the IT Project Success Funnel, and the quality of the outputs to be produced are defined within the parameters of this same funnel (Figure 3). The funnel serves as an orienting device used to narrow the range of possible inputs and focus the desired results of the OD practitioner's work.

In practice, this model provides a foundation for each step of the action research process. In entry and contracting, the OD practitioner and IT project manager already have a mutual understanding of the environment in which the IT project operates, and of its goals and staff responsibilities. The OD practitioner collects data that fall within the boundaries of the IT Project Success Funnel and provides group feedback within these same parameters. The IT project team and OD practitioner can jointly decide

Figure 3. Combining the IT Project Success Funnel with the Action Research Process to define input and output quality

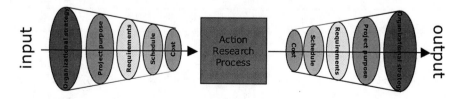

how to proceed with the validated data, and the action plan and goals they create can be compared against the funnel to ensure that the OD-related effort is compatible with the imperatives of the IT project. Subsequent evaluation and contracting can be conducted, with the funnel continuing to set context.

The action research process works in this context as a process within a process; Burke's teambuilding process serves as a preparatory, orienting process to the action research process, focusing it toward the level and IT project team processes offering the most opportunity for improvement and innovation. This combination of approaches involves the IT project team, not just in getting to the issue or opportunity, but also in agreeing about the environment in which the issue or opportunity exists.

Once the OD practitioner and IT project team have reached the process level and begun mutually deciding what to work on and how to do it, the IT Project Success Funnel and Burke's teambuilding model continue to provide the background and much of the OD practitioner's data (which tends to abbreviate the time-consuming data collection part of the action research process). Together the OD practitioner and the IT project team can apply the action research process to improve the effectiveness of meetings, resolve tensions between different but interrelated functions, guide planning efforts for the project's completion and implementation, identify developmental needs, and any number of other interventions the team finds appropriate and useful. So long as participation, leadership, and a shared understanding of the IT project boundaries are present, the opportunities presented by this structured OD approach are limitless, as are their results.

In actually implementing changes proposed by the team, it is a good idea to break large change into smaller, more manageable phases separated by time for reflection and team discussion (Freedman, 1997; Schaffer, 1997; Lippitt & Lippitt, 1986). In any OD intervention, and especially to one in the high-stakes environment of the IT project, the Hippocratic Oath applies: First, do no harm. OD is a difficult enough sell with a driven IT team; any approach that disrupts the requirements, schedule, or cost of the project will create animosity toward the OD practitioner. Conversely, smaller phases with time for evaluation and reflection give the team the opportunity to create change, learn from the change, and apply the lessons of the change to the next phase. Smaller phases also divide the risks of change, moving them from the all-or-nothing realm of wholesale transformation to the manageable parameters of incremental implementation and evaluation.

- **The human element:** The element of Burke's model most associated with the OD field and least associated with IT project teams is its fourth level, interpersonal relationships. Weisbord (1987, p. 258) lists three powerful levers in every workplace for turning anxiety into energy: purposes, structure, and relationships. The IT Project Success Funnel and the process-focused action research process offer powerful tools for leveraging purpose and structure to focus the IT project team's energy. This alignment and shared momentum create a fertile environment for building positive interpersonal relationships. Weisbord (1987) advocates guided team development, and his recommendation depends on developing awareness, skills, and cooperation within a natural workgroup against a social and business backdrop. Using as a guide the context and progress created by the work at the process level, and encouraging the democratic behaviors fundamental to that work, IT project team members can among themselves (or with the help of the OD practitioner as a coach) begin to identify and develop the healthiest, most harmonious behaviors and norms for the IT project team.

Resistance is a topic never far from the IT project, and an important consideration at the interpersonal and individual levels. The recipients of the IT project team's products and services in the customer organization (whether internal or external) may be expected to resist the changes technology demands, and the IT project team can certainly be expected to resist changes in their own familiar processes. McGregor and Knickerbocker addressed the very opportunities and challenges the IT-focused OD practitioner will face:

"We want to encourage enthusiastic cooperative effort, we want to increase efficiency to the utmost. These things we can accomplish only if the changes which are made in technical processes are perceived as necessary and reasonable by those whom the changes affect." (1941, p. 57)

Arthur Freedman (1997) notes the tendency among consultants and organizational leaders not to anticipate and prepare for difficulties in accepting and adopting change. If the OD practitioner and her IT project manager counterpart use the models described here to focus the IT project team's improvement but fail to anticipate and plan for those difficulties, IT project teams will likely be worse for having wasted precious time, and the OD practitioner will likely be out of work.

Putting Theory into Action

The teambuilding approach, when practiced within the framing and formalization of the model and charter, provides a structured approach to diagnosing and improving the cooperative, interdependent process behaviors required to deliver the IT project on time, within budget, and according to requirements. It would be a mistake to assert that this approach is a panacea for the universe of pitfalls that can happen in an IT project. IT projects concentrate complexity into narrowly defined windows of time, tasks, and funding, bringing together diverse people and disciplines to achieve a common goal without the luxury of extended reflection and experimentation. IT projects move quickly, and they create complex dynamics within a temporary organization. The approach and models presented here are not a universal cure, but rather one specific way to define and engage in the work of developing the IT team without impeding its work. In practice this approach is best used as a guide and a framework within which to apply the specific OD and project management knowledge most appropriate to a given situation and team. Rick Freedman (2000) warns about the double-edged sword of methodologies and best practices: While having a defined process for performing a complex task is clearly an advantage, that process should not be so rigid as to stifle innovation and impose uniformity on the creative process of developing the IT project team's effectiveness.

The following scenarios offer a glimpse of what this approach might look like in practice:

Scenario 1. An IT project is initiated for a telecommunications company to develop a system through which its customers can create Web pages about themselves, their hobbies, and their interests. These Web pages will be available to anyone with a Web browser, and they will be free to the customer. An internal IT team is formed to perform this project. In talking with the project sponsor for the project, the IT project manager learns that the site must go live in two months' time, and that it must offer features that its competitors in this market do not yet offer (though the competitors have been in this market for several years). While the tendency might be to ramp up this project quickly and burn as much midnight oil as necessary, the OD practitioner has two immediate concerns: First, the project does not appear to serve the strategy of a telecommunications company; and second, the requirements and schedule do not appear to be aligned (nor reasonable). Working with the IT project manager, the OD practitioner may facilitate additional discussions between the project manager sponsor before involving the team, ascertaining that the project is a good strategic fit and that the expectations of the team are reasonable, and saving considerable trouble in having a thinly stretched team and a dubious product.

Scenario 2. A government agency is engaged in a large project to enable Web-based records management among several thousand geographically dispersed employees. The project supports the organizational strategy by enabling more responsive service to citizens through the use of this system. A team of several different contractors representing various specialty firms is managed by an IT project manager, also a contractor. The schedule and budget appear reasonable for the requirements of the system, but skirmishes between various functions are causing the schedule slips and turnover among the team. The database analysts and the programmers are unable to agree on the proper ways to pass information back and forth between the interface and the database, and the requirements analysts and testers are sparring over what specific requirements mean in practice. In this scenario, the OD practitioner can work with the IT project manager to examine the barriers to collaboration and provide opportunities for the teams to make changes in their approaches. A possible approach might be a series of short workshops providing opportunities for mutual definition of norms and goal setting. Note that this scenario begins with tests of alignment between organizational strategy, project purpose, and requirements, schedule, and cost.

Future Trends

IT projects will continue to consume organizational energy, time, and money. Yet, the approach to managing and learning in IT projects can, with incremental adaptations, result in far greater effectiveness and organizational impact in IT projects. With hundreds of billions of dollars in waste being chalked up each year, IT projects are going to face increasing scrutiny before they are started and throughout their life cycles. With some incremental change, IT can continue its growth with less of the burden of failure it bears today.

The model and approach presented here provides a framework for planning, implementing, and evaluating OD efforts in an IT environment, allowing organizations to envision success and make course corrections as necessary. As this model becomes more common, it will be useful and informative to perform benchmarking within and among organizations in order to assess effectiveness and illustrate the possibilities presented by this approach. It will also be useful to track organizations using this approach over a period of years, and to compare their performance to those with different approaches. Organizations might also consider augmenting this approach with a system for capturing and reinvesting IT project savings in a measurable way.

IT and the projects that create it are going to be an increasingly integral part of modern life in the years to come. Most organizations already depend upon a robust IT infrastructure. The challenge in the coming years will be to integrate rather than compartmentalize, building the capacity of human systems and technological systems in tandem to produce the most effective collaboration between people and technology. The IT environment of the future must embrace the concept of the learning organization, "where people continually expand their capacity to create the results they truly desire, where new and expansive patterns of thinking are nurtured, where collective aspiration is set free, and where people are continually learning how to learn together" (Senge, 1990, p. 3).

Conclusions

This chapter has explained the common issues causing IT failure and waste, and it has described the magnitude and consequences of the problem. OD is a field uniquely qualified to collaborate with IT to address these issues. This chapter has presented a model for managing and practicing OD in an IT environment. Using this model, the OD practitioner or team can establish a collaborative, mutually beneficial relationship with the IT project manager. The outcomes of this partnership will be more effective teams, better organizational alignment both within the team and with the organization it serves, and the promotion of results-oriented organizational learning.

This is one of the first efforts to address the persistent problem of waste in the IT environment by codifying the relationship between OD practitioner and IT project team, and it is only the beginning. Some other issues to be explored are:

- how to gain entry into IT projects;
- specific techniques for negotiating the roles and expectations between the OD practitioner and the IT team;
- which techniques are more appropriate than others in improving IT project team communication and performance;
- possible areas of focus beyond the IT project team's effectiveness;
- how to establish a baseline for measuring results of interventions; and
- what the differences between various types (software development, upgrades, off-the-shelf product implementation) and stages of IT projects (requirements analysis, development, implementation) imply for the OD practitioner working to create the most useful outcomes for the IT project team.

What this chapter has established is a general context for and overview of work for OD professionals in an IT environment. While establishing the technical context of the IT project is an important step in enabling team development, Lewin's core principle for OD ultimately still applies: *We are likely to modify our own behavior when we participate in problem analysis and solution and likely to carry out decisions we have helped make* (Weisbord, 1987, p. 89). Yet, participation alone will not solve the issues of IT project waste. Participation requires *goal focus* and *active leadership* (Weisbord, 1987, p. 85). The two are brought together through a structured collaboration between the IT project manager and the OD practitioner. The opportunities for each are bound only by their mutual will and discipline in creating IT project success.

References

Beckhard, R., & Harris, R. (1987). *Organizational transitions: Managing complex change* (2nd ed.). Reading, MA: Addison Wesley.

Block, P. (2000). *Flawless consulting: A guide to getting your expertise used* (2nd edition). San Francisco: Jossey-Bass/Pfeiffer.

Burke, W. (1982). Team building. In W. Reddy & K. Jamison (Eds.), *Team building: Blueprints for productivity and satisfaction*. Alexandria, VA: NTL Institute for Applied Behavioral Science.

Cummings, T., & Worley, C. (1997). *Organization development and change* (6th ed.), St. Paul, MN: West Publishing Co.

Dyer, W. (1995). *Team building: Current issues and new alternatives* (3rd ed.), Reading, MA: Addison Wesley.

Executive Office of the President, Office of Management and Budget. (2003). *Report on information technology (IT) spending for the federal government*. Washington, DC: OMB. Retrieved September 9, 2003, from *www.whitehouse.gov/omb/budget/fy2004/sheets/itspending.xls*

Freedman, A. (1997). The undiscussable sides of implementing transformational change. *Consulting Psychology Journal: Practice and Research, 49*(1), 51-76.

Freedman, R. (2000). *The IT consultant: A commonsense framework for managing the client relationship*. San Francisco: Jossey-Bass/Pfeiffer.

Knickerbocker, I., & McGregor, D. (1941). Industrial relations and national defense: A change to management. *Personnel, 1*(July), 49-63. In M. Weisbord (1987), *Productive workplaces: Organizing and managing for dignity, meaning and community*. San Francisco: Jossey-Bass.

Lippitt, G., & Lippitt, R. (1986). *The consulting process in action* (2nd ed.). San Francisco: Jossey-Bass/Pfeiffer.

Microsoft Corporation. (2002, April 16). Q&A: Information technology: An engine for global economic growth. Seattle, WA: Microsoft Corporation. Retrieved July 1, 2003, from *www.microsoft.com/presspass/features/2002/apr02/04-16glcqa.asp*

Pande, P., Neuman, R., & Cavanagh, R. (2000). *The six sigma way: How GE, Motorola, and other top companies are honing their performance*. New York: McGraw-Hill.

Project Management Institute. (2000). *A guide to the project management body of knowledge* (2000 ed.). Newtown Square, PA: Project Management Institute.

Roethlisberger, F.J., & Dickson, W.J. (1939). *Management and the worker.* Cambridge MA: Harvard University Press.

Schaffer, R. (1997). *High-impact consulting: How clients and consultants can leverage rapid results into long-term gains.*

Schein, E. (1988). *Process consultation, Volume I: Its role in organization development* (2nd ed.). Reading, MA: Addison Wesley.

Senge, P. (1990). *The fifth discipline.* New York: Doubleday.

The Standish Group. (2003, March 25). Latest Standish Group CHAOS report shows project success rates have improved by 50%. West Yarmouth, MA: The Standish Group. Retrieved July 1, 2003, from *www.standishgroup.com/press/article.php?id=2*

Thorp, J. (1998). *The information paradox: Realizing the business benefits of information technology.* Toronto: McGraw-Hill Ryerson Limited.

Trist, E. (1981). *The evolution of socio-technical systems: A conceptual framework and an action research program.* Occasional Paper No. 2, Ontario Quality of Working Life Centre, City, June.

Verzuh, E. (1999). *The fast-forward MBA in project management.* New York: John Wiley & Sons.

Weisbord, M. (1987). *Productive workplaces: Organizing and managing for dignity, meaning and community.* San Francisco: Jossey-Bass.

About the Authors

Teresa Torres-Coronas earned her PhD from the Universitat Rovira i Virgili, Spain, where she currently is Professor in the Engineering School. Her research interests are in creative management, organizational development, and TICs and information systems. She is one of the Spanish associates of the Center for Research in Applied Creativity, Canada. She is interested in using creative systems thinking approaches to improve organizational development. She has experience in conducting consultancy projects with private-sector organizations in the area of applied creativity (building creative thinking, innovation, and problem-solving capabilities within organizations). She is also interested in promoting the understanding, development, and practice of managing information resources as key business assets. Since 2003 she has been acting as World Wide Representative for Spain for the Information Resource Management Association (IRMA-USA). She is a research member of the E-Business Research Group and main researcher in the Organizational Development Research Group, both within the Rovira i Vigili University. Dr. Torres won first prize in the 2000 edition of EADA-related management research for her work, *Valuing Brands* (Gestion, 2000). Dr. Torres has also published other books, journal articles, chapters in collective works, and international conferences in creative management, information systems, and other research fields such as management education and intangible asset management.

Mario Arias-Oliva holds a PhD in Management from the Rovira i Virgili University, Spain. His PhD thesis focused on virtual organizations, taking all doctoral courses at Erasmus Universiteit Rotterdam in Holland. He lectures at the Rovira i Vigili University in the Information Management area. Dr. Arias collaborates as International Research Associate with the Center for Computing and Social Responsibility, De Montfort University, UK. He has conducted several research projects including "Self-Employment Analysis in Spain" (Spanish Finance Ministry) and "The Relationship Between Training Consultancy Organizational Design and Strategy: The Effects on Quality and Performance of Training Services" (Unión General de Trabajadores, UGT, a leading Spanish trade union federation). He has been an invited speaker to several MBA programs, seminars, and courses, including at the Autonomous University of Madrid, Vigo University, the Rey Juan Carlos University of Madrid, the Polytechnic University of Madrid, De Montfort University (UK), Unisinos (Brazil), Autónoma del Sur (Chile), and Atacama University (Chile). In 2003 he received the Spanish education ministry's award for quality and innovative projects in Spanish universities. He worked as Consultant for some of the most important Spanish firms, including the BBVA Bank, National Institute of Social Affairs, and Bankinter group. Dr. Arias has participated in several international conferences, presenting papers in the fields of Human Resources and Information Technology.

*   *   *

Mousumi Bhattacharya, an Assistant Professor at Fairfield University, teaches strategy and human resource management at the Charles F. Dolan School of Business. She has a PhD in Strategy and Human Resource Management from Syracuse University. She has worked for the largest steel manufacturer in India in human resource management and strategic planning. Dr. Bhattacharya's research interests include strategic human resource management, social networks, flexibility, and risk. She has presented her research at national and international conferences of the Academy of Management, Strategic Management Society, and Eastern Academy of Management. Her research has been published by theses organizations, as well as by the Global Business and Technology Association. She has been nominated for an Outstanding Empirical Paper Award at the Eastern Academy of Management, 2004. She is a member of the Academy of Management, Society for Human Resource Management, and Strategic Management Society.

Constant D. Beugré is an Associate Professor of Management in the School of Management at Delaware State University (USA), where he teaches courses in organizational behavior, human resources management at the undergraduate level, and organizational leadership at the graduate level. Prior to joining Delaware State University, Dr. Beugré was an Assistant Professor of Management and Information Systems at Kent State University, Tuscarawas Campus. He has been a Visiting Fellow at Harvard University, and a Fulbright Scholar at the University of Indiana, Bloomington and Rensselaer Polytechnic Institute. He has also taught at the National University of Ivory Coast. Dr. Beugré holds a PhD in Management from Rensselaer Polytechnic Institute and a doctoral degree in Industrial/Organizational Psychology from the University of Paris X/Nanterre. His research interests include organizational justice and the organizational impact of information technology. He has published two books and more than 30 articles.

Robert F. Calderón is a Senior Associate for Caliber Associates. He received his BA degrees (1991) from Northwestern University in Psychology and Statistics, and his MA (1994) and PhD (1998) degrees from the Ohio State University in Industrial/Organizational Psychology. His research interests include performance management, occupational analysis, training, training evaluation, and personnel selection.

Anna Comacchio earned her PhD in Management from the University Ca'Foscari, Venice, Italy, where she is now Associate Professor of Organizational Behavior and Human Resources Management. Her areas of interest are organizational behavior, organizational structures, and human resources management, with main focuses on e-HRM, HRM competence-based organizations, human capital, innovation and organizations of SMEs, and people management in the tourism sector. She has written several articles and books including *The Competent Middle Manager: Framing Individual Knowledge in SEMs of North-East of Italy* (co-authored with A. Camuffo, to be published in *International Journal of Innovation and Learning*, 2004) and *Automation in the Automotive Industries* (co-authored with G. Volpato & A. Camuffo, 1998, Springer-Verlag).

Scott A. Davies is Manager of Research and Development for Hogan Assessment Systems in Tulsa, Oklahoma (USA). He previously served as a Senior Research Scientist with the American Institutes for Research in Washington, DC. He received his BS (1997) from Missouri Western State College in Psychology, and his MA (1999) and PhD (2002) from the Ohio State University in Industrial/Organizational Psychology. His research interests include personnel selection, ability test issues, application of IRT models to personality assessment, and strategic human resource management.

Elaine Farndale is currently a researcher at the Erasmus University Rotterdam, The Netherlands. Her research interests lie in the field of international HRM, with particular emphasis on the role of the personnel department, its professionalism in organizations and the impact of new technology on the profession.

Elizabeth Jones is a Senior Lecturer in the School of Applied Psychology at Griffith University, Brisbane, Australia. Her main research interests are in organizational communication and employee well-being during organizational change. She also publishes in the areas of stress at work, and gender and work.

Paul Hawking is Senior Lecturer in Information Systems at Victoria University, Melbourne, Australia. He has contributed to the *Journal of ERP Implementation and Management, Management Research News, Virtual Education, ERP & Data Warehousing in Organisations,* and many conference papers on IS theory and practice. He is responsible for managing the university's strategic alliance with SAP and is Coordinator of the university's ERP Research Group. Professor Hawking is Immediate Past Chairperson of the SAP Australian User Group.

Christopher L. Huntley holds a PhD in Systems Engineering from the University of Virginia. Prior to completing his PhD, he worked in the Information Systems and Service Design departments at Conrail, a Class I railroad in Philadelphia. He is an Assistant Professor of Information Systems and Operations Management in the Charles F. Dolan School of Business at Fairfield University. His research and teaching interests include organizational learning, software development processes, and metaheuristic search applications in system design. He has published articles in various refereed journals, including *Interfaces, Computers & Operations Research,* and *IEEE Computer.* Dr. Huntley is a member of the Decision Science Institute and INFORMS, where he serves as the Web master for the INFORMS Information Systems Society.

In Lee is an Associate Professor in the Department of Information Management and Decision Sciences in the College of Business and Technology at Western Illinois University (USA). He received his MBA from the University of Texas at Austin and his PhD from the University of Illinois at Urbana-Champaign. His current research interests include e-commerce technology development and management, agent-oriented enterprise modeling, and intelligent simulation systems. He has published his research in such journals as *IEEE Transactions on Systems, Man, and Cybernetics, Computers and Operations Research, Computers and Industrial Engineering, Business Process Management Journal, Journal of Applied Systems Studies, International Journal of Simulation and Process Modeling,* and the *Journal of Electronic Commerce in Organizations.*

Joseph Logan is a Senior Business Analyst for Performance and Organization Effectiveness in the IS organization of AstraZeneca Pharmaceuticals. Prior to joining AstraZeneca he was involved in enterprise-level strategy and performance consulting for over a decade for several large organizations in the public and private sectors. Mr. Logan is a member of the adjunct faculty at Boston University and American University, and he is a frequent contributor of articles on the convergence between information technology and organizational behavior. He is currently working on a field guide for organization development professionals with information technology clients. Mr. Logan is a graduate of the AU/NTL Master's of Science in Organization Development program at American University, Washington, DC.

Jaap Paauwe is Professor of Management and Organization. His research interests focus on corporate strategy, human resource management, organizational change and industrial relations. He is a co-founder of the Dutch HRM Network, an association of academics in the area of the employment relationship. He is currently Fellow of the Erasmus Research Institute in Management (ERIM) and responsible for the research program Managing Relationships for Performance. Paauwe is the author of several books and articles in international journals in the field of organization and HRM. His latest book is titled *HRM and Performance: Achieving Long-Term Viability.*

Annachiara Scapolan is a PhD student in Business Economics and Management at the Ca' Foscari University of Venice, Italy. Her research areas are organizational behavior and human resource management, with main focuses on e-HRM, intellectual capital, and organizational complementarities.

Gavin M. Schwarz is a Lecturer in the School of Industrial Relations and Organizational Behavior, The University of New South Wales, Sydney, Australia. He received his PhD in Management from the University of Queensland (2001). His current research interests include structural inertia and information technology change, virtual and distributed team change, and technology strategy.

Timothy Shea has spent his career in the information technology field – first in industry, developing large systems applications, and more recently as an information systems faculty member. He received his DBA in Management Information Systems from Boston University, his MBA in Management Information Systems from Indiana University, and his BS in Operations Management and Computer Science from Boston College. His numerous journal publications, conference presentations, and consulting activities focus on corporate universities, implementation issues around ERPs, e-commerce in the grocery industry, and the effective use of learning technologies. He is Associate Professor of Information Systems at the University of Massachusetts Dartmouth (USA), where he teaches courses in project management, database, and networking.

Pamela D. Sherer received her PhD in Management from the Isenberg School of Management at the University of Massachusetts Amherst. She has an MBA from Clark University and an MS in Higher Education from Southern Illinois University. Her numerous publications and consulting activities focus on human resource development in both industry and higher education settings. She is an Associate Professor of Management at Providence College, where she teaches courses in human resource management, international human resource management, managing workplace diversity, and organizational change and development. She was the Founding Director of Providence College's Center for Teaching Excellence and has led faculty development workshops on a broad spectrum of technology-related topics at colleges and universities in the United States and internationally. Her research on faculty development and online learning has appeared in *College Teaching, Innovative Higher Education, To Improve the Academy,* and *The Journal for the Art of Teaching.*

Andrew Stein is a Lecturer in the School of Information Systems in the Faculty of Business and Law at Victoria University, Melbourne, Australia. He has contributed to the *International Journal of Management, Journal of Information Management, ERP Implementation and Management, Management Research News, Virtual Education, ERP & Data Warehousing in Organisations,* and many conference papers on IS theory and practice. His research interests include enterprise systems, e-procurement applications, e-marketplace business models, and reverse auction systems. He is a member of the university's ERP Research Group and the Australian SAP user group.

Bernadette M. Watson is an Australian Research Fellow at the Centre for Social Research in Communication at the University of Queensland, Brisbane, Australia. Her key research areas are health communication, intergroup and interpersonal communication social identity, and organizational change.

Roger Williams is an Emeritus Professor of Organization and Management at Erasmus University Rotterdam. His field of interests are among others human resource management, management development, individual and organizational learning, organizational change, and continuous improvement.

Index

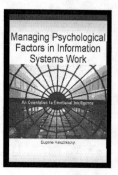